Risk

Risk

Edited by

Edward J. Burger, Jr., M.D., Sc.D.

Ann Arbor

The University of Michigan Press

First published by the University of Michigan Press 1993

Published in the United States of America by
The University of Michigan Press
Manufactured in the United States of America

1996 1995 1994 1993 4 3 2 1

LIBRARY OF CONGRESS CATALOGING-IN-PUBLICATION DATA

Risk / edited by Edward J. Burger.
p. cm.
"Originally published as the Fall 1990 issue of Dædalus, Vol. 119, no. 4, of the Proceedings of the American Academy of Arts and Sciences"—Galley.
Includes bibliographical references.
ISBN 0-472-08222-1
1. Health risk assessment—Social aspects—United States. 2. Risk perception—Social aspects—United States. 3. Risk—United States—Sociological aspects. I. Burger, Edward J., 1933–
RA427.3.R56 1993
614—dc20 93-13401
CIP

A CIP catalogue record for this book is available from the British Library.

This volume was originally published as the Fall 1990 issue of *Daedalus*, Volume 119, Number 4, of the *Proceedings of the American Academy of Arts and Sciences.*

Contents

Introduction

THIS PROJECT BEGAN with the overarching goal of examining how Americans think about risk—especially risk to health—and how these views shape our personal and political behavior. Both as a figure of speech and as an instrument of political momentum, risk has assumed an unusual prominence on the American scene. Over the course of the past two decades, private interests and public institutions have been profoundly altered as a reflection of attitudes toward perceived riskiness of products and practices of the manufacturing industry, of the community environment, and of others' behavior. Beginning in the late 1960s, the federal government—at both ends of Pennsylvania Avenue—embraced concerns for the environment with spectacular political enthusiasm. New regulatory agencies were born. Old statutes were rewritten, and new ones were created. There occurred a virtual explosion of governmental effort—legislative and administrative—toward regulation and enforcement, nominally aimed at reducing risks or at shifting responsibility and accountability for risky behavior. Theodore Lowi points out in one of this book's essays that this "regulatory binge" was even more extensive than that of the earlier wave of regulation in the New Deal. However extensive and dramatic this binge, Lowi contends that regulation has not been the effective instrument of societal control of risks that it was nominally intended to be as regulatory agencies could never fulfill but a fraction of goals set for them by the Congress. Whereas Lowi questions whether or not the Congress might have been naively unaware of these shortcomings, the more cynical are persuaded that the legislators fully understood what they were creating.

On one level, the background for this project was exceedingly simple. It seemed reasonable to ask what the dimensions were of the American concern for risk, what its origins were and its consequences. The concept of risk has come to occupy what appears to some as an unusually prominent place in American life. It has influenced private behavior. Along the way, public views about risk have colored political and, therefore, governmental activity (in all three branches) in many and diverse ways. Its effects are seen in policies governing energy production and use, agricultural programs, import and export policies, as well as direct regulation of industrial products and practices.

Yet this inquiry was explicitly *not* directed at the details of analysis of specific risks. Neither did it seek to examine the instruments and methods used by the growing community of analytically minded students of risk analysis. Its aim was a broad one. The purpose was to step back from the fray and examine the character of the present public views about risks and consider systematically the factors which have fostered those views. Have Americans changed (retreated) from risk taking to risk averseness? Have we altered our national views concerned with personal versus collective responsibility for our actions and mishaps? To the extent that the nation has altered its feelings about these matters, what cultural or economic or other factors have led to these changes?

An important part of this challenge has been to determine which factors are the most important independent and which are the most important dependent variables. Has life, in fact, become riskier? What do the assembled vital facts indicate? Have our trends of longevity been reduced by an overlay of chronic degenerative disease or has increasing longevity, by its nature, made cohorts of individuals "available" to become the victims of maladies characteristic of older age? What is the real contribution of exogenous agents to the human disease burden, alongside all of the other forces affecting health?

Whether or not life is truly riskier, are we more aware of risks than ever before? Several observers have remarked on a national preoccupation with health—with what contributes to health, with what might improve it and what factors might harm it. Lewis Thomas had spoken much earlier about "a nation of healthy hypochondriacs."[1] William Lowrance has referred more recently to the "medicalization of life."[2]

If there is greater awareness of or sensitivity to matters of health and risk, what has brought this new level of perception? Here one inevitably inquires of the intermediaries and messengers—principally the members of the fourth estate. Again, it is fair to inquire about how this fraternity accurately reflects facts and news about risks and to what extent its reporting drives the news. Stephen Klaidman's commentary on the imperatives of journalism indicates the inevitable combination of motivations operating in this sector. Closely related to the reporting of health- and risk-related news is the question of the public's capacity for understanding technically complex issues. Here as elsewhere, the subject of scientific literacy is much on our minds. Commonly held logic would dictate that a scientifically more literate society would tend to act and vote more rationally regarding risks. In this regard, some surveys, at least, are discouraging, suggesting that perhaps 39 percent (66 million American adults) give some credibility to astrology reports and about 7 percent of the population change their behavior because of the advice offered in those reports. In the same vein, about 40 percent of American adults persist in the belief of lucky numbers.[3]

There are important contrary views on this matter. One contends that public attitudes toward risks are not simply matters of perception. Rather, it is suggested, they strongly reflect underlying fundamental attitudes with which people approach risk taking. It is Mary Douglas who discounts the entire notion of the importance of objective fact in considering risks and, therefore, in the public's understanding of those facts. For her, risk is no longer a neutral or "innocent" word denoting probability of outcome. In the new litany, it means only danger—a conceptual role which indicates a fundamental shift in American culture toward protection of the individual rather than of the community. In that setting of opposing goals and desires for power, she contends, no effort at improvement in the public's understanding of what is supposed to be the technical underpinnings underlying risk estimation would make any difference in political behavior or outcome.

An important step in this book's creation was the consideration of our democratic institutions in the face of challenges brought by concerns for risk. Are those institutions up to the task of dealing with risks, with our concerns about risk, and with the complex technical detail we have brought to the risk table? Does the open texture of this society severely limit our ability to deal effectively with risks? Perhaps even more provocatively, to what extent is the open texture *responsible* for how we view risks? Are democratic structures capable of accommodating our views about risks and our expectations for resolving the challenges they bring? We seem to have a further complication in this country. From its beginnings, the nation has always entertained an underlying distrust of government. In recent years since Watergate and the Vietnam War period, we have overlaid that with a further and more general antiestablishmentarian view. There is said to be a reduced respect for institutions of all types—public and private. It was precisely this sentiment—citizens could no longer trust the federal Environmental Protection Agency to prevent harm from pesticides and chemical components in food—which persuaded the voters of California to pass the referendum initiative, Proposition 65, a few years ago.

A great deal of attention has been given to the role and behavior of the courts in risk matters—both in general and in this inquiry. Two classes of cases have come before the judiciary in overwhelming numbers compared with earlier years. One concerns the almost assured challenge by appeals courts of important federal regulatory agency decisions. Federal agencies, such as the EPA and the FDA, prepare their own "decisions" with an expectation that they will inevitably have to defend them in court. This pattern of "judicial regulation" has become a fact of life and is *the* factor which distinguishes American from Western European regulatory patterns.[4]

The other class comprehends the very large number of cases brought to trial courts by claimants for monetary damages and compensation for defective products or harm imputed to other private behavior or actions. As George L. Priest describes here (and, before him, so many others as well), there has occurred an enormous expansion of the civil justice system to become the most important and powerful institution both for regulating risk and for compensating for its consequences. Underlying this change has been a fundamental shift in the purpose of the workings of the civil law—from determination of negligence and resolution of disputes between individuals to a highly aggressive if, perhaps, inefficient vehicle for allocation of risks and the internalization of costs. Many have commented on the large and rapidly rising specter of court decisions for compensation and product liability, on unpredictable but sometimes unusually large financial judgments rendered by the courts, and on the large sums flowing to "transaction costs." George Priest goes further. To the extent that the civil justice system has been redesignated as an insurancelike compensation system, it is also a highly inefficient and regressive one.

A particularly fascinating aspect of contemporary risk matters concerns the scientific factual basis for estimating risks and for determining their importance or degree of seriousness. Risk estimates from putative environmental hazards or therapeutic drugs or the products of recombinant DNA technology, for example, are universally backed by volumes of detailed technical analysis. I don't consider here the components of those bodies of information or the methods used to analyze them. Rather, I refer to the ways in which science and scientists articulate with the public policy process. Discussion of this matter has many parts and points up important fundamental currents of how we have chosen to accommodate to risk challenges in recent years. The scientific factual fabric proffered by supplicants for permission to market a new product, for example, has become enormously more elaborated in the past 20 years. In part, this is because more scientific understanding has been generated. More important, it is a reflection of the new currency which scientific factual material has assumed in political bargaining. Not only the quantity but the quality and interpretation of scientific data have become the centerpieces of adversarylike proceedings—both in regulatory agencies and in the courts. In the United States, a remarkable amount of attention has been focused on what one senior British scientist recently described as the "new American Book of Genesis—carcinogenesis, mutagenesis and teratogenesis." The power of the factual fabric in political bargaining has been recognized by all hands—those bent on protecting and those determined to relax standards. Any rearrangement of the fund of factual and analytic assets and of the forum in which those assets are introduced and discussed is seen as perturbations in the political bargaining process.

Thus, proponents of the public's welfare complain that more scientific information and more rigorously interpreted and judged science stand in the way of protection of health and block the awarding of deserved or just compensation.[5] Critics of the imprecise or distorted use of factual material scream "junk science." Much political attention is focused on health and protection of health as these are possessed of unusual political attractiveness. Honest differences of interpretation of the rough edges of scientific understanding, wrongly considered the frontiers of science, are intensely debated in the agencies and in the courts, commonly as proxies for the real or core social dispute in each case. Groups deeply interested in agency business or in the outcome of toxic tort or product liability litigation are intent overwhelmingly on seeing their point of view prevail. Their interest is in winning. The weight of technical information and its interpretation becomes, in that context, an instrument of political power in a formal setting where bargaining, in the usual sense, is not permitted. In the absence of the ability to bargain, some notable compensatory moves have been taken in recent years. One of these is the increasing role of expert advisory committees. They have become gradually more prominent, formalized, and influential in EPA and FDA affairs, borrowing on long-standing experience in the United Kingdom and elsewhere in Western Europe where scientific experts sit very close to the political process. Scientific advisors and panels of experts are beginning to be appended to the court process—to supplement if not to compensate for the influence of the parties' partisan expert witnesses. A third has been an extraordinary drive toward increasing quantification of risk information. This numerology or "quantitative risk analysis," which gives the appearance of increased accuracy, has been correctly described by some of its critics as a "refuge in objectivity."

There is a counterpart in the court, as well. Much attention has been devoted to how scientific material is brought into the courtroom as product liability and "toxic tort" litigation have become increasingly technically complex. Frequently, in the adversary proceeding of the courtroom, each side tends to treat uncertainties and disputed areas of complex technical material as proxies for the core social dispute before the court.

Science has become the vehicle for argumentation over core social disputes, and uncertainties in scientific understanding have been the terms of dispute seized upon by those intent upon seeing their position prevail. Some unusual paradoxes have emerged. For example, it has been not uncommon for physicians and scientists, trained in preventive medicine, to find themselves in the unexpected role of arguing against the political momentum of the environmental or consumer movement where proponents of that movement appear to offend the integrity of the factual basis for national decisions.

The idea of this inquiry into risk originated many months before this publication as a collaborative effort between *Daedalus*, the *Journal of the American Academy of Arts and Sciences*, and the Institute for Health Policy Analysis, Georgetown University Medical Center in Washington. Many of the essays were eventually published in a special issue of *Daedalus*. Professor Stephen Graubard, editor of *Daedalus*, is due high praise and acknowledgment for both wisdom and perseverance in pursuing the original publication to its endpoint.

The *Daedalus* issue on risk was particularly well received by its readers. Several urged that the material and ideas be made available to a wider audience. Hence, this somewhat expanded version.

Edward J. Burger, Jr., M.D., Sc.D.
Washington, D.C.
July 20, 1992

ENDNOTES

[1]Lewis Thomas, *The Medusa and the Snail* (New York: Viking Press, 1974).

[2]William Lowrance, *Modern Science and Human Values* (New York: Oxford University Press, 1985).

[3]J. Miller, "Some New Measures of Scientific Literacy" (Paper presented to the Annual Meeting of the American Association for the Advancement of Science, Philadelphia, Pa., May 28, 1986).

[4]R. Brickman, S. Jasanoff, and T. Ilgen, *Controlling Chemicals: The Politics of Regulation in Europe and the United States* (Ithaca, N.Y.: Cornell University Press, 1985).

[5]D. A. Stone, "Physicians as Gatekeepers: Illness Certification as a Rationing Device," *Public Policy* 27, no. 2 (1979).

Mary Douglas

Risk as a Forensic Resource

FROM "CHANCE" TO "DANGER"

THE WORD *RISK* HAS ACQUIRED NEW PROMINENCE. One popular explanation is that risks from technology have greatly increased. They have indeed, in all the industrial world. But some other risks have decreased, at least if the figures for mortality and morbidity mean anything. So perhaps what needs to be explained is the greater political awareness from technology in America, greater awareness than in France,[1] and presumably greater than in Russia before Chernobyl. Some would explain the new use of the vocabulary of risk in American politics by the revival of laissez-faire liberal economics. In this volume Theodore Lowi shows how the nineteenth-century idea of the merits of individual risk taking have been reintroduced into American politics. Praise of risk taking invokes the virtues of frontier morality to interrupt the long, slow move to establish collective responsibility for accidents. However, this ideological change itself needs to be explained. American political history does not account for the market ideology renascent in Britain, and in China, and more recently in Russia and Eastern Europe. The question is why a changed political debate goes across national boundaries, couched in terms of risk. The answer here suggested is that a culture needs a common forensic vocabulary with which to hold persons accountable and further that *risk* is a word that admirably serves the forensic needs of the new global culture.

The object of this essay is to situate the notion of risk by comparing its current usage with similar concepts in other times and places. In

Mary Douglas is Retired Professor of Anthropology at University College, London.

becoming a central cultural construct in America, the word has changed its meaning. It has entered politics and in doing so has weakened its old connection with technical calculations of probability. In the nineteenth century, when the theory of risk taking became important in economics, humans were thought to be risk averse, because they were supposed to be making their choices according to the hedonic calculus. The owner of a firm needed a special profit incentive for risk taking or he would not invest. Going further back, in the eighteenth century the analysis of risk had important uses in marine insurance. The chances of a ship coming safely home and making the fortune of its owner were set against the chances of its being lost at sea, bringing ruin. The idea of risk in itself was neutral; it took account of the probability of losses and gains. Going further back still, the concept originally emerged in the seventeenth century in the context of gambling. For this purpose a specialized mathematical analysis of chances was developed. *Risk* then meant the probability of an event occurring, combined with the magnitude of the losses or gains that would be entailed. Since the seventeenth century the analysis of probabilities has become the basis of scientific knowledge, transforming the nature of evidence, of knowledge, of authority, and of logic.[2] Any process or any activity has its probabilities of success or failure. The calculation of risk is deeply entrenched in science and manufacturing and as a theoretical base for decision making. Clearly, probability theory has provided a modern way of thinking.

According to Ernest Gellner, the course of transition to modern industrial society imposes cultural homogeneity "by objective, inescapable imperative":

> Culture is no longer merely the adornment, confirmation and legitimation of a social order which was also sustained by harsher and coercive constraints; culture is now the necessary shared medium, the lifeblood or perhaps the minimal shared atmosphere, within which alone the members of the society can breathe and survive and produce. For a given society it must be one in which they can *all* breathe and speak and produce; so it must be the same *culture* . . . it can no longer be a diversified, locality-tied, illiterate little culture or tradition.[3]

On this line of argument the risk concept would have come to the fore in politics because probabilistic thinking is pervasive in industry, modern science, and philosophy. Risk would have become the idiom of politics as part of the homogenizing process of moving to a new world level of interaction. However, the risk that is a central concept for our policy debates has not got much to do with probability calculations. The original connection is only indicated by arm waving in the direction of possible science: the word *risk* now means danger; *high risk* means a lot of danger.

In this essay Gellner writes particularly about the role of education and shared culture as part of the necessary infrastructure of nationalism. He does not say how the "inescapable imperative" imposes its commands, or where it finds its authority: the homogenizing process results in the production of key words which cover agreed concepts. But why should this process prize risk away from its original meaning to become one of the key words?

The answer is that the fulcrum of change is a debate about accountability that is carried out incessantly in any community. This dialogue, the cultural process itself, is a contest to muster support for one kind of action rather than another. Decisions to invest in more technology, or less, are the result of the cultural dialogue. Decisions to invade, to refuse immigration, to license, to withhold consent, all these responses to claims need support from institutions of law and justice. The cultural dialogue is therefore best studied in its forensic moments. The concept of risk emerges as a key idea for modern times because of its uses as a forensic resource.

To perform well in a new culture, a word must have a meaning consistent with the political claims in vogue. When the direction of change is the shift from little local communities to a larger world community, the key words need to justify leaving the old constraints and commitments. The new sense of the word *risk* works because it can be strongly biased toward emancipation. The context of a shared commitment to emancipation bends its meaning to refer only to danger. Whereas originally a high risk meant a game in which a throw of the die had a strong probability of bringing great pain or great loss, now *risk* refers only to negative outcomes. The word has been preempted to mean bad risks. The promise of good things in contemporary political discourse is couched in other terms. The language of risk is reserved as a specialized lexical register for political talk about the undesirable outcomes. Risk is invoked for a modern-style riposte against abuse of power. The charge of causing risk is a stick to beat authority, to make lazy bureaucrats sit up, to exact restitution for victims. For those purposes *danger* would once have been the right word, but plain *danger* does not have the aura of science or afford the pretension of a possible precise calculation.

SINS AND TABOOS

All historical cultures are in transition. Cultural stability is short lived, homogeneity achieved with difficulty and always about to dissolve. Staying within his own culture, a person is apt to see no culturally standardized forms around him: transgression against the norm is more visible than conformity. The inside experience of culture is an experience of choice and decision, scrutinized and judged by neighbors and press. The local view obscures regularities, but as soon as the local moves abroad, he is forcibly struck by the standardized behavior of foreigners. The innocent view of culture is that we don't have it at home; it is only abroad that people are culturally hidebound. A special effort of sophistication is necessary to see our own culture. We normally operate within its unnoticed intellectual confines as we ourselves intervene passionately in the dialogue about justice and what the world is likely to do to people if they disregard its real conditions. One way to overcome culture blindness is to be attentive to the way that claims of authority and solidarity are being treated. In the regular ongoing cultural debate about justice and the world, some idea of danger is usually invoked. The debate sways between pressures for emancipation from the old institutional constraints and pressures to sustain the institutions in which authority and solidarity reside. The claims of justice and danger are rhetorical resources for all parties. On this fulcrum concepts of liability and tort are continuously at stake, always in process of revision. In this respect moderns should not think themselves different from anyone else. They are inescapably in a cultural debate and pressuring one another to cultural conformity.

Most little local cultures develop some common term that runs across the gamut of social life to moralize and politicize dangers. In the preindustrial West, Christianity used the word *sin*. The fact that a word like *sin* would be commonly understood is a sign of the cultural homogeneity achieved. A major sin would be expected to unleash dangers on the community at large, or to afflict the sinner's nearest and dearest. Before the bad event the sinner on the brink of transgression could be reminded of his responsibilities and checked in time; when the bad event happened, it would be traced back to the known sin. Before Christianity, the Bible is full of such interpretations: the defeats of the Israelites by foreign armies, destruction by earthquake, plague, and drought, were attributed to God's anger for sins. The public discourse on sin's dangers mobilized a moral community. This would seem to be a far cry from the modern, sanitized discourse of risk.

Taboos and sins belong to the discourse of religious faith. Because it promotes the opening of closed communities and the free movement of individuals, industrialization also promotes religious skepticism as part of that same cultural homogenizing process. The two cultural contexts for risk and sin would seem to be quite incompatible. If Western industrial democracy were ever to build a homogeneous culture using a uniform vocabulary for moralizing and politicizing the dangers around, it could not use the vocabulary of religion. The neutral vocabulary of risk is all we have for making a bridge between the known facts of existence and the construction of a moral community. But this is why the public discourse about modern risks has fallen into an antique mode. Risk, danger, and sin are used around the world to legitimate policy or to discredit it, to protect individuals from predatory institutions or to protect institutions from predatory individuals. Indeed, risk provides secular terms for rewriting scripture: not the sins of the fathers, but the risks unleashed by the fathers are visited on the heads of their children, even to the *nth* generation.

Risk is certainly not the same as sin or taboo. The differences are not quite what they would seem at first sight. From our modern, skeptical, secular standpoint we have the illusion that taboos and sins work backwards: first the disaster, then the explanation of its cause in an earlier transgression. By contrast, risk seems to look forward: it is used to assess the dangers ahead. This is not a real difference between the discourses about risk and sin. The observer's standpoint deceives. Looking from a secular perspective at sin and taboo, we draw upon our own knowledge about the lack of connection between moral misdeeds and the weather or the spread of disease. The connection the religions used to make between the sins and the disasters is given to them along with the rest of their construction of nature. The model of how the world works is in continuous production and sins work forward just as well as risks. The very name of the sin is often a prophecy, a prediction of trouble. So for the people living together first comes the temptation to sin, and then the thought of future retribution, then warnings from friends and relations, attacks from enemies, and possibly a return to the path of righteousness before the damage is done. The big difference is not in the predictive uses of risk, but in its forensic functions.

As a community reaches for cultural homogeneity, it begins to signpost the major moments of choice with dangers. The signs say that certain kinds of behavior are very dangerous. That means that the community has reached some (probably temporary and fragile) consensus in condemning the behavior. Ready examples would be blasphemy, perjury, treason, sedition, disrespect to elders. A climate of disapproval grounds the belief that certain deeds are dangerous. The foreigners' gullibility for taboo which we find strange arises where information about causes is least coordinated. Without professional institutions to narrow enquiry and sustain it on empirical tracks, the forensic uses of disaster triumph. We have similar gullibility for forensic explanations on the outlying fringes of the professional world. This is why the fringes are innovative, and why so little of the innovation can get translated into establishment practice.

There is another reason for the credibility of danger in its forensic uses. Who is going to get caught? The victim is going to have done something unpopular when disaster strikes. There has to be some match between the scale of the disaster and the wickedness of the perpetrator who unleashed it. The risk warning lists a condign series of bad outcomes for the transgressor and his family and friends. If a district is thought to be politically disloyal, the chief and his supporters may lay responsibility for a local drought at the door of local treason. A woman who dies in childbirth is an example of the dangers of promiscuity. The danger itself accuses the defecting individual. There is nothing *post hoc* about a connection that is always there, working in both directions. Only when the community consensus weakens in its commitment to political loyalty, or when kinship obligations or marital fidelity weakens, does the weakness of the causal connection come to view.

Danger in the context of taboo is used in a rhetoric of accusation and retribution that ties the individual tightly into community bonds and scores on his mind the invisible fences and paths by which the community coordinates its life in common. By grace of their concern for these lines and boundaries they can share their territory and muster resources to protect it. The modern risk concept, parsed now as danger, is invoked to protect individuals against encroachments of others. It is part of the system of thought that upholds the type of individualist culture which sustains an expanding industrial system. This is why risk is such an important subject for America. The expansion has been enormous; there is some retrenchment; more expansion beckons. The dialogue about risk plays the role equivalent to taboo or sin, but the slope is tilted in the reverse direction, away from protecting the community and in favor of protecting the individual.

This does not give a fair picture of taboo: it does not work only against the individual. The taboo concept may support the popular voice against the power of government, just as well as the risk concept. So long as there is a consensus that individuals need to be protected, there is usually a list of dangers cited to restrain abuse of power. It was the Israelite kings who were accused of bringing defeat, enslavement, and drought, by their dilution of the cult. The Shakespearian cycle of historical plays dealing with kingship during the Wars of the Roses draws on similar ideas about the punishment of royal oppression and arbitrariness. Nonetheless, it is still true that there is asymmetry in the usages. Being "at risk" in modern parlance is not the equivalent but the reciprocal of being "in sin" or "under taboo." To be "at risk" is equivalent to being sinned against, being vulnerable to the events caused by others, whereas being "in sin" means being the cause of harm. The sin/taboo rhetoric is more often used to uphold the community, vulnerable to the misbehavior of the individual, while the risk rhetoric upholds the individual, vulnerable to the misbehavior of the community. Edward Burger's essay in this volume ("Health as a Surrogate for the Environment") describes how political actions to protect the environment have to be proposed as if they were to protect the personal health of individuals. They look like "political actions taken under the wrong banner," but they are taken under the only banner that will rally support: protection of the individual. The new dialogue about risks normally does not protect the collective good, and the old dialogue about sins normally did. Burger's essay suggests why France and Russia and England have been less politically alert to risks from technology: it is not directly connected with technology or with danger, but rather implies that America has gone farther down the path of cultural individualism, and so can make more use of the forensic potential of the idea of risk.

RISK AND REALITY

Note that the reality of the dangers is not at issue. The dangers are only too horribly real, in both cases, modern and premodern. This argument is not about the reality of the dangers, but about how they are politicized. This point cannot be emphasized too much. It is astonishing how many intelligent reviewers of *Risk and Culture,*[4] even anthropologists, fell into the trap of thinking that the argument cast doubt on the reality of the dangers.[5] In the preindustrial world life expectancy is short, often not more than 48 years; mortality rates are high for everyone, but infant deaths may be over 25 percent. Death of women in childbirth is very high. Starvation, blight, and famine are perennial threats. It is a bad joke to take this analysis as hinting that the dangers are imaginary. The risks in the industrial world are equally real. The cross-cultural argument would not work if the dangers were fictive. The culturally innocent debate would not work if the dangers were not real. The debate always links some real danger and some disapproved behavior, coding the danger in terms of a threat to valued institutions. For us the valued institution is the liberty of the individual. If heavy taboos hold a woman to her marriage, you will find that the marriage is not a simple partnership of a man and a woman, but a complex series of alliances, the central institution governing processes of production and reproduction. If sedition is thought to unleash climatic disorders, then you can be sure that political solidarity is both precarious and desired.

Standing outside their community as we do, it is easy to see that dangers (real dangers) are being used to give automatic, self-validating legitimacy to established law and order. We see their punitive or deterrent function. But that is only half of what is happening. Those who fear the taboos see dangers and their connection with morality as part of how the world works. If they shake their heads and say of a woman who has died in childbirth that she got what was coming to her, it is because adultery is connected indefeasibly with reproductive disorders as fire is with burning. Taboo works because a community of believers has developed a consensus on the kinds of solidarity that will help them to cope collectively with their environment of disease, accident, and war. They deal with their risks by mustering solidarity, invoking danger to maintain difference. It may be that solidarity is more of a problem for them,[6] or it may be that defection and loss of solidarity affect us less. This would explain why it is so difficult to see ourselves in the same perspective: the sin/taboo discourse is aimed at conserving solidarity, while the risk discourse aims to disperse it and to dissolve distinctions.

Within the cultural debate about risk and justice opponents seek to inculpate the other side and exonerate their own supporters from blame. *Risk* is unequivocally used to mean danger from future damage, caused by the opponents. How much risk is a matter for the experts, but on both sides of the debate it has to be taken for granted that the matter is ascertainable. Anyone who insists that there is a high degree of uncertainty is taken to be opting out of accountability.

THE INNOCENT MODEL

The innocent model of risk works well when disputants are agreed on the kind of accountability they want to enforce in their community. Questions of fact will suffice to guide on questions of moral preference when goals are not in dispute. Risk analysis can tell you to very fine degrees the probability of a particular event happening, with a one in a million chance, one in a thousand, one in a hundred, and so on. Similar analysis can tell you the costs of averting the event, the costs of insuring against it, the costs of compensating for it, or even the scale of benefits that the event would engender. All of this information is necessary if the parties agree on community goals; none of it will reconcile to a decision that one party fundamentally disapproves.

Consensus does not depend on the facts being recognized. And consensus among a group of scientists does not guarantee consensus among the public. The profession of psychologists which has grown up to study risk perception takes the culturally innocent approach by treating political dissension as intellectual disagreement. Aiming to disregard the contests over power which give rise to differences of opinion about risks, the profession neglects the central issue. It seeks to bring to the assessment of public perceptions the same degree of objectivity aimed at in risk analysis itself, and by similar methods. Unfortunately, the effort is skewed by the culturally innocent assumption that cultural bias is irrelevant for us at home, that culture is something that starts with the Wogs, abroad.

Using the innocent model of risk perception generally leads to the conclusion that there should be more education of the misguided public. But in a democracy education is not expected to change political commitments. It is proper for professionals operating within their own culture to find that the public needs to be better instructed in particular kinds of information, as do Roy Widdus, Andre Meheus, and Roger Short in their account of public misunderstanding of sexually transmitted diseases, and Kathy Helzlsouer and Leon Gordis in their essay on risks to health. It would obviously be helpful for policy on risk if the public were better instructed in many subjects. (For instance, it would be easier to discuss energy problems if many people did not believe that acid rain is caused by nuclear power stations.) But it is most unlikely that better communication and more education would reconcile differences of opinion on risks.

A risk is not only the probability of an event but also the probable magnitude of its outcome, and everything depends on the value that is set on the outcome. The evaluation is a political, aesthetic, and moral matter. In practical life private decisions about risk are taken by comparing many risks, and their probable good and bad outcomes. No risk item will normally be considered in isolation. Nor does intellectual activity happen in isolation. As Aaron Wildavsky and Karl Dake find in their essay in this volume, political bias is the strongest predictor of attitudes toward risk. Essentially, a theoretical framework is needed to transcend the culture in which the risks are being debated.

Cultural theory starts by assuming that a culture is a system of persons holding one another mutually accountable. A person tries to live at some level of being held accountable which is bearable and which matches the level at which that person wants to hold others accountable. From this angle, culture is fraught with the political implications of mutual accountability. Instead of imagining the isolated individual testing every piece of news without bias or moral commitment, the person is assumed to be sifting possible information through a collectively constructed censor set to a given standard of accountability. It is as if a kind of constitutional scanning device inside the person's head were busy testing incoming news. The criterion for assimilated knowledge or rejecting mere noise is whether the new idea or fact will reinforce the subject's preferred political scheme. On this assumption it is futile to study risk perception without systematically taking the cultural bias into account. The subjects of psychological enquiry take into the experimental booth with them an idea about what constitutes a long term, a sense of whether the respondent will be there to enjoy a long term, and a practical experience of long and short odds in everyday life. It would be very feasible to develop questionnaires that sorted experimental subjects according to their cultural bias before embarking on their response to probabilities of loss.

CULTURE AND KNOWLEDGE

Several important essays in this volume indicate that knowledge is falling apart. Alternative knowledge in medicine and law has successfully jostled for a place beside establishment knowledge. No one offers us certainty, even in science. When we lived in a hierarchical culture, we used to think that either a thing was known to be true or it was wrong; a fact was a fact, and as such it guaranteed deductions made from it. Now that we are committed to an individualist culture, the competition is on; knowledge has to be defended at every point; the open society guarantees nothing. Each type of culture is based on a distinctive attitude toward knowledge. Hierarchy, both as a system of governance and a type of culture, assumes that the world is up to a point knowable, and that itself, the hierarchy is organized according to the principles which run the universe. Consequently, the consensus that upholds the political system upholds the authority of facts. Its self-protective political effort goes into protecting the system of knowledge with which it is identified. Confidence in its old knowledge is its hallmark. Individualism as a type of culture pays rewards to new knowledge. Individualism is not a formal system of governance so much as a competitive market system; even for ideas and facts its controlling principles are embedded in market exchange; characteristically the community arbitrates what is permissible through price. New knowledge must perforce discredit old knowledge. Knowing very well why we want new knowledge, we should not be surprised at the uncertainty that is generated.

As Theodore Lowi has outlined here, competitive market individualism needs a political base to assure its basic security. In the same way the hierarchical culture needs an economic base. There cannot be a market without an accompanying political culture and there cannot be hierarchy without economic exchange. This said, the culture of individualism severely constrains how and what the government can do and the culture of hierarchy severely constrains the market. Though they must coexist, the balance is so different in each case that each requires a different worldview to sustain it. The homogenizing educational process that Gellner describes as the infrastructure of nationalism is also the necessary infrastructure of cultural bias, but the effective locus of transformation is the law court, not the schoolroom.

Appealing to degrees of risk, assessed by accredited experts, is appealing to an external arbiter, an independent, objective judge of the rights and wrongs of the case. Normally the appeal to professional experts to settle questions of accountability works when their methods and their results are backed by authority. There has to be a Solomon to judge; the evidence does not provide the judgment by itself. In the present circumstances the appeal to science is made because of the absence of respect for any adjudicator. Solomon's role is not acceptable. The very idea that there could be a technical solution to a disagreement about goals and purposes shows that political reconciliation is rejected. The predictable consequence of using science in politics is that both sides consult their own scientific experts. Peter Huber describes how fringe calls to fringe: peripheral movements take technical advice from peripheral science and force a split between center and frontier. His own vivid warning that frontier science is barren is a form of modified discredit for science itself. When science is used to arbitrate in these conditions, it eventually loses its independent status, and like other high priests who mix politics with ritual, finally disqualifies itself. This process has been powerfully described in Brian Wynne's book on the connection between hazardous waste and the sociology of knowledge.[7]

If the scales of cultural change are tipping toward a more pervasive individualism, it is not because it is being imposed upon us. We who are the debaters in the forum of culture bring it about because we wish it. If the foundations of knowledge have come to seem more precarious, it is because we have been quietly undermining them. In doing so we are responding to the opportunities of the global industrial system. Every small shift in the legal structure can be assessed for its preserving or dismantling the edifice of structured solidarity. Pushing toward the culture of individualism puts knowledge into the forefront of political competition, just because that culture is incompatible with either authority or structure. Whoever bewails the results should consider the alternatives. Harvey Sapolsky's depiction of the political system itself as a health hazard for Americans is wonderfully to the point, but notice that in this perspective every political system is a health hazard, one way or another, for someone or other. The best way to stay cool about health and other hazards is to be self-aware about the choice between cultures.

MINORITY RISKS

One of the major policy issues that emerges from a survey of the debates on risk is the fear that those who are already disadvantaged will suffer more. The poor who carry the brunt often carry the blame for epidemic disaster. According to Paul Slack, in the Great Plague the majority of the English well-to-do saw the incidence of plague as the sign of God's judgment directed against the sins of the poor:

> The danger of contagion was employed to justify the new social policies of sixteenth century municipalities . . . . the isolation procedures taken against the plague would not have been so savage if the poor had not presented a conspicuous target which was subject to attack for other reasons. It is significant that plague regulations were most clearly and strictly formulated when the socially discriminatory disease became conspicuous.[8]

It may be a general trait of human society that fear of danger tends to strengthen the lines of division in a community. If that is so, the response to a major crisis digs more deeply the cleavages that have been there all the time. This will mean that if there is a big inequality of wealth, the poor will suffer more than if the distribution were more equitable. If there is violent xenophobia, the foreigners will be blamed and pogrommed more. Today there is concern about the political scapegoating of homosexuals.

Widdus, Meheus, and Short ask whether, if marginal groups and poor inhabitants of inner cities are specially at risk from sexually transmitted diseases, there may be a tendency to forget about them. The answer emphatically is yes, if the culture is individualist. Since it is inherently difficult to be aware of liminal groups in a society organized under the principles of competitive individualism, it is easier to write them off as human derelicts. Hierarchy does not necessarily perform better, but it is capable of being more aware of minority interests, because it is a political system for incorporating subgroups. Each culture discriminates, but the hierarchical one does it overtly, handing out group badges of difference; the individualist one does it covertly, by ignoring the powerless. If the existence of the minority is not acknowledged, even the scale of its problems is not assessable: the figures are not there. A minority in a well-run hierarchy should find it easier to organize its own consciousness of difference. It must be harder to become a vote to be reckoned with in a system that withholds overt recognition to minority segments. For us it is hard to imagine beggars organizing their own union, but in Islamic cities in Africa that is normal practice.

David Richards says of the age-old tendency to moralize danger from AIDS that it:

> adds a patina of public-health justification to what is essentially a kind of heresy persecution of homosexuals as moral heretics to the family. . . . The idea of moral plague is today a morally inexcusable failure of elementary standards of intellectual and moral responsibility.[9]

The word *today* in that sentence implies that persecution of moral deviants in the name of the dangers they spread is a primitive form of behavior which does not belong in the modern world. Similarly, Dorothy Nelkin and Sander Gilman explain stigmatizing of deviants by an individual need to escape reality. Like Richards, they also find it old-fashioned and inappropriate today to moralize and politicize danger:

> Despite the sophisticated scientific understanding underlying conceptions of disease in the late twentieth century, we still seek explanations based on behavior, ethnicity, or social stereotypes.[10]

There is nothing old-fashioned or exclusively primitive about social stereotyping. To assert that it is anomalous in our day is sheer cultural innocence. They are objecting to culture; they are saying that it should not still be with us. In asking for the discourse on danger to unload its ancient moral freight, they are innocently asking for the community of perfect love. Are they asking us outright to stop all exclusionary behavior, or are they asking us to try not to notice the stigma?

An individualist culture finds ways of making its disadvantaged members disappear from sight. To stop stigmatizing would be another way of making them invisible. It would only help the stigmatized if there was a welcoming community into which they could be incorporated. In default of that welcome and alleviation of wrong, removing stigma could only make the privileged members of the community feel more comfortable. It would have the effect of drawing a veil over the sorrows of aliens and the poor and the deviants. For them to be unclassified would result in their being unrecognized[11] but then their harms would remain unremedied. In a society organized by wealth, how hard it is to bring down barriers between rich and poor, to propose laws against residential zoning or to find work for the unemployed. There are real wrongs, and stigma is not the worst of them.

Stigma is interesting as a self fulfilling prophecy. Prejudiced and exclusionary behavior validates itself. The urban poor are housed in crime-infested districts with unpoliced subways, ill-lit streets, damp walls, and malodorous drains. They are more infectious in their bodies, more exposed to disease and mutilating accidents at work, with a shorter life expectancy. The stigma is not a false symbol of contamination: the sign is true and it is the condition of the stigmatized to be contaminating.

The underlying problem in talking about exposure to risk is still justice. Cultural analysis is a countervailing vision which warns what categories in each kind of culture are most likely to be at risk, who will be sinned against, and who will be counted as the sinner exposing the others to risk. It is true, as Charles Rosenberg says:

> Cultural values and social location have always provided the materials for self-serving constructions of epidemiological risk. The poor, the alien, the sinner have all served as convenient objects for such stigmatizing speculations.[12]

What is not true is that the same speculations are found in all cultures. In an individualist culture, the weak are going to carry the blame for what happens to them; in a hierarchy, the deviants; in a sect, aliens and also faction leaders. It behooves us therefore to try to know as much as possible about the different cultures in which the idea of risk is put to use even if it is only in order to know whether we are saying the same as everyone else.

ENDNOTES

[1]Denis Duclos, *La Peur et le Savoir: La Société Face à la Science, la Technique et leurs Dangers* (Paris: Editions de la Decouverte, 1989).

[2]Ian Hacking, *The Emergence of Probability, a Philosophical Study of Early Ideas about Probability, Induction and Statistical Inference* (Cambridge: Cambridge University Press, 1975).

[3]Ernest Gellner, *Nations and Nationalism* (Oxford: Basil Blackwell, 1984), 37–38.

[4]Mary Douglas and Aaron Wildavsky, *Risk and Culture* (Berkeley: University of California Press, 1982).

[5]Langdon Winner, "Pollution as Delusion," *New York Times Book Review* (August 1982): 8, 18; M. Kaprow, "Manufacturing Danger: Fear and Pollution in Industrial Society," *American Anthropologist* 87 (1985): 357–64; Brandon Johnson and Vincent Covello, "The Social and Cultural Construction of Risk: Essays on Risk Selection and Perception" (Netherlands: Reidel, 1987), viii: "According to this view, risk is not an objective reality."

[6]Mary Douglas, *How Institutions Think* (Syracuse, N.Y.: Syracuse University Press, 1986).

[7]Brian Wynne, *Risk Management and Hazardous Waste, Implementation and the Dialectics of Credibility* (Berlin: Springer, 1987).

[8]Paul Slack, "Response to Plague," *Social Research* 55 (3) (1988): 433–53.

[9]David A. Richards, "Human Rights, Public Health and the Idea of Moral Plague," *Social Research* 55 (3) (1988): 492–528.

[10]Dorothy Nelkin and Sander Gilman, "Placing Blame for Devastating Disease," *Social Research* 55 (3) (1988): 378.

[11]Paul Starr, "Social Categories and Claims in the Liberal State" (unpublished).

[12]Charles Rosenberg, "The Definition and Control of a Disease," *Social Research* 55 (3) (1988): 329.

Theodore J. Lowi

Risks and Rights in the History of American Governments

In their original letter of October 1988, our conveners observed, in good New England understatement, that "risk is something of a popular subject these days." Why? Our colleague Mary Douglas has her own explanation in our first article, but it can't be left to her alone because the explanation is part of the problem—and the problem is the politics of risk allocation. Risk has returned to the public policy agenda and to public discourse either because objective conditions affecting risk have changed significantly, or because ideology and values regarding the distribution of risk have changed. My explanation rests upon both, but more heavily upon the latter.

Three factors can be singled out. The first factor is the return of laissez-faire ideology to a place of respectability and influence in public discourse. The second is the democratization of risk-control and risk-indemnification policies, spreading advantages from the upper to the lower classes. Third is the still more recent movement toward public policies that convey the benefits of risk regulation as a matter of right.

As for the first, the societal benefits of individual risk taking is a well-known element of nineteenth-century liberalism. As that brand of liberalism (later erroneously relabeled conservatism) returned through the efforts of people like Milton Friedman to the inner circle of Republican administrations, the virtues of risk taking would

Theodore J. Lowi is John L. Senior Professor of American Institutions at Cornell University.

become well advertised once again. There is a self-evident relation among risk taking, profit, and productivity, and to deliberately eliminate the element of personal risk from economic endeavor would almost certainly affect the other two variables, profit and productivity. However, the extent and character of this relationship is heavily steeped in myth. When the Reaganauts came to power and looked with fear and loathing on the efforts of past administrations to create a "risk-free society," they were tapping deep wells of American emotion. No matter that those who spoke loudest against risk-alleviating policies were among society's most risk-insulated persons.

The second factor, democratization, is another ideological point, or, let us say, an objective fact magnified by ideology. The democratization of risk can happen at either extreme of the continuum of risk. At one extreme, risk can be democratized whenever every member of society is subject to the same dangers, as in the case of total war. Everyone is expected to pitch in, everyone puts everything up for sacrifice, including life itself, and, thanks to modern delivery systems, everyone has about an equal chance of being injured. Policy can move society away from democratization of risk at this extreme of the continuum by adopting policies exempting certain categories of persons from jeopardy, permitting the wealthy to pay for others to take risk in their place, and so on. At the other end of the continuum, risk can be democratized by policies that spread toward everyone the deliberate, collective protections from risk, or at least from the cost of injuries that mount as the level of risk increases. The welfare state itself can be defined as the partial democratization of risk in those terms. In response to the significant expansion of welfare state programs in the late 1960s, complaints began to emerge about the costs of risk control. As one critic put it:

> A new social order has evolved that started with a reliance by citizens on government for the solution to certain . . . problems and has grown to include pressures on government to mitigate almost every risk any individual might be asked to bear. . . . [There is a movement] away from reliance on the rational individual as a . . . bearer of the consequences of his choice to a socially determined allocation . . . designed to shift responsibility for both new and existing risks from individual to society.[1]

This is the stuff myths are made of. It suggests that there was a time when all individuals were the sole bearers of the consequences of their own choices. But the fact remains that risk shifting through collective means is as old as government itself and that what appears new is the effort to spread some of the advantage of risk shifting to the lower classes.

The third factor is the most relevant and the most true, yet the least appreciated. Recent policies reallocating risk and the responsibilities and costs of risks have been framed in such a way as to convey rights to the beneficiaries. Thus, where once the distribution of risk was a political question—whether in the hands of governments or private institutions—these questions have been increasingly taken out of the political process. This has rigidified the work of governing institutions and has become a means of delegitimizing politics itself, first by narrowing the universe of politics and second by creating expectations that cannot possibly be met. Each of these factors will be taken in turn.

BALANCING THE BOOKS ON RISK TAKERS AND PRIVATE MARKETS

In the 1880s, Illinois adopted a statute which, among other things, provided for regulation of rates charged by interstate railroads for that segment of the trip taking place within the state of Illinois. The Supreme Court held that the statute was unconstitutional on the grounds that the interstate trip could not be arbitrarily broken up into segments and that, therefore, the Illinois law was an unconstitutional burden on interstate commerce.[2] Within a decade the Supreme Court invalidated still other state efforts to regulate the conditions (risks) of work, the safety (risks) of plants and their machines, the working hours of women, and the working conditions of children. The Court held that, although the Constitution reserved all powers to the states that were not explicitly delegated to the national government, the states could not adopt "unreasonable" regulations and certainly could not interfere with the right of individual employees and individual employers to negotiate individual contracts for labor.[3] During this epoch of more than forty years, the United States was clearly the least regulated of any major industrial nation. The states could not regulate and the national government would not. It was the golden age of the myth of the free market, of freely operating entrepreneurs, and of voluntarily assumed risk.

But risk taking was counterbalanced by a wide variety of public policies dedicated to risk control, risk reduction, and risk shifting. These policies were not fully seen or appreciated as the debit side of a fully balanced accounting of the history of risk, because we were a strict federal system, and because virtually all of these interventionist policies were products of state legislatures.

People who embrace the myth of free markets driven by risk takers operate on the general assumption that if government would leave things alone, people using reason would risk what they have in order to get more, and in the process would produce more for society than if politicians ordained the outcome. But if, as observers, we use an equivalent amount of reason to analyze the behavior of risk takers, we would recognize fairly quickly that few people will habitually take risks to improve on what they have unless certain minimum conditions are met beforehand. Sociologists would call them functional prerequisites. A more accessible term would be *presuppositions*—that is, holders of wealth would be unwilling to put it voluntarily at risk unless they could presuppose certain states of affairs in advance of their entry to the market.

The following is a list of some of those presuppositions that have in fact been met historically and frequently by governments. The listing does not pretend to be an exhaustive or a logical scheme. Its purpose is to balance the books on the history of risk in America.

Provisions for Law and Order

Predictability in human affairs obviously precedes everything else. Risk itself is a probability statement about the extent of danger in an otherwise orderly environment. Although market regularities may contribute to social order, markets cannot exist in the first place without it. And the social order is more than the order imposed by military means, important as that is. Max Weber, in his important *General Economic History* (published in English in 1927), observed that an important presupposition for the existence of modern capitalism is what he called "calculable law." As he observed, "The royal 'cheap justice' with its remissions by royal grace introduce continual disturbances into the calculations of economic life." In a word, precisely the heavy hand that Adam Smith was objecting to. This bleeds over into the next several points.

Provisions for Property

Property is a legal fiction. It is a synthesis word for all the laws against trespass. Through this process, the government renders highly probable that we can enjoy real dominion over that which we claim as our own. Philosophy and ideology may guide legislators, courts, and citizens in the policies and provisions they support regarding property; and an unregulated free market may set the price of property. But property itself is nothing more than a residuum of all the things that the state does to permit me to call something my own and to have a reasonable probability of making it stick. "The market" comes after the risk of property ownership itself has been close to eliminated.

Provisions for Contract Enforcement

One of the world's great social revolutions, first described by Sir Henry Maine, was the transformation from status to contract. Contract became increasingly necessary for an economic system as people dealt increasingly with strangers, involving exchanges beyond their communities and their statuses. A contract is simply an agreement to control some specified aspect of the future. In other words, a contract is a means of controlling and channeling the risk inherent in every exchange. But just as it is impossible to imagine transactions today without contracts, it is impossible to imagine contracts without some close-to-absolute assurance that "the state" will make breach of contract more expensive than observance.

Honoring contracts, of course, has become a habit in advanced industrial societies. This is definitely an aspect of civil society. But it is a habit derived from routine enforcement by governments. There are some absolutists who would argue that free markets are enough in themselves to establish and maintain contracts without state intervention. There are two things wrong with that argument. First, when pushed, such an argument reveals an assumption that courts will be involved and that somehow courts are not part of the state. Second, it tends to play down the category of persons who don't care about reputation because they don't care about making a second contract after the first one in which they can make a large killing and then escape a particular market altogether. There is probably no half way in a matter of this importance: *either* entrepreneurs must be able to assume that mechanisms for contract enforcement work, *or* modern private markets won't work.

Provisions for Exchange

Although contract is at the very center of any conception of exchange, there are still other matters that lie behind contract, making contract itself possible. In brief, there has to be an agreed-upon language or terms by which contracts are written. The best simplification of this very complex process can be provided in the concept of *standardization*. This comes in at least two forms.

First, there has to be a legal language, a very formalized, conventionalized, in a word, standardized, set of references, to eliminate as many ambiguities as possible that are likely to arise between and among people who haven't lived a lifetime together or who would like to gain some advantage later by words that may have special and advantageous meaning.

The second form of standardization is provision for a technical language. Law itself is technical; the distinction intended here has to do with those concepts and terms that precisely describe qualities of the goods of services to be exchanged by the contract. Standards for establishing universal weights and measures are the most fundamental, and the most likely to be provided by government. Although a lot of standardization nowadays is accomplished by private means, mainly through trade associations, these trade associations are themselves private governments which exist outside the market in order to shape the market in one way or another; moreover, their standards are validated and upheld by governments through the statutory route and through the application of those standards in adjudication.

Provisions for Conveyance of Public Domain to Private Hands

The United States has gone so far in conveying public domain to private hands that few Americans are aware of the historic, market-creating role played by government through the subdivision and "privatization" of domain that was in public hands by right of conquest. It is also not generally appreciated in the United States the degree to which any government maintains the right to set conditions on conveyance of ownership and on the use of that which had been conveyed. There is in fact a continuum of private ownership, ranging from freehold to leasehold; and there is a continuum of ownership depending on what proportion of mineral rights, rights-of-way, or air rights have been retained as public domain. Many countries with as good a record of free-market capitalism as the United States set far more strict public limits, in these terms, on the degree to which private property is really private. From public health to public order, all of these conditions on conveyance are risk related.

A still less appreciated category of conveyance of public domain to private hands—and one highly related to risk control—is the conveyance of *privilege* rather than of real estate. This kind of conveyance is best known as licensing. A license is a grant of a privilege by a sovereign to do something that is otherwise illegal. Licensing, with all its abuses, is a quintessential public function in virtually all sectors of the private sphere from private professional services, such as law and medicine, to the key institution of capitalism itself, the corporation. Licensing and risk reduction are so closely associated as to be almost synonymous. Governments use licensing to restrict entry into particular markets in order to limit the number of participants to a level that will help keep prices stable and at a level higher than unrestricted markets might provide. Licensing is also used to redirect entry into a particular market in order to keep it limited to safe competitors and to qualified persons, thereby protecting all consumers from risk in their use of essential services. The corporation itself is a form of license, and it has been sought as a privilege—that is, "limited liability," which is a governmentally protected limit on the risk of all the stockholders. Historically, the corporation was a still more valuable privilege because it was a grant of immortality; a corporation is a fictitious person who can hold property, can sue and be sued, and can perpetuate all of the interests of the stockholders completely independently of their own life spans. The corporate charter was once used as a means of imposing detailed regulations; that is, the state implanted in a specific corporate charter certain limits and obligations on the conduct of that corporation. In that sense, the conveyance was a much more limited one than the present, virtually unconditional corporate charters. But any government could return to the practice of limited corporate charters anytime its legislature chose to adopt such a policy. The fact that governments could use the corporate charter as a means of imposing risk reduction to favor all consumers is an aspect of the democratization of risk that we can look at a bit later.

Provisions for Social Overhead Capital

Social overhead capital refers to the media of exchange, the media of transportation, the media of communications, and the means of national defense. These are also called "public goods" and are generally public functions because the benefits of each cannot be limited to those who paid for them.

Although the phenomenon of public goods or social overhead capital is well understood, it has, to my knowledge, not been sufficiently included in discussions of risk. Yet, nothing comes closer to government involvement in risk control or risk allocation than the provision of social overhead capital. Here is a case where the risk of a bad outcome is virtually certain. Moreover, those with the biggest incentive to take risks in society—e.g., entrepreneurs—are the ones with the greatest incentive to governmentalize these capital functions, in order to guarantee their provision at all and in order to force even the most casual, sporadic, and unlikely users to share the cost. Thus, one of government's core functions can be understood in the context of government and risk control.

Provisions for Meeting the Requirements for Work

This is the regulatory part of social overhead capital. In effect, there would be little risk taken in the private sector, particularly in manufacturing, if entrepreneurs could not assume the availability of workers. Enough people must be available at the appropriate places with appropriate incentives and appropriate skills to work. As literacy became essential for most forms of work, the public had to take this on, and in a virtually universal way, because no industry, regardless of its relative size in a particular community, could afford to provide this public good in order to meet their own particular needs as employers. Before compulsory public schooling, public policies provided sanctions for apprenticeship training and certification where skills were concerned. For the unskilled, laws also provided for control of vagrancy, including forced labor. And just as universal compulsory schooling was the appropriate and logical step to meet the needs of corporate risk control beginning in the late nineteenth century, the welfare state can be seen in the same light a bit later on. The welfare state is a recent effort to solve the ancient and perennial problem of how to save people from starvation without lowering their incentive to work. Workers have used their numbers in politics to reduce their risk of starvation. Their political success got for them what Piven and Cloward call a "right of subsistence" that has enabled marginal workers to refuse certain types of employment or not to work at all. This adds a great deal of uncertainty to employers, but can be balanced by other public policies, ranging from occasional severe retrenchment in welfare to relaxed immigration regulations and to union busting. All three of these reactions to welfare advances have had an important place in recent American history, and all of them can be seen as the intimate involvement of American government in regulating the risks that are peculiar to an industrial/proletarian economy.

Some Reflections on Traditional Risk-Control Policies

Review of these categories of traditional public policies motivated by risk control turns up some interesting impressions. First, modern economies would be unimaginable without provisions of the sort outlined above. Second, the role of government in the United States is comparable to that of any Western government. We must quickly add a third observation, which is that the U.S. is close to unique in the degree to which the public policies that are involved are not the policies of the national government but are those of the state governments. This is surely an important reason why we have been able to maintain an anti-state, free-market ideology and self-conception. Much of the traditional government activity, particularly in the area of risk regulation, simply escaped notice. And since, until quite recently, Americans tended to view common-law courts as umpires in the private markets rather than as instruments of "the state," Americans were all the more able to develop the myth that we had a risk-taking market system free of government.

Fourth and finally, a review of these traditional risk-control policies tends to lead toward a conclusion virtually opposite prevailing wisdom, which holds that there is an inverse relationship between risk control and risk taking, as though people become more and more risk averse as risk-control policies spread. Many's the best seller that pumps up entrepreneurial egos with the argument that people get soft if they are protected, that willingness to take risks is built into a person's character, and that risk aversion is for sissies. Yet, the long history and extent of public risk-control policies—and especially their continuation and expansion during the great epoch of nineteenth-century American risk taking—suggest that the relationship between risk control and risk taking, rather than being inverse, is direct, the one depending upon the other. This will be put in proportion in the next section.

DEMOCRATIZATION

One additional category of public policies toward risk remains to be identified: provision for the allocation of responsibility for the injuries attributable to risk taking.

The Allocation of Responsibility

This category is as old as the others; nevertheless, it is a category apart from the others. The seven identified above are categories of risk control which introduce the indispensable element of predictability in human affairs, and each of the categories controls risk in ways that permit the channeling of risk taking into their most productive directions for the society. But all that leaves one vast source of danger to risk takers, most particularly in highly developed market economies. That danger is the responsibility for the unintended consequences of risk taking in ordinary economic activity. No sane person would enter a market conscientiously if all responsibility for injury were personal and if there were no limit to that responsibility as identifiable products or services passed through the economy.

Western law is rich in public policies allocating responsibility for injuries attributable to risk taking. In the precapitalist epoch of American law, which lasted well into the nineteenth century, the pattern of allocation of responsibility was basically communitarian. Those were simpler times, where dealings were mainly among people in the same community and where agreements were consensual rather than contractual. Morton Horwitz, in his masterful book on this period, quotes an 1816 treatise to the effect that "the master's relation to the apprentice stood '*in loco parentis.*' "[4] Richard Epstein, perhaps the most righteous of laissez-faire legal historians, agrees with the liberal Horwitz that "accidents arising out of [these] consensual arrangements . . . rested, if at all, upon [an implicit] promise by the defendant employer to compensate the plaintiff employee for the injuries sustained."[5] In another essay, Epstein goes on to generalize that the pre-1840s theory was one of "strict liability [which] holds the defendant [the risk taker] *prima facie* liable for the harm caused. . . ."[6] And he defines strict liability as holding "the defendant *prima facie* liable for the harm caused whether or not . . . the defendant intended to harm the plaintiff or failed to take reasonable steps to avoid inflicting the harm." Cases that went to court were generally treated with such communally oriented rules as: the passive party has the stronger right; conversely, responsibility should be borne by the party who set the action in motion; or, who can best bear the cost of the innovation? Communal solutions such as these tended to be conservative, indeed anticapitalist, since the burden of risk fell most often on the innovator, the entrepreneur, the risk taker.

Reference to this earlier period is made primarily in order to underscore two points: first, that the approach to responsibility for risk taking that most Americans profess—individual blame and fault—did not exist always and forever; and second, that questions of responsibility for injuries attributable to innocent risk taking are basic questions of public policy and are neither natural to the market nor generated directly by the market.

The 1840s turning of the corner into the epoch of tort can be summarized as "no liability without fault." As Horwitz defines it, tort law replaced the earlier "common law assumption that individuals were presumed liable for all injury resulting from risk-creating activity" with a new policy focusing responsibility "exclusively [on] the immediate question of which party's carelessness had brought the injury about."[7]

This may sound like a Magna Carta for risk-taking capitalists. Stress upon individual blame and fault required documentation and good lawyers to argue convincingly before courts, whose judges were either drawn from the class of risk takers or were committed to progress. Moreover, there were a number of legal principles developed in the tort field that would tend to give employers and operators and other risk takers the upper hand. Take, for example, the doctrine of "contributory negligence." Even where the employer/proprietor/risk taker was clearly the active party and could, especially under traditional understandings, be held responsible for the injury, he could win the case if the injured party contributed to the injury, even in a small way, for example by being in the wrong place, by a show of evidence of drinking on the job, by not paying attention, and so on.[8] Friedman identifies several other such methods by which the responsibility for injuries could be displaced by law from the risk taker to the victim of the risk taker's actions.[9] All of this led Friedman and Horwitz to the conclusion that the actual policy-allocating responsibility for injury that underlay the tort law was a policy of displacing onto the victim a maximum proportion of the risk of the industrial revolution.[10]

Although research by other scholars does not confirm this conclusion,[11] all the scholars tend to agree on the principle of allocation of responsibility that prevailed for the rest of the nineteenth century and on into the twentieth century: take your risks and accept responsibility for your negligence. However, myths to the contrary notwithstanding, this was not to remain fixed. Cases that cascaded before state courts during the high-growth period of industrialization and mechanization put every American judge and jury in conflict over the immediate consequences of any decision made about risk and injury. Verdicts consistently favoring entrepreneurs and risk takers would leave a lot of widows and orphans dependent on the community. Yet, verdicts consistently favoring victims would give a community the reputation of being against progress. Obviously, judges engaged in a lot of balancing between communal and individualist values. This surely helps explain why the analysis of tort cases will not present a clear picture of class bias in favor of the entrepreneur or in favor of the victims. But in addition, these efforts at balancing conflicting values over the allocation of responsibility for injuries drew the courts more and more into roles that were perilously like those played by state legislatures—ultimately contributing to the decline of the very ethic of individualism on which the tort system of responsibility was based. As courts became increasingly willing to take "community effects" into account, they were not only engaging in a form of policy making, they were softening the individualist ethic itself.

Courts were both a cause and a reflection of a fundamental change in the opinions held, as well as the policies adopted, by American society regarding the allocation of responsibility for the injuries that flow from ordinary risk taking.[12] As the courts were beginning to take community effects into account in the balancing of individual claims by injured plaintiffs against the offending defendants, the social sciences, for example, were beginning to define the individual in terms of a larger social matrix rather than as a freewheeling character in control of his or her own fate. Space limitations permit only a couple of brief passages from the social sciences and one passage from a court case to indicate the emergence of a new approach toward the allocation of responsibility for risk taking. The first is an observation by Richard Ely, one of the founding fathers of the American Economic Association (AEA). Claiming that the AEA was organized out of the rejection of laissez-faire, he observed that "more and more we are becoming increasingly dependent upon others, and more and more this dependence was becoming interdependence. The forces of life were getting beyond the control of individuals." Twenty-five years later John Dewey echoed this observation with his own, that it "is no exaggeration to speak of a 'new age of human relations' . . . . The invasion of the community by the new and relatively impersonal and mechanical modes of combined human behavior is the outstanding fact of modern life."[13]

Just under two decades after Dewey made his observation, the California Supreme Court confronted the following case: a waitress was injured when a Coke bottle exploded while she was handling it. Although she could show no sign of negligence on the part of Coca Cola Bottling Company, the Court accepted her claim on the basis of the following argument:

> I believe the manufacturer's negligence should no longer be singled out as the basis of a plaintiff's right to recover. . . . [I]t should now be recognized that a manufacturer incurs an absolute liability when an article he has placed on the market, knowing that it is to be used without inspection, proves to have a defect that causes injury to human beings. . . . Even if there is no negligence . . . public policy demands that responsibility be fixed wherever it will most effectively reduce the hazards to life and health inherent in defective products that reach the market . . . . The cost of an injury and the loss of time or health may be an overwhelming misfortune to the person injured, and a needless one, for the risk of injury can be insured by the manufacturer and distributed among the public as a cost of doing business. It is to the public interest to discourage the marketing of products having defects that are

> a menace to the public. . . . However intermittently such injuries may occur . . . the risk of their occurrence is a constant risk and a general one. Against such a risk there should be a general and constant protection and the manufacturer is best situated to afford such protection.[14]

The California case suggests that the ethical shift had gone far beyond what was necessary to handle the injury to the waitress. The ethical shift was virtually a rejection of the purely individual blame-and-fault policy of the nineteenth century. Tort is obviously a category of continuing importance in American law. But the general policy toward the allocation of responsibility for injury resulting from the normal process of market economics and risk taking in America has been reduced to a much smaller domain. To state the case conservatively, there is a new policy toward risk that is at least as important in American society as tort, and may indeed be more important. Putting it in the extreme, in order to clarify the more subtle distinctions that will be made below, the new policy is a no-fault policy. Through courts and through legislation, the issue of whether to favor the employer/risk taker or to favor the victim was obviated by accepting a certain level of risk, to permit injuries to happen, and then to indemnify the victim. This is virtually a universal policy in the industrialized economies, although countries can vary significantly in terms of the generosity of the indemnification or the method of financing it. To summarize, the direction of development was from individual responsibility to interdependence, from individual blame to distributional balance, from liability to risk, and from negligence defined as "no liability without fault" to the dropping of negligence altogether in favor of ability to pay, spread through insurance and through customer markup, toward the concept of "social costs." All of this can be understood as the socialization of risk and the democratization of the costs of risk taking. The very concept of risk is indicative of the new universe of ethics. Risk takes the emphasis off discrete acts and places it on the probability of occurrence.

Insurance is probably the ultimate statement of the new social policy toward risk and responsibility. Well into the nineteenth century, the general attitude in the law was that people should not be able to insure themselves for injuries caused by their own negligence.

The illustrious Chancellor Kent stated such a position in 1828, that "the better opinion [is that] the insurer is not liable for . . . damage [which] may be prevented by due care . . . ."[15] In other words, the attitude toward responsibility for injury in the middle nineteenth century was so individualized that the cost of an injury could not be displaced. Consequently, the first casualty insurance company in the U.S. was not founded until 1864, and by 1898, there were only fourteen companies sharing casualty premiums of a mere $11 million.[16]

The spread of liability insurance bears, in at least four ways, upon the phenomenon of the democratization of risk and of responsibility for injuries attributable to risk taking. First, liability insurance is a mechanism of risk management, and as such it confirms the earlier observation that risk control and risk taking are directly rather than inversely related. The fact that most liability insurance has been provided by the private sector is irrelevant to the point being made here, which is that risk and responsibility are being socialized. Second, insurance even more directly produces or contributes to the socialization of risk by blurring or requiring the blurring of the harsh contours of individual responsibility. To put this another way, insurance provides a direct route to socialization of risk (which is not intended to be a synonym for socialism) by translating moral questions of responsibility into instrumental questions of cost. Risk itself is a very instrumental concept which would have an entirely different meaning, if any meaning at all, in the earlier context of individual fault and blame. Third, once insurance is in the picture, a larger universe is greatly superior to a smaller one. This is the reverse of the situation with risk regulation that works through individual responsibility, where the universe must be narrowed successively until a particular person and particular set of causes are located. When the question is one of probability, as it is in insurance, the universe is best extended to all past and future injuries, however classified. This is desirable so that everyone can help pay the indemnity; and it is necessary if statistics are to produce dependable predictions and equitable premium payments. Fourth, once injury becomes a matter of indemnification and insurance, and once it is recognized that the larger universe is to be preferred for the purpose, the step to governmentalization of part or all of the responsibility—or, underwriting part or all of the risk—is not a very big one at all.

The welfare state was America's most advanced and mature expression of the shift of ethic or policy toward allocation of responsibility for injuries attributable to risk taking. And although a metaphor, the welfare state is an appropriate metaphor. Welfare as a state enjoyed legitimacy across all classes of people. It had its own sources of revenue. It had its own means of coercion. And the members of the welfare state were citizens with rights—legislative rather than constitutional, but rights nevertheless. Almost exactly forty years after its founding, the welfare state seemed to come unstuck, and popular consensus seemed to collapse because of the democratization of the welfare state in the 1960s; the "safety net" was extended to and expanded for people who were completely outside the capitalist system—particularly to poor blacks, poor women, their children, and the dependent elderly. This gave rise to a new theology—or the revival of an old one—which rested on the gospel of hard work and the faith that to protect people from risk is to damn them to perdition. The risk-free society could be a form of hell on earth.

But the new theology didn't work. The welfare state was here to stay. President Reagan vowed to honor the safety net. David Stockman, the radical made wise by his disappointment, reflected on his experience in his remarkable memoir: "The abortive Reagan Revolution proved that the American electorate wants a moderate social democracy to shield it from capitalism's rougher edges."[17] The welfare state had been institutionalized. It was institutionalized by the acceptance and eventually the embrace of a succession of Democratic and Republican administrations, and it was institutionalized by the broad acceptance of the new social ethic: the very concept of risk had already taken the morality out of responsibility and had made the consequences of risk—injury—a merely instrumental matter. Risk had been socialized—or, to put it more pointedly, risk had socialized capitalism. But a third factor behind the institutionalization of the welfare state was that it had proven itself immune to the sermons of the lay ministers of the old middle-class Protestant ethic. The sermons of the rich are not very meaningful to the poor as long as the rich are themselves so well protected against risk. Successful people do take risks in America, but in a very carefully constructed, minimax framework. Dramatic examples of governmentally sponsored risk management for the well-off are as recent as the $500 billion cost of the savings and loan safety net.

Risk theologists were sending the wrong message. Columnist Ellen Goodman once observed that, in America, to get people to work we provide punishments for the poor and incentives for the well-off. *Incentive*, being derived from the Latin *incinere,* refers to anything that arouses feeling. America should be thinking about the democratization of incentives. Risk may then take care of itself.

RISKS AND RIGHTS

The 1980s attack on the welfare state was a tale of a tub. Safety nets for the poor, as for the rich, posed no serious threat to American character, family ties, or the work ethic. Yet meanwhile, there was a real threat to the legitimacy of risk and of risk management, and it has received almost no attention at all. I refer to the efforts arising out of the late 1960s to bring the concept of risk into the making of regulatory laws concerning the prevention of harm.

Between 1969 and 1974, the United States Congress went on a regulation binge. Depending on the method of enumeration, one could say that the number of important regulatory programs enacted during those five years exceeded those enacted during the seven premobilization years of the New Deal. And beyond any question of enumeration, the scale and coverage of the regulatory programs adopted during this second period of regulatory creativity greatly exceeded the first. This is an opening insight into why observers sought to distinguish this period from the New Deal by labeling the policies of the second period "social regulation." What was special about the policies and why did they contribute to the delegitimization of all regulatory policies and help put laissez-faire and the ideology of risk back up high on the public agenda?

First, then, why the adoption of regulatory programs on such an expanded scale? Twenty years ago I addressed this question and came up with a partial answer. I recognized that there had been a secular trend beginning early in this century to delegate more and more discretion to agencies in the exercise of regulatory powers. The movement was from concreteness to abstraction, and the definition of the problem tended from specific to general in the designation of conduct to be included, and from closed- to open-ended, verging on the universal, in the possible causes or sources of the injuries to be prevented.[18]

This pattern continued to hold through the 1970s and helped explain the collapse of public support for public regulation. However, my earlier treatment failed to recognize the underlying forces that drove this development. Since that time, I have been able to identify three highly relevant factors. The first of these is the insurance base of the American philosophy of welfare.[19] As observed earlier, insurance, in contrast to regulation, works best in the largest possible definition of the universe of conduct. But going beyond that, an insurer, including a government insurer, develops a very special point of view. Insurance may be the only enterprise where the patron is more concerned than the client for the welfare of the client. This is not for reasons of altruism but out of a keen concern for keeping costs under control. Consequently, as the United States government expanded the policies for indemnifying victims of risk taking in the economy, concern for the absolute level of injury and for the cost of injury spread at the same rate, if not faster. Except for maximum hours and minimum wages legislation in the 1930s, the national government did little through policy to abate risk of injury to workers until the late 1960s, culminating in the 1970 Occupational Safety and Health Act (OSHA). Incredibly large in scope and in expectation, the law provided that "each employer shall furnish to each of his employees employment and a place of employment which are free from recognized hazards that are causing or likely to cause death or serious physical harm to his employees." Moreover, this protection was intended to cover employees throughout their careers and presumably from substances and experiences (such as noises) whose harmful effects might come only from slow accumulation, long after severance or retirement. The OSHA statute is as broad as it is largely because it had to be co-extensive with the welfare state itself. This is precisely why the term *social regulation* is an appropriate one. But once again it must be said that the reason for extending the scope of the new regulation to the whole society was not sentimentality but cost control, which followed logically the welfare state's acceptance of injury as a system for purposes of indemnification.

This leads to the second factor driving the extension of the scope of regulation to the breadth of the whole society. This factor is the rise of professional knowledge. Amateur knowledge is knowledge arising out of sensory experience. Professional knowledge is knowledge based on formal agreements about experience. Professional knowledge is formal knowledge that is organized around concepts and definitions of reality agreed upon in advance. Though tied eventually to the senses, every effort is made to transcend the senses. This formalization is extremely powerful for analysis of complex problems—that's the secret of its development and enhancement by all the academic disciplines, and also the secret of its success in the bureaucracy. Modern administrative agencies are under particular pressure to routinize information because their broadly delegated responsibilities require constant input of data on all persons and phenomena defined as related to the agency's mission, no matter how remotely. But the same agencies are required to pin down concrete causes for specific effects: this is what regulation is all about, and this is what the rule of law requires. Identifying a specific cause for a specific effect is difficult even in the most advanced sciences. There is more power and efficacy at the system level, where patterns of behavior and causal relations can be dealt with in the aggregate and by probability. This is ideal for insurance and indemnification, as in the welfare state. But it creates fundamental problems in regulation. Defining the jurisdiction of a regulatory agency as a system and obliging the agency to formulate rules and standards for the possible causes of the identified effects produces an explosion of demands for rules—as manifest by the explosion of the number of pages in the *Federal Register.* This leads to the third and most compelling cause of the expanded scope of regulation, and it points to why regulation needs urgently to be reconsidered. When specialists from the agencies and from congressional committee staffs and interest group staffs bring to Congress a proposal for legislation, it is usually based upon lawlike patterns (in the scientific, not the legal sense) drawn from professional knowledge, derived artificially, and confirmed both by statistics and by causal theories with good scientific standing. Members of the relevant congressional committee recognize the described pattern as unanswerable and undebatable (e.g., the relation between a toxic substance and cancer). Although some members of Congress will oppose taking action at all, they will all tend to recognize that no amount of added knowledge can deny the pattern as such. But rather than reject the whole-system, whole-pattern approach and revert to piecemeal legislation on the specific aspects of the problem that are known and directly experienced by amateur members of Congress, Congress will instead enact the pattern as law (in the legal sense). In effect, Congress ordains as a goal the pattern determined by the systems analysis. The following is a paraphrase of the results in law:

> Whereas the best estimates show dirty air [defined in parts per billion], and whereas such air is harmful [defined by a biomedical theory estimating increased lung cancers], now therefore let there come to pass clean air [defined very precisely in parts per billion]. In pursuance of this goal, the agency will make whatever rules and whatever precise standards, using the best available technology, that will give us clean air by [whatever precise date is provided].

This is a new kind of law in the American experience. It calls for the distinction made most clearly by Professor David Schoenbrod of New York Law School between "rules statutes" and "goals statutes," where a rules statute identifies a particular conduct and either restricts or encourages it, and a goals statute ordains the outcome and leaves the rules to the agency.[20]

I take Schoenbrod's distinction a step further with the following two propositions: *Rules statutes convey obligations; goals statutes convey rights.* It is my contention that when Congress enacts a goals statute ordaining a desired outcome—such as clean air, safe consumer products, or safe working conditions—it is conveying a right to that outcome, whether that was intended by Congress or not. The responsible agency will later make rules restricting or encouraging the relevant conduct, but the goals in a goals statute remain as criteria by which agency action is judged, and as a cause of action in the courts against the agency. Since no agency rule can attain more than a tiny fraction of a legislated goal—especially given the grandiose rhetoric by which these goals were expressed in the 1970s statutes—each rule amounts to an inadequate remedy for the right denied by continued lack of the full attainment of the benefits inherent in the legislated goal. The right conveyed by a legislated goal is, of course, not a right in the constitutional sense; it is a legislated right that can be terminated by later legislation. But as long as it stands, the goals statute conveys rights.

This has had a devastating effect on the regulatory agencies, on the federal courts, and on public confidence in government. It has a twofold effect on the agency. First, there is a strong tendency for the agency to turn out rules, rules by the dozens. Here is a second cause of the explosion in the number of rules and rule proposals generated in the 1960s and 1970s. After all, since Congress delegated in the statute the responsibility for a whole, abstractly defined, open-ended system, the agency has no priorities, and everything becomes compelling for them to do. The second effect on the agency is one that is contradictory with the first: a tendency to engage in new research. This is the only way to locate the priorities and to translate the systems concept into concrete situations for purposes of regulation. This delays agency *action* even as it increases agency *activity*. People who are concerned with the activity of that agency will grow impatient and cynical, comparing the grandiose goals with the post-statutory research and comparing the grandiose goals with the flow of relatively trivial rules that seem to bring the agency no closer to the attainment of those goals. As people grow impatient with the lack of real agency progress toward the statutory goals, they can claim the goals as a matter of right and proceed to sue in court for a remedy. This leads to the effect of the goals statute on the courts.

There has been an explosion of litigation in the past couple of decades that has alarmed students of the judicial process and has mobilized conservative critics to attack the federal courts as an "imperial judiciary" operating under the influence of the new "public interest" groups bearing a left-wing program of class legislation and frivolous briefs aimed at changing the capitalist system. The conservative argument strengthened in intensity and in cogency as the federal courts began to liberalize their rules of standing, of class-action suits, and third-party suits, making it possible to sue the United States government (that is, the agency) even when the individual or group did not satisfy the Article III requirement that there be a real "case or controversy" in which the plaintiff had a substantial personal stake in the outcome of the case. It is not necessary, nor would it be possible, to demonstrate that the judges who comprise the federal district and appellate courts are, down to the last soul, eager to seize the kind of power implied by the accusation of being an imperial judiciary, or that these same judges have come under some kind of a left-wing spell. The simpler explanation is that the federal judges are responding to their natural calling: wherever and whenever a right has been denied, there has to be a remedy. If the statute ordains safe factories, that leaves the agency—the government—vulnerable when the safety is not forthcoming. The government is even more vulnerable when the goal is so specifically defined—*x* parts per billion—that the absence of the benefits may be clear for every plaintiff's lawyer literally to see, or smell. If members of Congress do not realize they are conveying rights when they ordain goals, then that is evidence, not that the courts are imperial or that these public-interest-group litigants are socialists, but that the members of Congress are, to be kind, lacking in appreciation of what they are doing.

CONCLUSION

Thus by a long succession of steps have we come to the real reason for the decline of popular support for regulation and the rise of the mythology about the virtues of risk taking and the evils of attempting to create a risk-free society. The problem is not with the welfare state as such, and it is not with the imperial judiciary or with a left-wing plot to subvert capitalism. Nor is the problem with the American people having grown soft and unwilling to work or to save or otherwise to take risks. The problem arose as the national government attempted to adopt policies aimed at dealing with risk and its costs at the level at which risk occurs—the system level. Risk, after all, is a system phenomenon. Risk doesn't really exist at all. Risk is a name we give to unwanted outcomes, and probability is a number we assign to risk. But only about half the problem of what we call risk can be reached at all at the level of risk itself. That half is the welfare state half, or the insurance state, or whatever it might be or become. That half is the effort in the last forty years to democratize the burden of bad outcomes by removing most of the blame and indemnifying as many of the victims as possible. But this half of the public policy approach to risk works precisely because the welfare state, functioning as it does through the reality and the conceptualization of insurance, works best at the level of the largest possible universe. The welfare state was, in effect, made to order for the emergent systems approach to public policy.

The other half of the public policy problem doesn't work at this level, and the persistence of Congress in trying to make it work has not only led to failure of specific programs but also seriously undermined government efforts to deal with the allocation of the burdens of risk or with the overall incidence of bad outcomes attributable to the taking of risks in the society. This is the regulatory half. Regulation requires the imposition of specific rules on specifically defined types of conduct. As far as I can determine, regulation is derived from or is closely related to the French *règle*, rule, and *réglementation,* the imposition of rules upon. These rules have to be general in nature, applying to a category of conduct relating to a particular category of injury or nuisance. But the application of the rule—that is to say, the regulatory process—has to come into focus on quite specific types of conduct. And this means that, almost by nature, regulation cannot be defined in systems terms. In effect, the only real regulatory statute is a "rules statute." And each rules statute has to be piecemeal. It cannot grapple with the system at all but only with specific conducts that may, cumulatively, improve the system someday, somewhere down the line.

In other words, regulation can't deal directly with risk at all. Risk is a system concept, and regulation has to concern itself with specific conduct. The job of determining whether that conduct has altered the level of risk in the society at large is the job of an economist or a statistician, not a policymaker. And if it is the finding of a committee of experts that the level of risk in a given situation—on the highways or in the factory or in the environment—is too high or has been increasing, the worst thing the policymaker can do is to ordain this finding as policy.

This conclusion is paradoxical only to those who can do sophisticated analyses of risk but who, rather than analyze government, merely harangue against it. Everyone wants a safer society. And almost everyone accepts the value of a society of risk takers. But these two values are competitive, and government will inevitably be drawn in to iron out the wrinkles. But government will fail unless policy evaluation precedes risk analysis. And by policy evaluation, I do not mean cost-benefit analysis. I mean *real* policy evaluation, understood as the study of legally definable possibilities, institutional limits, and unanticipated consequences. If there are risks in the society that government may be able to control or reduce, there are risks in the use of government itself. That is the study of risk that has been most neglected.

ENDNOTES

[1]Yair Aharoni, *The No-Risk Society* (Chatham, N.J.: Chatham House, 1981), 1–2.

[2]*Wabash, St. Louis and Pacific Railroad Co. v. Illinois*, 118 U.S. 557 (1886).

[3]*Lochner v. New York*, 198 U.S. 45 (1905).

[4]Morton Horwitz, *The Transformation of American Law, 1780–1860* (Cambridge: Harvard University Press, 1977), 208.

[5]Richard Epstein, "The Historical Origins and Economic Structure of Workers' Compensation Law," *Georgia Law Review* 16 (Summer 1982): 780.

[6]Richard Epstein, *A Theory of Strict Liability: Toward a Reformulation of Tort Law* (San Francisco: Cato Institute, 1980), 5.

[7]Horwitz, 95–96.

[8]Lawrence Friedman, *A History of American Law* (New York: Simon & Schuster, 1973), 409.

[9]Friedman, 409–27 and 262–63.

[10]Horwitz, 210; and Friedman, 416–17.

[11]See, for example, G. Edward White, *Tort Law in America* (Stanford: Stanford University Press, 1980); and Robert Rabin, "The Historical Development of the Fault Principle: A Reinterpretation," *Georgia Law Review,* 15 (1981): 925–61.

[12]Theodore J. Lowi, "The Welfare State: Ethical Foundations and Constitutional Remedies," *Political Science Quarterly* 101 (2) (1986): 197–220.

[13]Quoted in Thomas Haskell, *The Emergence of Professional Social Science* (Urbana: University of Illinois Press, 1977), 252–53.

[14]*Escola v. Coca Cola Bottling Company,* 24 Cal. 2D453 (1944).

[15]Quoted in Horwitz, 202.

[16]Daniel J. Boorstin, *Democracy and Its Discontents* (New York: Random House, 1971), 82.

[17]David A. Stockman, *The Triumph of Politics: Why the Reagan Revolution Failed* (New York: Harper & Row, 1986), 394.

[18]Theodore J. Lowi, *The End of Liberalism* (New York: Norton, 1969), chap. 5.

[19]For an account of this basic insurance point of view among the original participants, see J. Douglas Brown, *An American Philosophy of Social Security* (Princeton: Princeton University Press, 1972).

[20]David Schoenbrod, "Goals Statutes or Rules Statutes: The Case of the Clean Air Act," *UCLA Law Review* 30 (April 1983): 740–828.

Karl Dake and Aaron Wildavsky

Theories of Risk Perception: Who Fears What and Why?

How odd it is that anyone should not see that all observation must be for or against some view if it is to be of any service.

—Charles Darwin

IN SOCIAL SCIENCE RIVAL THEORIES seeking to answer the same questions rarely confront one another. Indeed, a variety of perspectives has been employed in research on public perception of risk, but alternative formulations remain largely untested. Missing most of all is a focused comparison of rival hypotheses.

One could hardly find many subjects that are better known or considered more important to more people nowadays than the controversies over harm to the natural environment and the human body attributed to modern technology, whether this be from chemical carcinogens or nuclear power or noxious products introduced by industry into the land, sea, or air, or into water or food supplies. Thus we ask: Why are products and practices once thought to be safe (or

Karl Dake is Research Associate at the Institute of Personality Assessment and Research, University of California at Berkeley.

Aaron Wildavsky is Professor of Political Science and Public Policy, University of California at Berkeley.

safe enough) perceived increasingly as dangerous? Who (what sort of people) views technology as largely benign, and who as mostly dangerous? To what degree are different people equally worried about the same dangers, or to what extent do some perceive certain risks as great that others think of as small? And how do concerns across different kinds of risk—war, social deviance, economic troubles as well as technology—vary for given individuals? Only by comparisons across types of danger can we learn whether individuals have a general tendency to be risk averse or risk taking, or whether their perceptions of danger depend upon the meaning they give to objects of potential concern. The test we shall put to each theory of risk perception is its ability to predict and explain what kinds of people will perceive which potential hazards to be how dangerous.

The most widely held theory of risk perception we call *the knowledge theory:* the often implicit notion that people perceive technologies (and other things) to be dangerous because they *know* them to be dangerous. In a critical review of *Risk and Culture,*[1] by Mary Douglas and Aaron Wildavsky, for instance, John Holdren's belief that perceivers are merely registering the actual extent of danger to themselves—the of-course-people-are-worried-they-have-lots-to-worry-about thesis—comes out clearly:

> A much simpler description might suffice: people worry most about the risks that seem most directly to threaten their well being at the moment; environmental concerns predominate only where and when people imagine the risks of violence and economic ruin to be under control. . . . What is wrong, after all, with the simple idea—paralleling Maslow's stages of wants—that worries about more subtle and complex threats will materialize if, and only if, the most direct and obvious threats are taken care of?[2]

If Holdren is correct, perception of danger should accord with what individuals know about the risk in question. But do risk perceptions and knowledge coincide?

Another commonly held cause of risk perception follows from *personality theory*. In conversations we frequently hear personality referred to in such a way that individuals seem to be without discrimination in their risk-aversion or risk-taking propensities: some individuals love risk taking so they take many risks, while others are risk averse and seek to avoid as many risks as they can. We will test this common, if extreme, view. We will also examine a more moderate theory of personality: that stable individual differences among persons are systematically correlated with their perceptions of danger. Leaving aside the extraordinary Oblimov-like characters staying in bed all their lives, or Evel Knievels breaking bones on too-daring feats, this version of personality theory suggests that individuals are so constituted as to take or reject risks in an enduring manner.[3] But do traditionally assessed attributes of personality such as intrapsychic dynamics and interpersonal traits relate to risk perceptions and preferences in predictable ways?

The third set of explanations for public perceptions of danger follow two versions of *economic theory*. In one, the rich are more willing to take risks stemming from technology because they benefit more and are somehow shielded from adverse consequences. The poor presumably feel just the opposite. In "post-materialist" theory, the rationale is reversed, however: precisely because living standards have improved, the new rich are less interested in what they have (affluence) and what got them there (capitalism), than in what they think they used to have (closer social relations), and what they would like to have (better health).[4] Is it true, however, that the newly affluent aspire to post-materialist values, such as interpersonal harmony, and hence fear environmental pollution and chemical contamination?

Other explanations for public reactions to potential hazards are based on *political theory*. These accounts view the controversies over risk as struggles over interests, such as holding office or party advantage. The view of politics as clashing interests connects conflicts to different positions in society. The hope for explanatory power in such approaches to risk perception is thus placed on social and demographic characteristics such as gender, age, social class, liberal-conservative ratings, and/or adherence to political parties.[5]

Viewing individuals as the active organizers of their own perceptions, *cultural theorists* have proposed that individuals choose what to fear (and how much to fear it), in order to support their way of life.[6] In this perspective, selective attention to risk, and preferences among different types of risk taking (or avoiding), correspond to *cultural biases*—that is, to worldviews or ideologies entailing deeply held values and beliefs defending different patterns of social relations. *Social relations* are defined in cultural theory as a small number of distinctive patterns of interpersonal relationships—hierarchical, egalitarian, or individualist.[7] No causal priority is given to cultural biases or social relations; they are always found together interacting in a mutually reinforcing manner. Thus there are no relationships without cultural biases to justify them, and no biases without relations to uphold them.

Socially viable combinations of cultural biases and social relations are referred to in cultural theory as *ways of life* or as *political cultures*. More specifically, then, hierarchical, egalitarian, and individualist forms of social relations, together with the cultural biases that justify them, are each hypothesized to engender distinctive representations of what constitutes a hazard and what does not. Among all possible risks, those selected for worry or dismissal are functional in the sense that they strengthen one of these ways of life and weaken the others. This sort of explanation is at once more political (there is a political purpose to all of this perceiving—defending a way of life and attacking others) and less obvious (what has risk perception to do with ways of life?).

Since cultural biases are forms of ideology, there should be high correlations between certain biases and corresponding ideologies (e.g., egalitarianism and political liberalism). When we vary the kinds of possible dangers to which people react, however, we should see that the left-right distinction captures the cultural bias of egalitarianism but fails to distinguish between hierarchy and individualism. Hence we expect the three cultural biases to predict a broad spectrum of risk perceptions better than political ideology does.

According to cultural theory, adherents of hierarchy perceive acts of social deviance to be dangerous because such behavior may disrupt their preferred (superior/subordinate) form of social relations. By contrast, advocates of greater equality of conditions abhor the role differentiation characteristic of hierarchy because ranked stations signify inequality. Egalitarians reject the prescriptions associated with hierarchy (i.e., who is allowed to do what and with whom), and thus show much less concern about social deviance.

Individualist cultures support self-regulation, including the freedom to bid and bargain. The labyrinth of normative constraints and controls on behavior that are valued in hierarchies are perceived as threats to the autonomy of the individualist, who prefers to negotiate for himself. Social deviance is a threat to individualist culture only when it limits freedom, or when it is disruptive of market relationships. Our expectation is that individualists should take a stance between hierarchists, to whom social deviance is a major risk, and egalitarians, to whom it is a minor risk at most.

Egalitarians claim that nature is "fragile" in order to justify sharing the earth's limited resources and to discomfort individualists, whose life of bidding and bargaining would be impossible if they had to worry too much about disturbing nature. On the contrary, individualists claim that nature is "cornucopian," so that if people are released from artificial constraints (like excessive environmental regulations) there will be no limits to the abundance for all, thereby more than compensating for any damage they do. Hierarchists have something in common with individualists: they approve of technological processes and products, provided their experts have given the appropriate safety certifications and the applicable rules and regulations are followed. In hierarchical culture, nature is "perverse or tolerant"; good will come if you follow their rules and experts, bad if you don't.

People who hold an egalitarian bias (who value strong equality in the sense of diminishing distinctions among people such as wealth, race, gender, authority, etc.) would perceive the dangers associated with technology to be great, and its attendant benefits to be small. They believe that an inegalitarian society is likely to insult the environment just as it exploits poor people. Those who endorse egalitarianism would also rate the risks of social deviance to be relatively low. What right has an unconscionably inegalitarian system to make demands or to set standards? The perceived risks of war among egalitarians would be low to moderate: they are likely to mistrust the military (a prototypical hierarchy); they also believe that the threat of war abroad is exaggerated by the establishment coalition of hierarchy and individualism in order to justify an inegalitarian system at home.

Cultural theory's predictions for the individualist bias are just the opposite: its adherents perceive the dangers of technology as minimal, in part because they trust that their institutions can control or compensate for the severity of untoward events. These same predictions hold for the cultural bias of hierarchy. How then do we distinguish between the worldviews of hierarchists and individualists? By varying the object of concern. A study of technological risks alone would leave these two cultures hopelessly confounded. Both are technologically optimistic, individualists because they see technology as a vehicle for unlimited individual enterprise—to them risk is opportunity—and hierarchists because they believe that technology endorsed by their experts is bound to improve the quality of life.

Due to the emphasis placed on obedience to authority within hierarchy, its supporters scorn deviant behavior. In contrast, individualists, who prefer to substitute self-regulation for authority, are much more willing to permit behavior that is the product of agreement. And yet, here too, a distinction must be made. If the object of attention is personal behavior, such as sex between consenting adults, individualists will be against allowing government to intervene. But if the subject is crime or violence against established institutions, they will be more disposed to support a governmental crackdown. In other words, if "order" signifies support for the stability and legitimacy necessary for market relationships, individualists will support government action toward that end.

Economic troubles represent a different kind of risk than those of technology or social deviance, since almost everyone has a reason to worry about them—egalitarians because lower living standards are especially harmful to the poorest people, and adherents of hierarchy because it weakens the system they wish to defend. We would expect individualists to fear economic failure more than others, however, because the marketplace is the institution most central to their life of negotiated contracts.

To test these rival theories—knowledge, personality, economic, political, and cultural—we drew upon the risk-perception data archives established by Kenneth H. Craik, David Buss, and Karl Dake at the University of California's Institute of Personality Assessment and Research.[8] We used the *pro-risk* index of their *Societal Risk Policy* instrument to gauge the extent of an individual's endorsement of risk taking versus risk aversion in regard to technology. This pro-risk index assesses whether risk taking and risk management are viewed as opportunities for advancement, or rather as invitations to catastrophe at the societal level.

We assessed perceptions of risk associated with *technology and the environment, war, social deviance,* and *economic troubles* by using variables chosen from a list of 36 "concerns that people have about society today." Following procedures similar to those used in the most important pioneering study of risk perceptions, we selected average ratings of 25 technologies on *risk* and *benefit* for use.[9] These indices enable us to compare public responses to different kinds of dangers. Now we turn to the factors that have been used to explain such responses.

Knowledge. One measure of knowledge we have used is the individual's self-report of how much he or she knows about specific technologies. Another measure is self-report of educational level. Self-ratings are the simplest and best way to address some psychological phenomena (who knows better than the individual how much dread a perceived hazard evokes for him?), while in regard to other phenomena they are notoriously poor. To avoid the potential pitfalls of relying only on self-reported knowledge, we developed a measure of perceptual accuracy based on differences between public and expert judgments of annual fatalities associated with 8 technologies: contraceptives, nuclear power, diagnostic X rays, bicycles, lawn mowers, motor vehicles, home appliances, and commercial aviation.[10]

Personality. In order to explore the correlations among personality characteristics and risk perceptions, we have drawn upon a broad set of traditional personality measures, including the *Adjective Check List* and the *California Psychological Inventory.*[11]

Political orientation. To evaluate predictions of risk perceptions based on political variables, we utilize measures of political party membership and liberal-conservative ideology (both self-rated and calculated on the basis of 20 policy issue stances).[12]

Cultural biases. To test the relations among perceptions of danger and the worldviews justifying *hierarchy, individualism*, and *egalitarianism*, we developed new measures to assess individual endorsement of three cultural biases.

Our hierarchy index embodies support for patriotism ("I'm for my country, right or wrong"), law and order ("The police should have the right to listen in on private telephone conversations when investigating crime"), and strict ethical standards ("I think I am stricter about right and wrong than most people"). It also expresses concern about the lack of discipline in today's youth and supports the notion that centralization is "one of the things that makes this country great."[13]

Our index for the cultural bias of individualism expresses support for continued economic growth as the key to quality of life, and private profit as the main motive for hard work. It espouses the view that democracy depends fundamentally on the existence of the free market, and argues that "the welfare state tends to destroy individual initiative." The individualism scale also indicates support for less government regulation of business, and endorses private wealth as just rewards for economic endeavor: "If a man has the vision and ability to acquire property, he ought to be allowed to enjoy it himself."[14]

Our measure of egalitariansim is based on survey items written to assess attitudes toward equality of conditions. The egalitarianism scale centers on political solutions to inequality: "Much of the conflict in this world could be eliminated if we had more equal distribution of resources among nations," "I support federal efforts to eliminate poverty," and "I support a tax shift so that the burden falls more heavily on corporations and persons with large incomes." The egalitarianism index also covers perceived abuses by the other political cultures: "Misuse of scientific and expert knowledge is a very serious problem..." and "The human goals of sharing and brotherhood are being hindered by current big institutions . . . ."[15]

There are many theories that might account for the perceptions of risks, from those based on knowledge, personality, or economics, to those based on politics or culture. Our task is to discriminate among these rival theories by comparing their power to predict who fears what and why.

CULTURAL BIASES BEST PREDICT RISK-PERCEPTION FINDINGS

If it were true that the more people know about technological risk, or about technology in general, the more they worry about it, it should follow that risk perception goes along with such knowledge. Using the measure of self-rated knowledge about technologies, and self-rated education, we see quite the opposite.

Our findings show that those who rate their self-knowledge of technologies highly also tend to perceive greater average benefits associated with technologies than those who are less confident about their knowledge.[16] Those who report higher levels of education tend to perceive less threat from the risks of war. Otherwise, self-rated knowledge and education bear only weak (that is, statistically insignificant) relations to preferences for societal risk taking or to perceived risks associated with technology and the environment, social deviance, and economic troubles.

The more an individual's annual fatality estimates correspond to expert estimates, in addition, the more likely that person is to rate other risks as small—at least compared with those who are less accurate. While on the whole those who are more in accord with expert mortality estimates perceive less risk, they are also less optimistic regarding the benefits of technology. *Overall, the conclusion is compelling that self-rated knowledge and perceptual accuracy have a minimal relationship with risk perception.*

With regard to personality, we find that those who feel our society should definitely take technological risks can be described as patient, forbearing, conciliatory, and orderly (i.e., the pro-risk measure is positively correlated with the personality traits "need for order" and "deference").[17] Advocates of societal risk taking tend not to be aggressive, or autonomous, or exhibitionistic, but are more likely to be cautious and shy and to seek stability rather than change. *This pattern is suggestive of a technologically pro risk personality, which emerges as that of an obedient and dutiful citizen, deferential to authority.* Such a personality structure fits extremely well with the political culture of hierarchy.

By contrast, those citizens who perceive greater risk in regard to technology and the environment tend to turn up positive on exhibitionism, autonomy, and need for change, but negative on need for order, deference, and endurance (i.e., just the opposite of those who score as favoring societal risk taking). *This technologically risk-averse pattern of personality traits also holds for those who endorse egalitarianism.*

Those who endorse egalitarianism are also more likely to be personally risk taking, but societally risk averse, while those who favor hierarchy tend to be personally risk averse, but societally pro-risk with respect to technology and the environment. Thus, *we find no evidence for a personality structure that is risk taking or risk averse across the board.* Risk taking and risk aversion are not all of a piece, but depend on how people feel about the object of attention. Cultural theory would predict, for example, that hierarchists would be risk averse when it comes to taking risks with the body politic.

Relative to conservatives, those who rate themselves as liberals tend to be technologically risk averse at the societal level, are more likely to rate the risks of technology and the environment as very great, and are comparatively unconcerned about the risks of social deviance. As the self-rating of liberal increases, the average ratings for the risks of the 25 specific technologies increases, and the average ratings of their benefits decreases.

Political party membership is less predictive of risk perceptions and preferences than left-right ideology, especially on the Democratic side (undoubtedly because Democrats are the more heterogeneous party). When we ask what it is about thinking of oneself as a liberal or a conservative that makes such a big difference compared with thinking of oneself as a Democrat or a Republican, the findings are informative. Whether by self-rating or policy designation, *liberals have strong tendencies to endorse egalitarianism* (r=0.52 and r=0.50), *and to reject hierarchy* (r=−0.55 and r=−0.51) *and individualism* (r=−0.37 and r=−0.31). Likewise, membership in the Democratic party is correlated with egalitarianism (r=0.30), but is not predictive of agreement or disagreement with the hierarchical or individualist point of view. *Republicans have a penchant toward individualist* (r=0.31) *and hierarchical biases* (r=0.40), *and an equally strong proclivity for rejecting egalitarianism* (r=−0.45). These correlations among political party membership, left-right ideology, and cultural biases are huge by the standards of survey research.

How does cultural theory compare with other approaches to perceived risk? *Cultural biases provide predictions of risk perceptions and risk-taking preferences that are more powerful than measures of knowledge and personality and at least as predictive as political orientation.* We find that egalitarianism is strongly related to the perception of technological and environmental risks as grave problems for our society (r=0.51), and hence to strong risk aversion in this domain (r=−0.42). Egalitarianism is also related positively to the average perceived risks, and negatively to the average perceived benefits, of 25 technologies. One could hardly paint a worse picture of technology—little benefit, much risk, and the risks not worth taking.

Individualist and hierarchist biases, in contrast, are positively related to a preference for technological risk-taking (r=0.32 and r=0.43) and to average ratings of technological benefits (r=0.34 and r=0.37). Here the image is more sanguine: the benefits are great, and the risks small, so society should press on with risk taking to get more of the good that progress brings with it.

DISCUSSION

We have shown that whether measured by cultural biases or by political orientation, perceptions of technology are predictable given the worldview of the perceiver. But one should not conclude that the establishment cultures of individualism and hierarchy always favor risk taking, or that egalitarians are always risk averse. *Perception of danger is selective; it varies with the object of attention.* For we find that compared with advocates of egalitarianism, those in greater agreement with individualism perceive greater risk in respect to war (r=0.15 versus r=0.40 respectively). Likewise, it is the hierarchical bias that is most highly correlated with perceived threat of social deviance (r=0.35 compared with r=0.15 for egalitarianism). Nor is it always the adherents of establishment cultures versus those of egalitarianism. As predicted by cultural theory, *it is not that devotees of individualism and hierarchy perceive no dangers in general, but that they disagree with those who favor egalitarianism about how dangers should be ranked. Just as technological and environmental risks are most worrisome to egalitarians, social deviance is deemed most dangerous to hierarchists, and the threat of war (which disrupts markets and subjects people to severe controls) is most feared by individualists.*

It is obvious that culture neither causes nor influences demographic characteristics such as gender or age (though it may influence their social meanings). Thus we do not argue that the weak correlations we find between cultural biases and personal attributes like income or social class reveal the influence of political culture on those variables. Whether we look at knowledge, personality, political orientation, or demographic variables, however, we find that cultural theory provides the best predictions of a broad range of perceived risks and an interpretive framework in which these findings cohere.

The importance of using a wide range of risks in studying how people perceive potential dangers should now be apparent. Employing only dangers from technology, while better than nothing, is far less powerful than considering a panoply of dangers from the threat of war to social deviance to economic collapse. Broadening the spectrum of related questions to be considered allows for more discriminating tests of rival theories. With perceived dangers from technology as the only issue, moreover, one cannot tell whether the level of concern registered by an individual comes from aversion to or acceptance of risk in general, or is evoked differentially by various risks. By observing whether there is a variegated pattern of risk perception (now we know there is) and by ascertaining who rates each kind of risk in which way, we may study *patterns of risk perception*. Fitting these patterns to alternative explanations, we believe, is a superior test of competing theories.

Comparing rival theories, not just a single explanation, has similar advantages. Making the rival theories confront each other reduces the temptation to claim easy victories. It is not enough to show respectable correlations; it is also necessary to do better than the alternatives.

Viewed in this light, the cultural theory's greater power than alternative explanations is manifest in its ability to *generate* broader and finer predictions of who is likely to fear, not to fear, or fear less, different kinds of dangers. Having derived from cultural theory a number of explanations approximated in our findings, the next question is what this tells us about risk perception.

Our findings show that it is not knowledge of a technology that leads people to worry about its dangers. In the current sample, the difference between public and technical estimates of annual fatalities ranges up to several orders of magnitude in size. The enormous variation in these public perceptions is not accounted for by knowledge, leaving considerable room for other explanations. Indeed, if people have little knowledge about technologies and their risks, then public fears can hardly coincide with how dangerous various technologies have proved to be.

Wait a minute! Everyone knows that nuclear radiation and AIDS can kill. We agree. When these subjects become politicized, however, disagreement develops along the fault lines of policy differences, seizing upon whatever cracks of uncertainty now exist: What are the health consequences of prolonged exposure to low levels of radiation? Is there such a thing as an amount of radiation so small that exposure causes no harm? Can AIDS be passed along by social contact? Should sufferers from AIDS be quarantined? Should their sexual contacts be traced and informed?

Our findings on personality raise the question of why there are such interesting sets of correspondence among traditionally assessed traits and cultural biases. Part of the difficulty in interpreting these findings is that personality entails such a wide set of characteristics—from intrapsychic to interpersonal relations—that virtually no aspect of individual life is left out. Were there theories connecting particular aspects of personality to patterns of risk perception, interpretation would be easier, for then we could test these hypotheses. One possibility is that personal orientations may guide individuals to make commitments consistent with specific political cultures, while at the same time, cultures may select from among individuals those that support their way of life. Since there are no such theories, however, we are left to explore among personality characteristics to see what fits.

Assuming both personality and political culture are operative, which is more powerful in predicting perceptions of danger and preferences for risk taking? Clearly, the closer one gets to asking questions about policy preferences, the better one's predictions of the selective perceptions of danger should be. Since our measures of cultural biases are closer to public policy than traditional measures of personality are, we should expect our measures (other things being equal) to predict better. And they do. But if that were all there were to prediction—proximity of the explanation to the explained—then we would expect assessments of political ideology to predict risk preferences far better than cultural bias does. As we have shown, however, public policy stances and self-rated political orientation do not do as well as cultural biases in predicting risk preferences and perceptions—even though they are the most proximal to risk policy of all the variables we test.

How then do cultural biases, which are so remote from the evidence regarding risks, guide people in choosing what to fear? A detailed answer is presented in *Risk and Culture*. Here, we can say only that hierarchists favor technological risk taking because they see this as supporting the institutions that they rely on to make good their promises, to wit: technology can promote a stronger society and a safer future provided that their rules (and stratified social relations) are maintained. Individualists also deem technology to be good. They hold that following market principles (and individually negotiated social relations) will allow technological innovation to triumph, conferring creative human value on otherwise inert resources. They also believe that the enormous benefits of technological innovation will convey their premise that unfettered bidding and bargaining leaves people better off. If they believed that free market institutions are intrinsically ruinous to nature, individualists could no longer defend a life of minimum restraints. By the same token, egalitarians are opposed to taking technological risks because they see them as supporting the inegalitarian markets and coercive hierarchies to which they are opposed.

By this time readers are right to wonder, in view of the assertions we are making, whether other surveys support our claims. A recent one to come to our attention is supportive in many ways. Its subject is the irradiation of food as a preservative process, widely considered safe by scientists, but a topic of considerable worry to concerned consumers. The participants were 195 adult women chosen from Pennsylvania women's groups of various kinds—religious, civic, professional, social, and political. The respondents were given a questionnaire to fill out, then were shown different kinds of information about food irradiation, then filled out another questionnaire, and finally were engaged in group discussion. The authors, Richard Bord and Robert O'Conner, find, as we do, that knowledge (based on the information given to participants) is inversely related to fear of a technology: "Having accurate knowledge about the food irradiation process translates into greater acceptance." They add significantly that:

> whether respondents received a technical or non-technical communication about the food irradiation process and whether they received a detailed discussion of the major arguments for and against food irradiation had no discernible effect on their judgments.

It is not knowledge per se, but confidence in institutions and the credibility of information that is at issue:

> Trust in business and industry in general, the food irradiation industry specifically, government regulators, and science as a provider of valid and useful knowledge is the major predictor of whether the respondent indicates she will or will not try irradiated food. . . . Learning that others have used food irradiation safely and of its approval by prestigious professional organizations enhanced its acceptability. . . .

> People who oppose big government and big business express greater fear of radiation.

> [One of the main topics of group discussion] was the respondents' view that complex technology bears a burden of too much uncertainty, too much greed on the part of its sponsors, and too little effective governmental control. The point was frequently made that even if the scientific-technical plan was flawless the people executing the plan and managing the technology would inevitably create serious problems.[18]

It is not only that "the facts" cannot by themselves convince doubters, but that behind one set of facts are always others relating to whether business and government can be trusted.

If there are any people to whom knowledge about hazards should make the most difference, it is those who are professionally employed in the analysis and management of risk. Yet a survey of risk professionals drawn from government, industry, environmental groups, and universities shows something dramatically different. Thomas Dietz and Robert Rycroft find that self-reported ideology:

> appears to have the strongest links to environmental attitudes and values of risk professionals.... For example, on the question of whether we are seeing only the tip of the iceberg with regard to technological risk, 88.5 percent of [the] very liberal ... agreed ... as did 74 percent of [the] liberals. Only 25 percent of [the] very conservative and 36.4 percent of [the] conservative respondents agreed.[19]

The more perceptions of contested subjects are studied, we believe, the more they will reveal the strong influence of cultural biases. In this respect, Paul Sabatier and S. Hunter's recent study of causal perceptions in belief systems is especially useful because, like the present analysis, it focuses on perceptual biases from more than one cultural direction:

> Environmentalists perceived water clarity to be getting worse, while those in favor of economic growth and property rights simply refused to believe the wealth of documented, and widely diffused, scientific evidence developed by one of the world's leading limnologists demonstrating statistically significant declines in water clarity over the previous 10–15 years. This suggests that in high-conflict situations, perceptions on even relatively straightforward technical issues can be heavily influenced by elites' normative presuppositions.[20]

This position reaffirming the importance of worldviews is bolstered by the "risk and benefit perceptions, acceptability judgments, and self-reported actions toward nuclear power" spoken of by Gerald Gardner and his coauthors. Their respondents were taken from environmental groups, blue-collar workers, college students, businesspeople, and technologists (scientists and engineers employed by a utility company). While education, sex, gender, religion, and other sociodemographic variables were not related to protests or other personal actions taken on nuclear power, Gardner et al. found that liberal-conservative ideology was predictive: "The most important correlate of reported action and 'acceptability' . . . appeared to represent a 'liberal/public interest group vs. a conservative/private enterprise' dimension."[21]

The power of the ideological explanation is strengthened further by Stanley Rothman and S. Robert Lichter, who analyzed questionnaires filled out by a sample of 1,203 congressional staff, civil servants, television and print journalists, lawyers, officials of public interest groups, moviemakers, military officers, energy and nuclear power experts. The results vary widely by group membership, with 98.7 percent of nuclear energy experts thinking nuclear power plants are safe, compared with only 6.4 percent of public interest officials, and 30.6 percent of journalists on television networks. Their major finding is that compared with a variety of demographic, social, and economic variables, political ideology was by far the most powerful predictor. "We hypothesize," they conclude, "that nuclear energy is a surrogate issue for more fundamental criticism of U.S. institutions."[22] This restates the thesis of *Risk and Culture* for nuclear technology.

Whenever other studies present comparable findings, they reveal that the most powerful factor for predicting risk perceptions is trust in institutions or ideology, which is largely about which institutions can be trusted. *Such findings show that, however conceptualized—whether as political ideology or cultural biases—worldviews best account for patterns of risk perceptions.*

In summary, the great struggles over the perceived dangers of technology in our time are essentially about trust and distrust of societal institutions, that is, about cultural conflict. Once we vary the object of concern, we do indeed discover that egalitarians (who fear social deviance less than hierarchists and individualists) fear technology a great deal—seeing in it, or so the cultural theory claims, the corporate greed they believe leads to inequality. Individualists, who believe in competition, and who are exceedingly loathe to place restraints on what they consider to be mutually profitable relationships, deem technology to be good. In contrast, hierarchists, who fear disorder and erosion of status differences, are more worried about social deviance and less worried about technological dangers than egalitarians.

We have shown that other surveys, with different assumptions, methods, and sample populations find, as we do, that risk perceptions and preferences are predictable given individual differences in cultural biases. It is the congruence of our analysis with others' that gives us the most confidence in our findings. We would have preferred to ask more subtle and differentiated questions about knowledge; but the other surveys we cite do that, and they also show the importance of cultural biases. Above all, we would have preferred more elaborate statistical analysis than small samples permit.[23]

Knowing what sorts of perceptions come from which kinds of people may allow for practical applications of cultural theory in a variety of policy contexts. Risk communication programs, for instance, might profitably focus on the underlying causes of risk perception—such as confidence (or lack of trust) in institutions, or the credibility of hazard information—rather than only on "the facts" regarding possible harms. Since cultural theory generates clues to the propensities of those with various worldviews to underestimate or overestimate specific kinds of risk, in addition, it can be used to tailor educational programs—say cigarette and alcohol warnings—to the plural rationalities represented in the general public.

It has been two decades since Chauncy Starr's seminal essay "Social Benefit versus Technological Risk" asked how much our society is willing to pay for safety.[24] Since then, a lively and spirited research community has grown up around the issues of technological risks.[25] We hope to have pointed the study of risk perception in the right direction by: (1) expanding the scope of the questions asked to include patterns of risk perception (not only technological hazard, but also war, social deviance, economic decline, etc.); and by (2) comparing rival explanations of public fears. As predicted by cultural theory, we find that individuals perceive a variety of risks in a manner that supports their way of life.

ACKNOWLEDGMENTS

The risk-perception data archives used in this paper were established in 1981 and 1982 by Kenneth H. Craik, with David Buss and Karl Dake, under National Science Foundation Grant PRA-8020017 to the University of California's Institute of Personality Assessment and Research. See David Buss, Kenneth H. Craik, and Karl Dake, "Perceptions of Decision Procedures for Managing and Regulating Hazards," in F. Homberger, *Safety Evaluation and Regulation* (New York: Karger, 1985), 199–208; "Contemporary Worldviews and Perception of the Technological System," in Vincent T. Covello, Joshua Menkes, and Jeryl Mumpower, *Risk Evaluation and Management* (New York: Plenum, 1986), 93–130. The writing of this paper was supported in part by the National Institutes of Health under Biomedical Research Support Grant 89–34 to the Survey Research Center. Acknowledgment is gratefully made to Dr. Kenneth H. Craik for his permission to use these data, and to Dr. Percy Tannenbaum for the support of the Survey Research Center.

ENDNOTES

[1]Mary Douglas and Aaron Wildavsky, *Risk and Culture: An Essay on the Selection of Technological and Environmental Dangers* (Berkeley: University of California Press, 1982).

[2]John Holdren, "The Risk Assessors," *Bulletin of the Atomic Scientists,* 39 (1983): quotation 36.

[3]K. R. MacCrimmon and D. A. Wehrung, *Taking Risks: The Management of Uncertainty* (New York: Free Press, 1986); R. G. Mitchell Jr., *Mountain Experience: The Psychology and Sociology of Adventure* (Chicago: University of Chicago Press, 1983).

[4]Ronald Inglehart, *The Silent Revolution: Changing Values and Political Styles among Western Publics* (Princeton: Princeton University Press, 1977).

[5]Stephen Cotgrove, *Catastrophe or Cornucopia: The Environment, Politics and the Future* (Chichester, England: John Wiley & Sons, 1982); Dorothy Nelkin and Michael Pollack, *The Atom Besieged: Antinuclear Movements in France and Germany* (Cambridge: MIT Press, 1981).

[6]Mary Douglas, "Cultural Bias," Occasional Paper 35 (London: Royal Anthropological Institute, 1978), republished in *In the Active Voice* (London: Routledge & Kegan Paul, 1982), 183–254; "Passive Voice Theories in Religious Sociology," *Review of Religious Research* 21 (1979): 51–56; *Essays in the Sociology of Perception* (London: Routledge & Kegan Paul, 1982). See also Douglas and Wildavsky, *Risk and Culture;* Michael Thompson, Richard Ellis, and Aaron Wildavsky, *Cultural Theory, or, Why All that is Permanent is Bias* (Boulder: Westview Press, 1990).

[7]Cultural theory delineates two additional cultures: fatalists and hermits; it also makes finer distinctions regarding nature, technology, and risk perception than are discussed here. Were it possible, we would prefer to measure cultural biases in

their social context. Instead, we have taken the approach suggested by the survey data at our disposal. We assess cultural biases as worldviews.

[8]Intensive assessments of 300 ordinary citizens were conducted, including measures of perceptions of technologies, preferences for societal decision approaches and societal risk policy, confidence in institutions, sociotechnological and political orientations, personal values, environmental dispositions, self-descriptions personal background, and more.

Two public samples were drawn from cities in the East Bay area of the San Francisco region: Richmond, Oakland, Piedmont, and Alameda. Stratified samples were selected on the basis of an analysis of social trends that provided detailed information regarding the median demographic characteristics of each postal zip code in the sample region. Participants were recruited via telephone directory sampling, letter of invitation, and telephone follow-up. Most, but not all, of the current findings are based on analysis of sample 2 (which had 134 participants), leaving sample 1 (which had 166 participants) available for replication of this study.

[9]Participants rated how risky, and how beneficial, they judged each of 25 technologies to be: refrigerators, photocopy machines, contraceptives, suspension bridges, nuclear power, electronic games, diagnostic X rays, nuclear weapons, computers, vaccinations, water fluoridation, rooftop solar collectors, lasers, tranquilizers, Polaroid photographs, fossil electric power, motor vehicles, movie special effects, pesticides, opiates, food preservatives, open-heart surgery, commercial aviation, genetic engineering, and windmills. See Baruch Fischhoff, Paul Slovic, Sarah Lichtenstein, Stephen Read, and Barbara Coombs, "How Safe is Safe Enough? A Psychometric Study of Attitudes toward Technological Risks and Benefits," *Policy Sciences* 9 (1978): 127–152.

[10]The measure of perceptual accuracy was motivated by Paul Slovic, Baruch Fischhoff, and Sarah Lichtenstein in "Facts and Fears: Understanding Perceived Risk," in R. Schwing and W. Albers, Jr., *Societal Risk Assessment: How Safe is Safe Enough?* (New York: Plenum, 1980), 181–216.

[11]Harrison Gough, *California Psychological Inventory Administrator's Guide* (Palo Alto: Consulting Psychologists Press, 1987); Harrison Gough and Alfred Heilbrun, *The Adjective Check List Manual* (Palo Alto: Consulting Psychologists Press, 1983).

[12]The measure of liberalism-conservatism based on policy preferences follows Edmond Costantini and Kenneth H. Craik, "Personality and Politicians: California Party Leaders, 1960–1976," *Journal of Personality and Social Psychology* 38 (1980): 641–61.

[13]Quotations, in order, are from Leonard Furguson, "The Isolation and Measurement of Nationalism," *Journal of Social Psychology* 16 (1942): 224; Hans Eysenck, *Sex and Personality* (London: Open Books, 1976), 153; Gough; David Buss, Kenneth H. Craik, and Karl Dake, *The IPAR Risk Perception Data Archives: Assessment II Instruments*, unpublished document, Institute of Personality Assessment and Research (Berkeley: University of California, 1982).

[14]Quotations, in order, are from Eysenck, 155, and from Furguson, 224.

[15]Quotations concerning a tax shift and the elimination of poverty are from Costantini and Craik; the balance are from Buss, Craik, and Dake, 1982.

[16]We report correlations throughout this essay, not means or mean differences. For sample 1 (134 participants), a correlation must be greater than 0.15 or less than −0.15 to be statistically significant. Nothing about average scores or group comparisons is implied.

[17]Gordon Allport, *Pattern and Growth in Personality* (New York: Henry Holt and Company, 1961); see also *Personality: A Psychological Interpretation* (New York: Henry Holt and Company, 1937).

[18]Richard Bord and Robert O'Conner, "Risk Communication, Knowledge, and Attitudes: Explaining Reactions to a Technology Perceived as Risky," (manuscript submitted for publication), quotations 14, 11–12, 14–15. Authors are at Pennsylvania State University.

[19]Thomas Dietz and Robert Rycroft, *The Risk Professionals* (New York: Russell Sage Foundation, 1987), quotation 47.

[20]Paul Sabatier and S. Hunter, "The Incorporation of Causal Perceptions into Models of Elite Belief Systems," *Western Political Quarterly* 42 (1989): quotation 253.

[21]Gerald Gardner, Adrian Tiemann, Leroy Gould, Donald Deluca, Leonard Doob, and Jan Stolwijk, "Risk and Benefit Perceptions, Acceptability Judgments, and Self-reported Actions toward Nuclear Power," *Journal of Social Psychology* 116 (1982): 116, quotations 194–95.

[22]Stanley Rothman and S. Robert Lichter, "Elite Ideology and Risk Perception in Nuclear Energy Policy," *American Political Science Review* 81 (1987): 81, quotation 395.

[23]Our findings call for multivariate statistical analysis of the interactions between cultural biases and the other classes of predictors. We are fully aware of the difficulties of regression or path analysis on small samples, so efforts are under way on larger samples. We are also sensitive to the fact that correlations do not necessarily imply causation. Cultural theory makes causal attributions, however, and the correlations we do find are consistent with its predictions.

[24]Chauncy Starr, "Social Benefit versus Technological Risk: What is Our Society Willing to Pay for Safety?" *Science* 165 (1969): 1232–38.

[25]National Research Council, Committee on Risk Perception and Communication, *Improving Risk Communication* (Washington, D.C.: National Academy Press, 1989).

Sheila Jasanoff

American Exceptionalism and the Political Acknowledgment of Risk

As the early morning commuter flight leaves Manchester for London, a carefully modulated voice announces that there will be no smoking in the cabin in deference to passengers' wishes. Smokers who board a plane in the United States are also out of luck, but in their case it is because federal law has decreed that smoking on any domestic flight is unsafe for all passengers. An executive of Dow Chemical, a major discharger of dioxin, wryly observes that if one wishes to eat fish caught in the Great Lakes, one had better do it in Canada. The fish is safe across the border, even though dioxin residues have led U.S. regulators to label it unfit for human consumption. A giant German chemical firm decides to build a new biotechnology facility in Massachusetts.[1] American citizens evidently welcome the investment, although the German public vehemently opposes such plants because of misgivings about the morality and safety of genetic engineering.

Such anecdotes can be multiplied many times over as one moves across countries enjoying remarkably similar levels of economic prosperity and technical sophistication, committed to similar forms of government, and linked to each other by myriad economic, social, and political ties. The implications are intriguing. It appears that citizens of Western industrial democracies create and exploit the same technologies, but without necessarily agreeing about their risks and benefits. Countries sharing an ostensibly rational approach to

Sheila Jasanoff is Professor and Director of the Program on Science, Technology, and Society at Cornell University.

policy formulation differ in the amount of risk they tolerate from a given technological activity. Even when a risk is perceived the same way in different countries, there are deep disagreements about how it should be controlled and who should control it.

In an era of rapidly increasing interdependence, this state of affairs raises interesting and provocative questions about humankind's capacity to take concerted steps toward managing risk. Are cross-cultural discrepancies inevitable in the perception and control of risk? If so, how can nations ever reach accord on solutions to global risk problems such as the greenhouse effect or ozone depletion? National disparities in risk regulation prompt us to rethink the connections between scientific knowledge, technological change, and public policy. A rigid belief in technological determinism has to be abandoned in the face of evidence that similar technologies do not induce the same political and policy responses among similarly situated people. But does this mean that the universality of science is a myth and that the accumulation of knowledge plays no part in bringing nations together in their actions against risk? Must we regard policy-relevant science, in particular, as a culturally dependent variable, taking form and content from its political and social context? If the evidence points in this direction, then how can we avoid the nihilistic conclusion that science does not matter in the management of risk, at least on an international scale?

Comparative policy studies offer a promising vehicle for clarifying how knowledge interacts with politics and culture in the way societies deal with risk. Both space and time are potentially fruitful dimensions of comparison. By looking at risk decisions across national boundaries, we can begin to sort out how different institutional and procedural traditions bear on the production and use of knowledge. By following such policies over time, we can trace how (and whether) changes in knowledge influence societal efforts to manage risk. Comparative research also furnishes an empirical basis for probing what is truly durable in any nation's strategies for confronting risks. We can begin to investigate on a comparative canvas whether risk eventually generates its own brand of politics regardless of national context. Are there distinctive political consequences that flow, in democratic societies, from the attempt to formulate policy for all on the basis of knowledge accessible only to the few? Alternatively, are there features in each country's approach to risk management that persist in spite of the homogenizing effects of shared knowledge?

In recent years, a small but steady stream of comparative research on health, safety, and environmental regulation has begun to shed light on similarities and differences in national approaches to managing risk. I use this body of work as a starting point for addressing the questions concerning scientific knowledge and its relation to politics that lie at the heart of this essay. My central focus is on risk in the United States. With the experiences of other nations as a backdrop, I reconsider and seek to refine the notion of American exceptionalism that is so frequently reiterated in the comparative policy literature. I conclude with a few brief reflections on the implications of the American case for future international efforts to cope with risks that cut across established geopolitical boundaries.

THE ROOTS OF DIFFERENCE

Studies of public health, safety, and environmental regulation published in the 1980s revealed striking differences between American and European practices for managing technological risks.[2] These studies showed that U.S. regulators on the whole were quicker to respond to new risks, more aggressive in pursuing old ones, and more concerned with producing technical justifications for their actions than their European counterparts. Regulatory styles, too, diverged sharply somewhere over the Atlantic Ocean. The U.S. process for making risk decisions impressed all observers as costly, confrontational, litigious, formal, and unusually open to participation. European decision making, despite important differences within and among countries, seemed by comparison almost uniformly cooperative and consensual; informal, cost conscious, and for the most part closed to the public.

Correlated with these differences were some marked disparities in the characterization of risk, especially with regard to toxic chemicals. Thus, U.S. agencies in the 1970s designated as carcinogens a number of substances that most European regulators did not believe presented a cancer risk to humans. The Environmental Protection Agency (EPA), for example, banned the pesticides aldrin and dieldrin as potential carcinogens,[3] and the Food and Drug Administration

(FDA) tried to ban saccharin on similar grounds but failed because of intense public and congressional opposition.

The special status of the United States was particularly apparent in the forms of evidence deemed suitable as a basis for policy. A noteworthy trend in the public justification of American regulatory decisions was the growing resort to quantitative representations of risk. Despite much controversy about their reliability, mathematical models came into widespread use in measuring and characterizing exposure to toxic substances, in extrapolating human risk estimates from animal studies,[4] and in establishing *de minimis* (that is, "no need for action") levels of risk. Even more controversial was a method developed by EPA for quantifying the degree of variation in expert judgments based on scientific uncertainty and multiple inferences.[5] The use of similar quantitative models was far less prevalent outside the United States. For purposes of regulating chemical products and pollutants, in particular, qualitative analyses of risk were generally considered sufficient, and few European governments endorsed the position that the benefits of quantitative risk analysis outweighed its not inconsiderable costs.

Paradoxically, however, there was much greater uniformity on the side of political action to curb risk. Though official bodies in the United States and Europe frequently differed in their assessments of scientific information, the decisions they took against particular hazards often seemed to converge. Thus, a study of actions taken against a group of fourteen suspected carcinogens in Britain, France, West Germany, and the United States showed a remarkable parallelism of policy outcomes, even though agencies in the four countries did not use the same principles of risk assessment and did not even agree in all cases that the substances presented a carcinogenic risk to humans.[6] Similarly, a comparison of regulatory responses to formaldehyde in several European countries, Canada, and the United States revealed many differences of detail in the way expert committees evaluated particular pieces of scientific evidence. Yet, in all these countries, standards for protecting workers against formaldehyde were eventually set at virtually the same numerical level.[7]

In seeking to understand this pattern of divergences and convergences, the scholarly literature focused on key differences in the political, legal, and scientific traditions of decision making in Europe and the United States. Under each heading, U.S. risk-management practices displayed a resistance to consensus building and closure that set them apart from approaches in leading European nations.

Political Competition

If the political environment for risk regulation in the United States had to be characterized in a single word, that word would be *competition*. Risk policies, like most of this country's major public policy initiatives, emerge from an interlocking series of competitive engagements among interest groups, between Washington and the states, and among the branches of the federal government. With power divided among so many actors, a wide variety of political viewpoints, including relatively marginal views about risk, can find ways of insinuating themselves into policy, albeit not usually at the national level. A notable exception is the Delaney clause of the Federal Food, Drug, and Cosmetic Act, which prohibits the addition of carcinogenic chemicals to food.[8] Written into federal law by a single concerned legislator, Congressman James Delaney of New York, this naively restrictive provision has haunted a generation of federal efforts to design a reasonable public health policy for carcinogens.

Political competition has put its distinctive stamp on U.S. laws aimed at controlling risk and on subsequent efforts to implement this legislation. Beginning in the 1970s, Congress enacted a succession of regulatory statutes that represented more a patchwork of unreconciled political differences than a fabric of compromise. The aspirational goals of committed environmentalists were married to ambiguous legal standards and to complex and constraining procedural requirements that virtually guaranteed policy stalemate. New regulatory agencies were granted broad discretionary powers to rid the environment of harmful chemicals, both old and new, and their resources for research and technical analysis were in some instances greatly expanded. But Congress refused to relinquish control over its creations. The agencies were required to show results within unrealistically constricted timetables and were held accountable to Congress as well as the courts. Citizen suit provisions gave the public extensive rights to sue regulators if they failed to comply with statutory requirements.

European politicians, too, responded to the onset of environmentalism in the early 1970s, but in a spirit of significantly greater caution.[9] Although new laws were enacted, often contemporaneously with U.S. legislation addressing the same issues, their scope was generally more modest and they were drafted with an eye to administrative feasibility. Thus, European statutes governing chemical regulation did not require systematic reevaluation of existing products and substances or the retrofitting of old plants to meet new standards. New responsibilities were divided among existing agencies, leaving established patterns of bureaucratic behavior largely untouched. Unlike American legislation of this period, European laws did not for the most part formally expand the right of citizens to participate in decision making or to gain access to expert documents. Accordingly, policy decisions about risk remained, as before, the preserve of experienced bureaucrats and their established advisory networks.

Legal Access

It takes little more than a nodding acquaintance with American politics to realize that courts in this country play a uniquely influential role in policy making. But even experienced U.S. court watchers could not have foreseen the impact that courts would have on administrative thinking about scientific uncertainty and on national policies for controlling risk. Comparative analysis revealed striking disparities between America and Europe with respect to the judicial control of administrative decisions. Whereas European agencies could generally count on their decisions as being final, no significant administrative action in America was assured of finality until it had undergone judicial review. Review by the courts not only delayed decisions relating to risk (as in licensing nuclear power plants or authorizing field tests for genetically engineered organisms), but also affected the character of administrative decision making in more subtle ways. The knowledge that their decisions would be subjected to judicial scrutiny drove agencies to adopt formal analytical procedures, such as quantitative risk assessment, and to build massive technical records to satisfy judicial demands for "reasoned decision making" and a "hard look" at the evidence. These records went far beyond any reports or explanations produced by European agencies concerned with risk.

Judicial review also played an important part in democratizing technical decision making in the United States: administrative agencies were forced to explain their actions in a manner comprehensible to lay judges—and indirectly to the public—no matter how technically complex the explanation. The results, however, were not always salutary. Litigation prompted an often unproductive deconstruction of scientific evidence, converting policy making into an endless technical debate.[10] The readiness of the courts to steep themselves in science, particularly the Court of Appeals for the D.C. Circuit, gave litigating parties an incentive to reframe fundamentally political cleavages over the acceptability of risk as disputes over scientific evidence. Though the courts were sensitive to, and generally sophisticated about, the nature of scientific uncertainty, the requirements they imposed on standard setting sometimes overestimated the power of science to determine policy;[11] at other times, they underestimated the need to involve scientists themselves in the resolution of policy problems at the frontiers of science.[12]

Although our concern in this paper is mainly with public risk policies—the focus of most comparative studies—we should note that U.S. courts were equally active in private legal disputes over risk. Judicial decisions in such areas as products liability, medical malpractice, and toxic torts not only helped to shape the nation's norms of risk acceptance, but challenged in their own way the finality of administrative decisions about risk. For instance, compliance with safety standards was not recognized as a defense in products liability actions; under doctrines of strict liability, injured plaintiffs could recover even if the manufacturer had met all applicable standards of safety. As a result, U.S. liability law provided an avenue by which individual victims of technology could challenge collective societal judgments about what levels of risk were "acceptable." Again, this legal development was unmatched in Europe.

Scientific Pluralism

A third key area of divergence between Europe and the United States in the aftermath of Earth Day and the Stockholm conference was the organization of scientific expertise relevant to policy making. While academic and industry scientists continued to serve as experts in all countries, two additional sets of actors with independent claims of expertise emerged on the U.S. scene: the regulatory agencies and public interest scientists.

Under U.S. law, much of the responsibility for gathering, interpreting, and, where necessary, generating scientific data relating to risk fell on the regulatory agencies, which began to develop distinctive precautionary policies for dealing with scientific uncertainty. Sensitive both to congressional supervision and to the omnipresent threat of litigation, U.S. regulators usually opted to draw conservative inferences when confronting imperfect data, that is, inferences more likely to overstate than understate the degree of risk. For example, federal risk-assessment guidelines for chemical carcinogens treated positive studies involving rodents as more significant than negative human epidemiological studies. Similarly, in interpreting bioassays, agencies uniformly endorsed the principle of high-dose testing despite the risk of false positives[13] and accepted benign as well as malignant tumors as indicators of a carcinogenic risk to humans.[14] Such assumptions prompted critics in and out of the United States to charge that this country's regulators were using "bad science" to further an expensive and unrealistic strategy of "zero risk."

Political circumstances in the early 1970s were also calculated to promote the growth of a new "public interest science" under the sponsorship of a newly attentive and active environmental community.[15] Centers developed where the uncertainties and ambiguities of policy-relevant science could be probed from a pro-environment, pro–public health perspective. A number of environmental, labor, and consumer groups, such as the Natural Resources Defense Council (NRDC) and Ralph Nader's Public Citizen, established themselves in the public eye as alternative sources of expert information on risk issues. To many chronically suspicious Americans, these "outsider" organizations seemed inherently more trustworthy than the regulatory agencies or their captive scientific advisers.

In most European countries, by contrast, regulators had neither the incentive nor the resources to develop an independent scientific persona. Politically, the factors that made American officials increasingly sensitive to carcinogenic risk found no exact parallels in Europe. Administratively, European agencies lacked the resources to mount their own research programs, and risk assessments continued to be performed as before in closed expert committees, shielded from public review and criticism. This sheltered environment was not calculated to promote the growth of public interest science with spokesmen who could challenge the rule of government experts. Consequently, most European regulatory agencies, unlike their American counterparts, felt little pressure to make explicit the principles they used in assessing risk or to lower the standard of proof (to suspicion rather than actual harm) for regulating toxic pollutants. Evidence judged by U.S. risk assessors as having crossed the threshold for action failed to arouse a similar level of concern in other countries, where the same evidence was frequently dismissed as flawed, inconclusive, or susceptible to other interpretations.[16]

THE DYNAMICS OF CHANGE

Risk decisions are made against a background of constant change in both science and politics. By looking at the impact of these changes on policy making, we can begin to see systematic and lasting connections between a nation's political culture and its actions to identify and control risk. Change, in other words, is the lens through which we can most clearly discern "national styles" of responding to risk.[17] Are there such styles, and how resistant are they to the march of technology and to the unifying forces of shared knowledge and economic interdependence?

How Special the United States?

The description I have given thus far of the distinctive U.S. approach to risk management is largely based on comparisons of American and European regulatory practices of the 1970s and early 1980s. This, however, was a period of unusual turmoil in the politics of risk. In the United States, increasing public concern about pollution and environmentally induced illness drove inexperienced government agencies into previously uncharted policy territory. The relatively sudden emergence of a broad band of environmental issues on the political agenda provoked novel and controversial attempts by regulatory agencies to link science with policy; generic risk-assessment principles for carcinogens were among the most visible and controversial results. These efforts, in turn, became the focus for an intensely confrontational brand of politics, marked by recurring legal attacks on agency decisions by industrial, labor, consumer, and environmental organizations.

But to generalize about American attitudes toward risk based solely on this period of upheaval and adjustment would be misleading indeed. With the advent of the Reagan years, many of the basic premises of the government's role in risk management were modified or rewritten. The new administration entered Washington with an explicit mandate to scale down the level of governmental intervention into business activity, even when the object was to safeguard public health and safety. EPA was a particular target for reform, and the appointment of Anne Gorsuch, a Republican loyalist, to head the agency delivered a forceful message about the turnaround in federal policy. At the same time, the increased prominence of the Office of Management and Budget (OMB) in regulatory proceedings signaled the White House's determination to keep a tight lid on the cost of the nation's risk-reduction policies.[18] With the White House clearly on the side of industry and asserting centralized control over rule making, the scope for adversarial clashes between regulators and the private sector, as well for independent action by mission-conscious agency heads, seemed to be greatly diminished.

To what extent did the distinctive characteristics of American risk management survive these political changes? One notes, to begin with, an across-the-board reduction in the adversarial and litigious ferment that had marked the 1970s. The Reagan years were characterized not merely by a commitment to deregulation, but by an active emphasis on cooperation between government and industry, with important ramifications for risk management.[19] In keeping with the theme of cooperation, EPA took the lead in applying techniques of mediation and alternative dispute resolution to rule making: agency experiments with "negotiated rule making" appeared to concede that the political cleavages separating major adversaries in the regulatory process could and, where possible, should be resolved without recourse to the courts.

The judiciary, for its part, adopted a markedly more deferential attitude in reviewing agency decisions based on scientific expertise. In a 1983 decision, the Supreme Court reemphasized that courts should be at their most deferential where an agency "is making predictions, within its area of special expertise, at the frontiers of science."[20] Although courts continued to overrule agency decisions concerning risk—as in the case, noted below, where FDA tried to apply the *de minimis* principle to several carcinogenic color additives—they did so for statutory reasons, or because the agency had changed course without explanation, rather than because of flaws in the agency's interpretation of technical data. Finally, there was a swing toward more expert-centered decision-making processes, as agencies increasingly began submitting their scientific determinations to outside expert bodies for peer review.

These events on the national legal and political arena coincided with a many-sided retreat from the concept of zero risk. Part of this evolution may be detected in judicial decisions. Federal courts, led by the Court of Appeals for the D.C. Circuit, announced as a matter of legal principle that some risks were too small for government to regulate without arbitrariness.[21] Confronted by statutory language that could be interpreted as mandating zero risk, both the Supreme Court and the D.C. Circuit concluded that Congress could not have intended so absolutist a reading of its intentions.[22] Regulatory agencies likewise indicated that they would develop principles for designating risks below a certain level as *de minimis*, that is, not meriting regulatory attention. In one of the most dramatic applications of this policy, FDA sought to exclude a number of potentially carcinogenic color additives from banning under the Delaney clause on the ground that, although they induced cancer in test animals, they presented only a *de minimis* risk to human health.[23]

EPA's philosophy of risk assessment also underwent notable modification. As the agency began revising its cancer risk assessment guidelines in the mid-1980s, it became clear that EPA's position was drawing perceptibly closer to that of counterpart agencies in Europe. For instance, EPA explicitly adopted the "weight of the evidence" approach to classifying carcinogens developed by the International Agency for Research on Cancer. More generally, the agency shifted away from the rigidly generic classifications of its earlier initiatives toward a more flexible policy, allowing more case-by-case consideration of available scientific knowledge. Thus, while EPA continued to accept the (relatively conservative) linearized multistage model for extrapolating risk estimates from high-dose assays, the new guidelines indicated that the agency would alter the choice of model if biological or other indications suggested a need for such deviation.[24]

With courts taking a backseat to regulatory agencies on matters of science, with agencies advocating cooperation and flexibility, with scientific advisory committees assuming greater importance in rule making, and with OMB aggressively counting the costs of regulation, the most salient differences between American and European policy making on risk seemed on the way to being leveled. Yet, a look at three controversies of the 1980s suggests that beneath the convergence of national styles of governance some of the factors that prompted the earlier "exceptionalism" of the United States remained very much alive. An important connecting thread in these cases was the reluctance of powerful social actors to accept "expert" knowledge as the basis for their own political acknowledgment of risk.

Cancer Risks and Proposition 65

My first example, concerning California's controversial right-to-know initiative for toxic chemicals, illustrates how changes in the risk strategies of federal regulatory agencies drove the politics of risk into decision-making forums subscribing to very different rules of the game. In 1986, California environmentalists, fed up with what they saw as the failure of traditional command and control regulation, called for a public referendum on a new approach to controlling carcinogens and reproductive toxins. The result, popularly known as Proposition 65, was voted into law by a nearly two-to-one majority and went into effect on March 1, 1987.

Proposition 65 played not only upon the American public's characteristic preoccupation with chemical hazards, but also on its traditional distrust of "expert" federal regulators and their rule-making practices. The law embodied a basically simple conceptual scheme. It called on the governor of the state to publish a list of known carcinogens and reproductive toxins. Manufacturers or dischargers of these chemicals were then required to follow two basic rules of the road: no discharges of listed chemicals into drinking water and no exposure of the public without warning. Citizens could sue to enforce the law, and successful bringers of such suits were to be rewarded with a "bounty" equal to 25 percent of the penalty collected from the violator.

Like the ingredients of a witch's broth, the elements comprising the early implementation of Proposition 65 had a familiar ring to them: a minimalist initial response by the governor, a lawsuit to compel more aggressive listing, appointment of a scientific advisory panel, charges that the scientists were biased, complaints and special pleading from industry, and hesitant progress by inexperienced state regulators trying to grapple with economic and political uncertainty. But Proposition 65 represented more than just the transfer of chemical risk politics from Washington to Sacramento. It articulated a deeply felt need to make policy making more responsive to public rather than expert perceptions of risk. No surprise, then, that Bruce Ames, California's most visible biochemist, said he knew of no toxicologist in the state who had been in support of Proposition 65.[25]

Alar and Public Interest Science

In our second case, the transformation of *Alar*, the name for an obscure chemical compound, into a household word in 1989 demonstrated the power of public interest science to capture the national agenda on risk. Alar, a plant-growth regulator, was widely used by the apple industry to increase yields and improve the appearance and keeping qualities of harvested fruit. But cancer studies carried out in the 1970s indicated that both the active ingredient in Alar (daminozide) and one of its breakdown products (unsymmetrical dimethylhydrazine, or UDMH) produced tumors in test animals and hence might present a risk to humans. On this basis, EPA tentatively decided to cancel the registration of Alar, though the agency was required by law first to consult its Scientific Advisory Panel (SAP) for pesticides.

At a hearing held by the panel, EPA and Uniroyal, Alar's manufacturer, presented sharply conflicting views of the risks of Alar, with Uniroyal arguing that the existing cancer studies were not of sufficiently high quality to justify withdrawing the product from the market.[26] SAP agreed with Uniroyal, and EPA was forced to retreat from its initial negative assessment of the compound. At this point, the debate on Alar might well have returned to bureaucratic oblivion in most European regulatory systems. Under U.S. law, however, EPA was authorized to ask Uniroyal to carry out more tests on Alar. Completion of these studies in early 1989 appeared to confirm the finding that UDMH caused blood vessel tumors in mice. EPA considered the data sufficiently alarming to speed up its regulation of Alar, although agency officials continued to state that the substance presented no immediate risk to the exposed public.

EPA's hopes for restoring a business-as-usual approach to Alar rapidly dissipated as NRDC, one of the nation's leading producers of public interest science, seized the opportunity to convey its own risk messages to the public. Following SAP's rejection of the early Alar studies, NRDC had commissioned its own study of risks to children from several pesticides and chemical products registered for use in the United States, including Alar. When Uniroyal published the results of the new Alar studies, NRDC thus was poised to go forward with its own interpretations of the data, which estimated the risk of Alar to be several hundredfold higher than calculated by EPA. Broadcast on the CBS news program "60 Minutes," the NRDC report caused a public outcry of such dimensions that neither EPA nor Uniroyal could regain control of the issue. Within months, Uniroyal concluded that it would no longer be profitable to keep Alar on the market and announced that it would voluntarily withdraw the product. In the end, then, it was NRDC's risk assumptions, not those of industry, EPA, or its prestigious advisory panel, that determined the commercial fate of Alar.

The Response to Global Warming

Does the American way with risk invariably lead to the rejection of centrist expert assessments in favor of more risk-aversive populist positions? And are American political responses more likely to err on the side of safety than those of other industrialized countries? The initial U.S. reactions to warnings of global climate change suggest otherwise.

By the late 1980s, climate researchers had concluded with surprising unanimity that increasing releases of greenhouse gases from human activity would raise the earth's surface temperature by 2° to 6°C in the next century.[27] They also agreed that uncertainties in climate modeling precluded an exact prediction of the impact on various regions of the earth. U.S. scientists were among the first to make these forecasts, and U.S. legislators, agencies, and environmental groups were in the forefront of those calling for a national policy on global warming. Displays of local activism were not uncommon; in one such initiative, the city of Irvine, California, voted to ban certain ozone-depleting chemicals.[28] Most policy analysts agreed that a global strategy would have to go much further. The most frequently broached proposal was for an initial decision to stabilize greenhouse gas emissions at near-current levels, followed by an international accord on stepwise cuts to be achieved worldwide.

At the Paris "environmental summit" of 1989, the United States and its six major industrial allies heeded the warnings of science and committed themselves in principle to limiting carbon dioxide emissions. Many in the United States hoped that President Bush would take the lead in proposing a framework for international policy. But in February 1990, the president indicated in an eagerly awaited speech to the Intergovernmental Panel on Climate Change that he had elected a different course. Specifically, he sided with those of his advisers who stressed the uncertainties of climate change against the certainties held out by climate experts. The speech, which disappointed scientists and environmentalists alike, emphasized how little we know, and the president's promises were directed primarily toward support for further research.[29]

By contrast, a closer nexus between experts and national policymakers developed in Europe, even under conservative political leadership. For example, Britain's Margaret Thatcher, hardly a committed environmentalist during her first ten years in office, appeared far more persuaded than George Bush of the risk of global warming and the need to act now. In a speech before the United Nations in November 1989,[30] Thatcher underlined how much science had already learned and made a commitment to having a draft convention on greenhouse gas emissions ready by the 1992 World Conference on Environment and Development.

KNOWLEDGE, PLURALISM, AND POLITICS

Seen against the backdrop of change, then, a feature of the U.S. risk-management culture that emerges as resilient is its capacity to generate competing yet credible representations of risk around which political action can crystallize. In all three of the preceding cases, the factor that made the greatest difference to the policy outcome was the presence in the public domain of alternative accounts of risk, each backed by sufficient authority to command political support. Was the public being adequately protected against carcinogens in its environment and drinking water? Was applesauce safe for children in spite of containing Alar residues? Is the evidence of global warming persuasive enough to justify immediate public investments in cutting back on greenhouse gas emissions? In each case, there were powerful social actors that believed the opposite, and the structure of the American political process enabled their views to prevail in one or another significant political arena.

Because of scientific pluralism, the prescription to "consult the experts and do as they say" has relatively little meaning in the context of American risk politics. Too many organized interests have both the incentive and the ability to pattern as experts and to create accounts of risk that find plausible support in the record of available information. The ambiguities and uncertainties of policy-relevant science undoubtedly facilitate the production of such alternate readings. But equally important to the politics of risk in America is the relatively nonhierarchical organization of science as well as politics. In the U.S. political setting, no single institution enjoys an exclusive right to speak for science, and when Americans seek scientific support for their risk perceptions, they seem prepared under appropriate circumstances to believe NRDC as much as EPA, Nader as much as the National Academy of Sciences.

Science clearly is a force to reckon with in the U.S. risk-management process. Claimed advances in knowledge by any of this country's multiple centers of expertise can play a decisive part in placing items on the regulatory agenda, in setting priorities, and in determining the boundaries of debate. When Uniroyal or NRDC produces new information on Alar, there may not be a consensus on what it means, but there is agreement that these claims must be addressed by policymakers if their decisions are to be perceived as legitimate. At the same time, the existence of competing scientific voices—regulatory agencies, scientific committees and societies, industry, public interest groups, even the courts—permits different constructions of risk to enter the debate; which one ultimately resonates most convincingly with the public depends on the political skill, credibility, resources, and occasionally even plain luck of its proponent.

CROSS-NATIONAL IMPLICATIONS

Returning to the theme of cross-national policy convergence and divergence, we are now in a position to say that differences in the societal responses to risk between the United States and other nations result in part from the relatively low level of scientific pluralism in countries with a more homogeneous or centralized culture of knowledge. The privacy of expert committee proceedings and the restrictions on access to information remarked by many comparative policy analysts act as brakes against the creation of alternate centers of technical expertise. Few other countries can claim to have nurtured as sophisticated a cadre of public interest scientists as the United States.

In countries with a tight centralization of the production and analysis of knowledge, there has been little opportunity for culturally different images and perceptions of risk to find acceptance as legitimate "science." Accordingly, it is easier in most countries to establish an expert consensus on risk and to use that consensus as a baseline for developing policy.

But U.S. exceptionalism on this score is beginning to show signs of impermanence. The risk constructs that the United States generates in such generous profusion are available to interested actors in other societies, and the literature on risk controversies already provides numerous examples of the successful exploitation of American public interest science by groups outside the United States. More important in the long run, however, is a discernible trend toward loosening the controls over knowledge in other industrialized nations. In Europe, for instance, new right-to-know laws adopted in the wake of the Seveso accident provided the public substantially liberalized access to information about toxic and hazardous substances. One finds, too, a renewed political interest in technology assessment and in other processes that are designed to make European governments more publicly accountable for their technological choices, including, importantly, their scientific assessments of risk. Some European countries, notably the Netherlands, Sweden, and West Germany, have already gone far toward institutionalized participation by major interest groups and the lay public in decisions related to the management of risk.

These developments provide a partial answer to our initial question about cross-national similarities in the politics of risk. An important, if unobtrusive, way in which risk is shaping politics in our time is by generating an impatience with the sequestration of knowledge. Citizens of Western democracies—and now their counterparts in Eastern Europe—appear increasingly uncomfortable with decision-making paradigms in which knowledge indispensable to policy is accessible only to the few who can claim to be truly expert.[31] The provision of expert information to the lay public on a widening scale may be the most significant contribution that risk makes to the politics of liberal societies over the next decade.

Does this mean that policy differences on particular risks and hazards will tend to disappear? I think not. While phenomena such as the conservative swing in U.S. regulation and the liberalization of information policies in Europe may erase some of the differences we currently see in the way nations manage risk, the uncertainty of our predictive sciences is such that citizens will always have scientific leeway to choose among alternate characterizations of risk. Important policy differences will still emerge, conditioned by basic national dissimilarities in the organization of political and legal decision making. In particular, our experiences to date suggest that new scientific knowledge about risk is most likely to arise in the United States, often accompanied by responsiveness at the level of local or regional politics. But national political closure, built around commonly accepted interpretations of knowledge, can sooner be expected in the more consensus-seeking politics of Europe.

These observations carry certain obvious implications for managing risks of global dimension. While the United States can be looked to for leadership in science and in policy innovation, the pressure to take action on transboundary hazards may have to come from less pluralistic societies. Current international efforts to control ozone depletion and climate change will shed light on the feasibility of such a division of labor. We shall see whether, when the stakes are high enough, nation-states are capable of overcoming their political and cultural divergences and agreeing to agree on risk.

If a workable formula can be found to address the catastrophic and global risks created by human activity, then we need not worry unduly about the culturally induced discrepancies that are sure to remain in societal evaluations of risk. Fish safe in Canada may well stay banned in the United States, while Germany allows unlimited speeding on its crowded highways, but rejects genetic manipulation in controlled laboratory environments. As long as these decisions do not jeopardize our common future, risk analysts can join with citizens of industrial societies to say, with reasonably clear conscience, "Vive la différence."

ENDNOTES

[1]BASF in 1989 announced plans to open a new biotechnology laboratory in Boston, and other German firms are following similar strategies. David Dickson, "German Biotech Firms Flee Regulatory Climate," *Science* 244 (1989): 1251–52.

[2]My characterization of cross-national similarities and differences is based on a number of works dealing with health, safety, and environmental regulation: Ronald Brickman, Sheila Jasanoff, and Thomas Ilgen, *Controlling Chemicals:*

The Politics of Regulation in Europe and the United States (Ithaca, N.Y.: Cornell University Press, 1985); Joseph Badaracco, *Loading the Dice* (Cambridge: Harvard Business School Press, 1985); Alan Irwin, *Risk and the Control of Technology* (Manchester: Manchester University Press, 1985); Steven Kelman, *Regulating America, Regulating Sweden: A Comparative Study of Occupational Safety and Health* (Cambridge: MIT Press, 1981); David Vogel, *National Styles of Regulation* (Ithaca, N.Y.: Cornell University Press, 1986); Graham Wilson, *The Politics of Safety and Health* (Oxford: Oxford University Press, 1985). Comparative studies focusing explicitly on the use of scientific information in policy making include Brendan Gillespie, Dave Eva, and Ron Johnston, "Carcinogenic Risk Assessment in the United States and Great Britain: The Case of Aldrin/Dieldrin," *Social Studies of Science* 9 (1979): 265–301; Frances McCrea and Gerald Markle, "The Estrogen Replacement Controversy in the USA and UK: Different Answers to the Same Question?" *Social Studies of Science* 14 (1984): 1–26; Sheila Jasanoff, *Risk Management and Political Culture* (New York: Russell Sage Foundation, 1986); Sheila Jasanoff, "Cultural Aspects of Risk Assessment in Britain and the United States," in Branden B. Johnson and Vincent T. Covello, eds., *The Social and Cultural Construction of Risk* (New York: Reidel, 1987), 359–97.

[3]Gillespie et al.

[4]Between 1978 and 1980, only eight chemicals were regulated in the United States on the basis of quantitative risk analyses. Between 1981 and 1985, the number had risen to 53. Curtis C. Travis et al., "Risk and Regulation," *Chemtech* (August 1987): 483.

[5]See, for instance, M. Granger Morgan et al., "Technical Uncertainty in Quantitative Policy Analysis—A Sulfur Air Pollution Example," *Risk Analysis* 4 (1984): 201–16.

[6]Brickman et al.

[7]Jasanoff, *Risk Management and Political Culture.*

[8]Enacted in 1958, this provision prohibited the addition to food of any substance shown to cause cancer in humans or animals. The Delaney amendment's significance for policy flowed not only from its explicit focus on carcinogens, but also from its endorsement of animal cancer studies as a suitable scientific basis for eliminating cancer-causing agents from the food supply.

[9]For a detailed account of the contrasts in legislative approach, see Brickman et al.

[10]This consequence is difficult if not impossible to avoid when using uncertain science as a basis for policy. See David Collingridge and Colin Reeve, *Science Speaks to Power* (New York: St. Martin's Press, 1986). See also Jasanoff, *Risk Management and Political Culture.*

[11]R. Shep Melnick, *Regulation and the Courts* (Washington, D.C.: Brookings Institution, 1983), 294–98.

[12]Sheila Jasanoff, *The Fifth Branch: Science Advisers as Policymakers* (Cambridge: Harvard University Press, 1990), 49–60.

[13]Cancer studies with laboratory animals must be carried out at high doses in order to magnify the response, so that statistically significant results can be obtained

using small numbers of animals. Such tests are controversial, however, because chemical exposure at high doses can overwhelm the body's natural immunological responses or produce metabolic changes that are not seen at lower exposure levels. Such effects, in turn, can increase the test animal's susceptibility to cancer.

14 For an account of the evolution of U.S. cancer risk assessment guidelines and the political battles they engendered, see Mark E. Rushefsky, *Making Cancer Policy* (New York: SUNY Press, 1986).

15 As originally proposed by Joel Primack and Frank von Hippel, "public interest science" was to be the product of a creative interaction—fostered by mechanisms ranging from government subsidies to voluntary activity by scientists—between the scientific and technical community and public interest groups seeking to participate in technological decision making. Such interactions, the proponents believed, would make transparent the uncertainties and assumptions buried in expert judgments about risk. This, in turn, would lead to a more comprehensive characterization of the unanticipated consequences of technological development and, ultimately, to more informed policy decisions. Joel Primack and Frank von Hippel, *Advice and Dissent: Scientists in the Policy Arena* (New York: Basic Books, 1974). In the activist environment of the 1970s, the scientific basis for regulatory decisions was indeed increasingly opened up to the public. One consequence, as I suggest below, was a push toward more conservative principles of risk assessment for chemicals.

16 The contrasts between British and U.S. risk assessments most strikingly illustrate this pattern. See Jasanoff, "Cultural Aspects of Risk Assessment in Britain and the United States."

17 David Vogel used the concept of "national styles of regulation" to explain differences that he, along with other comparative analysts writing in the early 1980s, identified between British and U.S. environmental policy making. See Vogel, *National Styles of Regulation.* Ironically, Vogel's own historical and cross-sectoral research did not fully support his argument about the tightness of the coupling between political culture and regulatory styles. For a critique of this part of Vogel's thesis, see Wilson, *Politics of Health and Safety.*

18 OMB's Office of Information and Regulatory Affairs kept a tight rein on EPA's decision making throughout the Reagan years. For example, OIRA carried out independent assessments of the scientific basis for EPA's cancer risk assessment guidelines and other substantial regulatory proposals. For a fuller account, see Jasanoff, *The Fifth Branch.*

19 Although my concern in this article is with cooperation in the specific context of risk management, the theme of government-industry collaboration was a pervasive one in the 1980s, extending well beyond questions of regulatory policy. The desire to lower barriers between the public and the private sector was evident, for example, in such legal developments as the Federal Technology Transfer Act of 1986, which encouraged government laboratories to enter cooperative research relationships with industry. Similar concerns prompted President Reagan in 1987 to issue an executive order requiring agencies to nominate individuals responsible for technology transfer.

20 *Baltimore Gas and Electric Co. v. Natural Resources Defense Council, Inc.*, 462 U.S. 87 (1983).

[21]*Monsanto v. Kennedy,* 613 F. 2d 947 (D.C. Cir. 1979).

[22]*Industrial Union Department, AFL-CIO v. American Petroleum Institute,* 448 U.S. 607 (1980).

[23]This attempt to reinterpret the law in the light of current wisdom about minimal risks proved too extreme for even the pragmatic Reagan judiciary. The D.C. Circuit reluctantly held that the language and history of the Delaney clause ruled out such a liberalized reading. *Public Citizen v. Young,* 831 F.2d 1108 (D.C. Cir. 1987).

[24]In other words, although EPA still favored a relatively conservative baseline position, the agency wanted greater scientific assurance that the use of these assumptions was warranted in individual cases. Terry Yosie, "Science and Sociology: The Transition to a Post-Conservative Risk Assessment Era," paper presented at Annual Meeting of Society for Risk Analysis, Houston, Tex., 2 November 1987.

[25]Eliot Marshall, "California's Debate on Carcinogens," *Science* 235 (1987): 1459.

[26]For a more detailed analysis of the Alar controversy see Sheila Jasanoff, "EPA's Regulation of Daminozide: Unscrambling the Messages of Risk," *Science, Technology, and Human Values* 12 (1987): 116–24.

[27]See, for example, Stephen H. Schneider, "The Greenhouse Effect: Science and Policy," *Science* 243 (1989): 771–81.

[28]"California City Votes to Ban Ozone-Depleting Chemicals," *New York Times*, 20 July 1989.

[29]Remarks by the president at the Intergovernmental Panel on Climate Change, Georgetown University, Washington, D.C., 5 February 1990.

[30]Address by Prime Minister Margaret Thatcher to the Forty-fourth Session of the United Nations General Assembly, New York, 8 November 1989.

[31]Sheila Jasanoff, "Public Participation in Science Policy," *Chemistry in Britain* 25 (1989): 368–70.

All life is an experiment.
The more experiments you make the better.

Ralph Waldo Emerson (1803–1882)
From "Experience," in *Essays*,
Second Series

Harvey M. Sapolsky

The Politics of Risk

ALTHOUGH IT DOES NOT CARRY A WARNING LABEL, our political system may be hazardous to our health. It hunts small risks ruthlessly while permitting much bigger ones to exist relatively unmolested. It invests billions, seeking unobtainable safety while failing to provide the resources necessary to protect our future. Hardly anyone is saved by the collective mania with risk; many may be harmed by what goes undone.

Scientists offer little solace in the quest for safety. On the contrary, they often stoke public fears with their ever-increasing ability to detect low levels of potentially dangerous elements in commonly used products and everyday experience. The attempts to calculate the consequences of these exposures do not enlighten because they are based on contested assumptions about the actual exposures and effects of low doses on human health.

Without the constraints of certain knowledge, the regulation of risk becomes intensely political. Most of the participants, locked as they are in separate contests for public support, find advantage in exaggerating potential harms. The result is an unending parade of health threats that confuse more than they guide behavior. Margarine may be better than butter, but it also has its risks. Driving without a seatbelt is dangerous, but eating apples is as well. Smoking kills, but so does nearly everything else.

The question then becomes why there is continuing demand for this confusing bad news about consumer products. American society more than any other is absorbed by the pursuit of minor risks,

Harvey M. Sapolsky is Professor of Public Policy and Organization at the Massachusetts Institute of Technology.

abetted no doubt by the responsiveness of its political institutions. Have we lost our sense of proportion? Is our political system inherently flawed? Are we being irrational or are we being driven to irrational behavior by our political institutions? An old and a new case help us understand the dynamics. But it is the incentives we cultivate that are a problem for society.

ONE OLD CASE

Efforts to promote the addition of fluoride compounds to the public water supply in order to reduce the incidence of dental caries became controversial in the late 1950s and early 1960s, much to the surprise of the proponents, who were mainly public health officials. To them, fluoridation was a major advance, similar to the chlorination of water, the iodizing of salt, and the enrichment of bread, which offered significant public benefits at low costs. Only the ignorant or the misguided could oppose such a gain, it was thought.

The ability of fluorides to prevent tooth decay in children was identified in observations of naturally fluoridated areas, initially undertaken to explain the mottling and discoloration of teeth that also often occurred. Tests were conducted in matched cities to determine the effectiveness on dental health of controlled doses of fluorides. When the results seemed to indicate important reductions in caries for the population under age 16, the Public Health Service with the support of other agencies announced a national program to encourage the adoption of fluoridation by local water authorities.[1]

Opposition to the program quickly developed, primarily but not entirely from the fringe right, which viewed fluoridation as mass medication possibly inspired by Communists. Fluoride compounds, it was noted, were also key ingredients in rodent poisons. Taken over time they could, it was alleged, cause cancer, kidney disease, left-handedness, and many other harms.

Fluoridation did spread rapidly in the United States, but not when the issue was put to a vote. Fluoridation was rejected in over two-thirds of the communities that held referenda to determine the outcome.[2] Adoption was much more likely in jurisdictions, usually larger ones, where the right to petition for a vote was restricted by governing charters and where the matter was settled by nonelected administrators or by powerful mayors persuaded to act by their health advisors. Thus Chicago, Illinois, had its water fluoridated, but not Fort Smith, Arkansas.

The controversies, often bitterly fought, attracted much attention from the social sciences. The common judgment was that rejection of fluoridation was a sign of public alienation.[3] Unquestioning of health officials who were convinced that fluoridation was safe as well as effective, social scientists viewed rejection as irrational. Their standard explanation for irrational behavior was alienation. The public, they claimed, in one of the few chances it had, was striking out against mass society, big government, and scientific authority.

However, on close scrutiny this argument is unpersuasive. Fort Smith, Arkansas, may have rejected fluoridation, but so did Wellesley and Cambridge, Massachusetts, hardly bastions of the weak, the oppressed, or the alienated. Fluoridation is at risk when there is a referendum, no matter what the demographic characteristics of the community. The only statistical relationship that is significant is a curvilinear one with education: the least and the most educated favor fluoridation.[4]

The referenda campaigns provide a clue to this result. Initially, most citizens surveyed favor fluoridation, generally confusing it with chlorination, the purification of the water supply. As the campaigns unfold, it is clear to those who pay some attention that there is opposition and that there are accusations that fluoridation may pose a health risk. The least educated do not follow the campaigns and may continue to confuse fluoridation with water purification. The most educated can distinguish between established health agencies, which generally favor fluoridation, and opponent organizations, which often use similar sounding names (for example, the National Institutes of Health and the National Health Federation). Those in the middle, the bulk of the population, know enough about the issue to be aware that it is controversial, but lack the time or the sophistication to decipher the sides. Voting against fluoridation becomes a thoroughly rational response to confusing information. Why endorse an experiment with your own health?

The behavior of public health officials provides additional evidence.[5] Among the opponents of fluoridation was an occasional physician or scientist generally lacking in national stature except for a strong antifluoridationist stand. Public health officials typically would refuse to debate them, not wishing to add legitimacy to their claims that fluoridation was a danger. At times, professional sanctions were applied to silence opponents of fluoridation. Most likely, though, citizens conditioned to expect two sides in every referendum found this behavior to be more worrisome than reassuring.

Out of the counterclaims some real risks to health could be discerned. Cosmetically unattractive mottling and discoloration can begin for about 10 percent of the exposed population, even at the controlled levels. In addition, fluoride compounds accumulate in the bones, causing them to be brittle, a hazard especially for the elderly. Kidney failure is also a danger. Perhaps one person in a million might die prematurely because of fluoridation. Those who drink large amounts of water, are dependent upon dialysis care, or consume foods naturally high in fluorides (fish, for instance) are particularly at risk.

More recently, some doubts have been cast about the benefit/cost trade-offs of fluoridation.[6] Improved diets and hygiene may be more the cause of the continuing decline in dental caries recorded in the United States than the diffusion of fluoridation is. Interestingly, the possible rate of one death in a million lifetime exposures that did not deter promotion of fluoridation by public health agencies in the 1950s now sets off regulatory alarms in the very same agencies, whose focus has shifted to protecting consumers from potential harms. The strange protests of the antifluoridationists of the 1950s seem much less strange today.

ONE AMONG MANY CURRENT CASES

Sometimes protective action begins when there is no knowledge of any actual victims. Such is the case with asbestos in the schools and other buildings. The hazards of occupational exposures to asbestos are well established and severe: lung cancer, mesothelioma, and asbestosis. But the health effects of episodic exposures to asbestos building materials are yet to be determined. Nevertheless, school districts across the country have been encouraged to consider removing the materials at great cost. Billions of dollars in expenditures are potentially involved. Ironically, these asbestos products became popular in large part because of their value in reducing fire risks and energy costs.

Concerns about the occupational hazards of mining and fabricating asbestos were expressed as early as the turn of the century, but it was not until the 1960s and 1970s, when the disease burdens of increased exposures resulting from the Second World War shipbuilding effort became visible, that they attracted much attention. Studies showed especially high rates of cancer and lung problems among workers. There were even indications of hazards to workers' families from fibers carried home in clothing used on the job.

In liability suits that followed, it was discovered that the mining firms were at least aware of the hazards, but sought to hide the knowledge rather than warn exposed workers.[7] To limit the punitive awards that quickly mounted on these revelations, Mansville, the leading asbestos producer, sought bankruptcy protection and further eroded public confidence in the industry. Critics, now marshalling wider support, pointed out the potential hazards of the continued use of asbestos in the manufacture of brake linings, fabrics, water pipes, building materials, and other products—the so-called second wave of the asbestos legacy. As a consequence, occupational standards have been greatly tightened over time, and most uses of asbestos have been restricted or banned. Clearly asbestos had become an endangered as well as an endangering product.

The question then arose about what to do with the millions of pounds of asbestos already embedded in society. Water damage and other abuses can cause asbestos materials to deteriorate and to release fibers into the environment. Extrapolations from occupational exposures convinced some that significant risks existed. Attention initially focused on the hazards in school buildings because children were thought to be especially vulnerable to asbestos-related health effects. However, regulators at the Environmental Protection Agency (EPA) envisioned the problem as larger than just that of the schools, likely involving hundreds of thousands of apartment buildings, factories, and office complexes as well as millions of homes. Discussions within the government about a course of action intensified just as the Reagan administration took office with its well-advertised intention to reduce the burden of regulation on business.

Asbestos was drawn into the deregulation debate that ensued because its removal from existing uses would likely be costly and could increase rather than reduce risk if poorly managed. Estimates of the possible harm from casual exposures were continually revised downward, eventually falling to one ten-thousandth that of occupational exposures. The administration's preference was to avoid mandating asbestos removal, but under pressure from the Congress, the EPA did issue a recommendation to the nation's school districts that buildings be inspected and parents and staff be notified of the existence of asbestos materials. Because asbestos was widely used as a fire retardant and heat insulator, there were soon thousands of frightened parents and school employees clamoring for a cleanup, even though only a relatively few districts actually followed the EPA's recommendation. The administration was unwilling to go any further, delaying promised regulations requiring complete inspections and the initiation of protective measures. Congress intervened to force the EPA to issue the regulations and to monitor the survey of school buildings and the training of inspectors.

Across America, school districts are now looking for friable asbestos and developing plans for its containment or removal. Many are choosing removal, an expensive and risky venture, as it gives the belief, if not the reality, of permanently ridding a site of the hazard. Despite certification programs, asbestos expertise is not very widespread or deep. Many removal efforts have been bungled, leaving school buildings more fiber-laden than they were before. Several billion dollars, most of which will be taken at least initially from local education budgets, will be required to complete the cleanup task. Because neither Congress nor state legislatures have appropriated significant funds for asbestos removal, many districts are suing the materials manufactures for costs and damages. And lurking in the background is an estimated hundred billion dollars in cleanup costs for nonschool buildings.[8]

Surprisingly, little research has been done on the actual hazards posed by asbestos building materials. Current assessments indicate that the most commonly used types of asbestos are not especially dangerous in their manufactured forms.[9] The risk to schoolchildren and other building occupants, but not to asbestos removers and others who poke at it, may be zero.[10] No one yet understands the hazards of the substitute materials. But the fear of asbestos in all its forms persists, as does the urge to poke and remove.

THE LOW-DOSE PROBLEM

We knew fluoride compounds to be poisonous long before their natural presence in water supplies was detectable. It took years for the risks of asbestos mining and fabrication, where the air was thick with dust and fibers, to be fully recognized. Improvements in measuring techniques now allow the identification of potential hazards in small doses, up to parts per billion. Thus we are aware of minute quantities of Alar in our apple juice and of EDB in our corn muffins. But what we do not know is what will happen to us in twenty or thirty years, the latency period for cancer and other serious disease, if we drink the Alar-spiked juice or eat the EDB-laced muffins.

The toxicity of substances is usually determined in animal studies. The doses in these studies are kept high because animals are normally short-lived and costly to maintain in laboratory settings. However, some results are species-specific and therefore of puzzling regulatory relevance. It was humans, not mice, that suffered from the effects of thalidomide. In contrast, dioxin is highly lethal to mice, but not necessarily so to humans.

To gauge the effects on humans of low to moderate doses generally requires epidemiological studies, but these are often difficult to conduct. For all except the most unusual populations, human experience is quite varied and hard to follow for long periods of time. Closed communities, like those in institutions or isolated occupations, can provide evidence of effects, but only the most severe. In everyday life there are many confounding variables to mask exposure effects. Mortality and morbidity reporting systems, although improving, are not yet sufficient to discover the consequences of low doses in unrestricted populations. Re-creating experience through interviews with disease victims to determine exposure levels is an art dependent upon fallible memories.[11]

Complicating the search for the health effects of chemicals is a number of unresolved technical issues.[12] Attempts to extrapolate from high-dose occupational exposures to low-dose experience are challenged by claims that there may be thresholds which need to be passed before effects occur. The utility of using bioassays for predicting human effects is debated among specialists. It is unclear how to deal with conflict between positive and negative studies, or with effects in one species or sex but not another. Some believe benign tumors are indicative of carcinogenic potential while others do not. There is room for much discretion in risk assessments.[13]

More and more the tendency is for regulators to favor the most risk-averse stance.[14] The Reagan administration's attempt to resist was easily overwhelmed by congressional maneuver and popular reaction. Although studies show a diminishing return to the regulation of product and environmental hazards, the desire to regulate remains unaffected.[15] The public's fear of these hazards is so great that officials dare not admit doubts about the need for the strictest controls. Only the occasional academic asks about the costs of excessive prudence in terms of progress foregone and of more important problems neglected.[16]

THE INCLINATION TO EXAGGERATE

Personal experience is usually sufficient to allow consumers to cope with the traditional hazards of the marketplace. Consumers learn quickly to count their change, to check package weights, and to discount the promises of salespeople. Consumers do not expect much from product warranties and are seldom disappointed. They are deluged by advertisements, but make their own choices. They either comparison shop or pay the price for convenience and full service.

But product health risks are a different sort of market hazard. Few consumers feel comfortable with the measure parts per million, let alone parts per billion. They cannot easily check what has been sprayed upon crops, dumped into the oceans, or fed to livestock. And how many know whether they should use margarine with monounsaturated or polyunsaturated fat? Personal experience affords no protection from products that may be slowly clogging arteries or producing cancerous lumps. Instead, consumers must rely upon the risk interpretations of intermediaries—scientists, government officials, reporters, policy advocates, and others—to guide their behavior.

The intermediaries often provide misleading advice. Their views on risks are shaped by professional and organizational interests that encourage, in most instances, the exaggeration of dangers. Their presentation of risk makes small risks become big and big risks bigger, but not proportionally. Consumers are easily confused, thinking health risks are bigger and more alike than they actually are.[17]

No one, of course, knows what are the true risks that consumers face. Lurking on pantry or bathroom shelves may be products that will someday be revealed as silent killers. But it is clear that the public has difficulty in distinguishing between the risks of cigarette smoking and failing to wear seat belts and those of consuming Alar-sprayed apples or living near a nuclear power plant. It is the prism of institutional interests that distorts risk perceptions.

It is not that consumers are intentionally misled. On the contrary, much of the distortion is the unavoidable consequence of professions and organizations competing with one another for scarce resources, in this instance the patronage of a population frightened by the recognition of its mortality. Scientists, individually and by disciplines, compete for recognition and reward; reporters must seek out audiences; public interest advocates need patronage; and government officials have to obtain budgets for their agencies. Even product manufacturers, who might be thought always to wish to underplay risks, can find market advantage in stimulating fears by heralding product versions free of suspect ingredients. Proportionality is easily lost in the clamor for attention and support.

RESPONSIVELY IRRESPONSIBLE

Government policies add to the confusion over risk. There are contradictory statements about particular risks and inconsistent rankings among them. This is not because agencies lack the capacity to establish coherent programs. Each usually has a long-term policy agenda from which it would prefer not to deviate. Most are closely linked to a profession which has predictable norms and predictable goals. That policies are contradictory within and between jurisdictions, and that they may change as does the calendar, is due to our structure of government and the fact that the agencies are subject to political masters who must respond to public pressures in order to retain office.

Convinced that they must appear willing to alleviate every product or environmental fear as it arises, officials make no effort to pursue consistent, carefully designed policies toward health risks. Whatever the scare of the day, officials stand ready to formulate quickly congressional testimony, briefing papers, news releases, and programs that demonstrate their unsurpassed commitment to protecting the public. Dare they hesitate, and an ambitious congressman armed with staff and a subcommittee will leap forward to take their place in front of the cameras. Thus, we are told that the fight to control AIDS is our number-one health priority, but so are the control of cigarette smoking, drunk driving, drug abuse, and teenage pregnancy.

If priorities are always changing, so too are the officials who proclaim them. Every change of leadership brings another shift in policy emphasis, a different personal interest requiring the attention of subordinates. One secretary of the Health and Human Services Department is a reformed smoker wishing to spread the word; another is a long-time civil rights advocate determined to improve the health services available to minorities. One commissioner of the Food and Drug Administration seeks the mantle of consumer advocate; another wants to be known as a friend to industry. Conservationists recapture the Environmental Protection Agency from the conservatives while a surgeon general makes an in-office conversion to liberalism. Only the publishers of Washington's hundreds of insider newsletters find pleasure in the never-ending parade of personal interest that passes for public policy.

The malleability of the policy-making process is not lost upon interest proponents. Each knows a circuit court that is likely to give a favorable ruling, a local jurisdiction that is inclined to be sympathetic, an academic report that legitimizes a position. State attorneys general, environmental commissioners, and consumer advocates find national reputation and career opportunities in pushing harder. Research institutes committed to support a particular ideology provide tailored studies whose results can be promoted via direct mail, planted stories, or news conferences.

The ability to influence policy outcomes gets increasingly diffused. Once we looked to politicians for policy direction and thought that their manipulative skills were so unusual as to be inborn. Now we know that politicians, or anyone else for that matter, need no special gene to be successful in shaping policy, but only the guileful advice on strategy and image that consultants can provide. The kind of media and campaign expertise that a few firms and trade organizations first developed to protect their interests in referenda is now both intensively studied and widely available.[18] And thanks to foundations and contingency fee arrangements, so too is the high-powered legal representation that once only the largest corporations could afford. For good or bad, almost everyone has a chance to make public policy in America.

The Alar controversy illustrates these points. In 1988 the EPA was laboring through a contended deregistration proceeding that challenged the safety of Alar, a growth-regulating product that keeps apples from falling prematurely off trees. The Uniroyal Chemical Company, Alar's manufacturer, had through the years used many technical consultants on various issues, including some scientists who had a role in advising the EPA on Alar. An advocacy group, the

National Resources Defense Council (NRDC), was a sponsor of a questionable study that found Alar's health risk for children to be several times that of the assessments that the EPA was using. Frustrated by the EPA's cautious, legally constrained response to the study, the NRDC hired a public relations consulting firm to promote its case before the public.[19]

Soon the NRDC's scary findings and the potential conflict of interests of the EPA's science advisors were national news. A "60 Minutes" story kicked off the campaign with cover articles in both *Time* and *Newsweek* following along with dozens of other media features. Meryl Streep, the Academy Award–winning actress, became a celebrity spokesperson for the NRDC, testifying at a hastily called but well-attended congressional hearing about the harm being done to children in the pursuit of Alar profits. Fearing the federal government would not act quickly enough to save a generation from cancer, state governments initiated their own restrictions. Apple sales declined immediately by over 20 percent, costing growers, even those not using Alar, millions of dollars. Before long, Uniroyal capitulated, withdrawing Alar from the market and signaling that it had been outmaneuvered in this round in the contest over food safety policy.[20] No other country has anything near the national tumult over risk issues that America has. Elsewhere governmental authority is more secure, policy-making proceedings more secretive, and official expertise more respected. There is less opportunity, but also less need, for organized interests to use the public's health fears for political advantage. Instead, associations of various types often are given a formal role in determining policy, reducing both the visibility of the process and its potential for inconsistency.

Of course, it is the responsiveness and openness of our political system that we value the most. Inconsistent and even foolish policies may be the consequence of our determination to avoid the centralization of power and to preserve the opportunity for any and all to press a point of view. We leave to the individual the responsibility to choose among them.

CONCLUSIONS

There is no shortage of advice about risks. Let a potential risk be identified and soon all possibly relevant professions, agencies, and trade groups will offer public positions in order to protect established interests or proclaim new ones. Add the news appeal of risk stories, the availability of advertising dollars to defend and promote products, and the ongoing flood of scientific reports and there is a flood of guidance for the concerned.

Unfortunately, most of the organizations (and individuals) that offer advice on risks are driven to exaggeration. The competition for the attention of peers, donors, editors, public officials, and customers is so intense that the irresistible temptation is to shout in order to be heard. Careers are as much at risk in risk controversies as is the public's health.

Because of the distortions that this competition produces, it is no surprise that consumers have difficulty in sorting out product risk. Some pay little heed to the warnings. Others, following the cautious calculus of the fluoridation referenda, support the strictest regulation of all potential harms and are careful about their own behavior. Still others may pick and choose among hazards, avoiding what they believe are the biggest while ignoring the rest. Likely there is a curvilinear relationship with education, as observed in the fluoridation controversy, and perhaps with income as well. The vast middle in education, income, and age worry the most about their fate.

Product liability laws and administrative action can protect us from some harms. The research investment to ferret out dangerous commodities is large. Despite the opposition of producers, we now have plenty of labels to read. Some products are no longer available for sale; others have their use restricted.

But in the end, there is little to protect against the exploitation of our fears of unknown or marginal harms. We want responsive organizations and professions. Competition keeps these institutions responsive, but at a cost. Americans are traditionally distrustful of government. We need now to be as skeptical of the behavior of research organizations, public interest groups, the news media, and businesses as we are of government behavior because they too find advantage in taking advantage.

Choice is what we desire: the opportunity to select our companions, our politicians, our causes, our entertainment, and our products. In the case of products, no less than in the others, the consequences of our choices can be disastrous. The information that we need in order to choose wisely surely is distorted, but not entirely absent. Amidst the competitive din there is guidance if we care to, and can, listen carefully. That we persist in ignoring safe pleasures or in reaching for dangerous ones is, however, to be expected, for we cherish the institutions that always permit, and at times even encourage, such errors.

ENDNOTES

[1]Donald R. McNeil, *The Fight for Fluoridation* (New York: Oxford University Press, 1957).

[2]Harvey M. Sapolsky, "Science, Voters, and the Fluoridation Controversy," *Science* 162 (25 October 1968): 427–33; R. L. Crain, E. Katz, and D. B. Rosenthal, *The Politics of Community Conflict: The Fluoridation Decision* (Indianapolis: Bobbs-Merrill, 1969); Diana Chapman Walsh, "Fluoridation: Slow Diffusion of a Proved Preventive Measure," *New England Journal of Medicine* 296 (19) (12 May 1977): 1118–20.

[3]For a summary and analysis of this perspective, see Brian Martin, "The Sociology of the Fluoridation Controversy: A Reexamination," *The Sociological Quarterly* 30 (1) (1969): 59–76.

[4]Harvey M. Sapolsky, "The Fluoridation Controversy: An Alternative Explanation," *Public Opinion Quarterly* 33 (1969): 240–48.

[5]Brian Martin, "Analyzing the Fluoridation Controversy: Resources and Structures," *Social Studies of Science* 18 (1988): 331–63.

[6]Bette Hileman, "Fluoridation of Water," *Chemical and Engineering News* (1 August 1988):26–41; Malcolm W. Browne, "Rat Study Reignites Dispute on Fluoride," *New York Times,* 13 March 1990; Eliot Marshall, "The Fluoride Debate: One More Time," *Science* 247 (19 January 1990): 276–77; "Weak Link on Fluoride and Cancer," *New York Times,* 27 April 1990. See also Tom Christoffel, "Fluorides, Facts, and Fanatics: Public Health Advocacy Shouldn't Stop at the Courthouse Door," *American Journal of Public Health* 75 (8) (1985): 888–91.

[7]Paul Brodeur, *Outrageous Misconduct: The Asbestos Industry on Trial* (New York: Pantheon, 1985); Thomas H. Murray, "Regulating Asbestos: Ethics, Politics, and the Value of Science," in R. Bayer, ed., *The Health and Safety of Workers* (New York: Oxford University Press, 1988), 271–92.

[8]Pamela S. Zurer, "Asbestos: The Fiber that's Panicking America," *Chemical and Engineering News* (4 March 1985): 28–41; Louis S. Richman, "Why Throw Money at Asbestos," *Fortune* (6 June 1988): 155–70; Claudia Copeland, *Asbestos in Buildings: Current Issues,* Congressional Research Service Issue Brief (Washington, D.C., 2 February 1990).

[9]Richard Doll and Julian Peto, *Asbestos: Effects on Health Exposure to Asbestos* (London: Her Majesty's Stationery Office, 1985); B. T. Mossman, J. Bignon, M.

Corn, A. Seaton, J. B. L. Gee, "Asbestos: Scientific Developments and Implications for Public Policy," *Science* 247 (19 January 1990): 294–301.

[10]William K. Stevens, "Risk Is Seen in Needless Removal of Asbestos," *New York Times,* 19 January 1990.

[11]For more on the hazards of epidemiology see Alvan R. Feinstein, "Scientific Standards in Epidemiologic Studies of the Menace of Daily Life," *Science* 242 (2 December 1988): 1257–63.

[12]These issues along with an analysis of their involvement in the development of policy are effectively examined in Mark E. Rushefsky, *Making Cancer Policy* (Albany, N.Y.: State University of New York Press, 1986). See also Kenneth W. Wachter, "Disturbed by Meta-Analysis," *Science* 241 (16 September 1988): 1407–8; John D. Graham, Laura C. Green, and Marc J. Roberts, *In Search of Safety: Chemicals and Cancer Risk* (Cambridge: Harvard University Press, 1988); Malcolm Gladwell, "Risk-Assessment Techniques Throw Researchers a Curve," *The Washington Post National Weekly Edition,* 2–8 April 1990.

[13]Compare Michael Gough, "Environmental Epidemiology: Separating Politics and Science," *Issues in Science and Technology* (Summer 1987): 22.

[14]Sheila Jasanoff, "Cultural Aspects of Risk Assessment in Britain and the United States," in B. B. Johnson and V. T. Cavello, eds., *The Social and Cultural Construction of Risk* (Boston: Reidel, 1987), 388.

[15]John F. Morrall III, "A Review of the Record," *Regulation* (November-December 1986): 25–34. See also Janice Long, "EPA Focuses on Environmental Problems Posing Least Health Risk," *Chemical and Engineering News* (15 January 1990): 16–17.

[16]Albert L. Nichols and Richard J. Zeckhauser, "The Perils of Prudence," *Regulation* (November-December 1986): 13–24; Aaron Wildavsky, *Searching for Safety* (New Brunswick, N.J.: Transaction Books, 1988).

[17]Harvey M. Sapolsky, ed., *Consuming Fears: The Politics of Product Risks* (New York: Basic Books, 1986).

[18]Larry J. Sabato, *The Rise of Political Consultants* (New York: Basic Books, 1981).

[19]"How a PR Firm Executed the Alar Scare," *Wall Street Journal,* 3 October 1989.

[20]Cristine Russell, "As American as Alar Pie," *The Washington Post National Weekly Edition,* 19–25 March 1990. Also Malcolm Gladwell, "A Consuming Matter of Apples," *The Washington Post National Weekly Edition,* 1–7 May 1990; Ann M. Thayer, "Alar Controversy Mirrors Differences in Risk Perception," *Chemical and Engineering News* (28 April 1989): 7–14; Leslie Roberts, "Alar: The Numbers Game," *Science* 243 (17 March 1989): 1430.

Peter W. Huber

Pathological Science in Court

"THE RAW MATERIAL OF SCIENCE IS FULL OF ERRORS." Says who? Well, all sorts of disgruntled chiropractors, of course, along with astrologists, the mothers for peace, *New Yorker* journalists, and assorted believers in homeopathic medicine and the curative powers of crystals and pyramids. And lots of lawyers, too. These critics, from the fringes of science and beyond, must discredit orthodox science to build their own cases for unorthodox nostrums, their own indictments of hitherto unrecognized techno-terrors. But this particular comment happens to come from Robert K. Adair, an eminent particle physicist at Yale University.[1]

So let us begin where Adair begins, in particle physics. Almost no litigation muddies the waters in this neck of the scientific woods. And particle experiments, though they can be extraordinarily complex in execution, are conceptually simple. Best of all, as Adair points out, "[t]he results are highly falsifiable—a wrong answer will be discovered promptly and definitely by others." Which means that it is far easier to distinguish good and bad particle physics than to separate good and bad medicine, biology, or epidemiology. Nevertheless, says Adair, the field, like the rest of science, is "full" of errors. There are many false starts, many conjectures that end up being disproved, many suggestive data points that end up in the oubliettes of scientific history. Mistakes are common.

This is convenient. Not for those who seek the truth about elementary particles, of course, but for those who wish to reflect on

Peter W. Huber is Senior Fellow at the Manhattan Institute, and of Counsel at Mayer Brown & Platt.

the science of nonscience. What another great scientist, Nobel chemist Irving Langmuir, called in a famous 1953 lecture "pathological science," "the science of things that aren't so."[2]

Langmuir started with the Davis-Barnes effect—experimental observations on the combination of alpha particles and electrons. The claimed effects seemed to match Bohr calculations of electron energies with great accuracy. Other researchers soon replicated or explained the phenomenon. Yet in the end, it became clear that all were "counting hallucinations." So were the discoverers of N rays in 1903. Mitogenetic rays emitted by onion roots proved equally unreal. So did the Allison effect, which allowed the identification of now long-forgotten new elements (Alabamine, Virginium) and a slew of nonexistent isotopes; the effect is remembered today as "Allison wonderland." Time and again, many believed, many tested, many published. But in the end, there was nothing.

Langmuir went on to itemize characteristic features of pathological science. Effects are often independent of intensity, or better still, almost inversely related to intensity, so that the worst effects come from the most diffuse excitations. Why should this be? Because increasing intensity is the easiest, most definite sanity check in real science. With N rays, mitogenetic rays, and the rest, the stimulus "had to be low intensity. We know why it had to be of low intensity: so that you could fool yourself so easily. Otherwise it wouldn't work."

For similar reasons, pathological science often depends on experiments at the threshold of detectability, or at the lowest margins of statistical significance. The claims frequently emerge from a body of data that is selectively incomplete; wishful researchers unconsciously discard enough "bad" data to make the remaining "good" points look important. That the measurements are at the very threshold of sensitivity is an advantage, not an obstacle. Data that don't fit the theory are explained away; those that fit are lovingly retained.

Pathological science often needs claims of great accuracy as well, to convert random noise into an apparently meaningful pattern. Observed effects rise and fall as the intensity of the field (or the alpha rays, or the ambient traces of dioxin, or whatever) are steadily increased. The skeptic concludes: "There is no effect here at all." "Oh no," says the believer. There are "windows" of sensitivity and response here. Resonances. The effects are highly sensitive to the precise frequency of the electric field, or dosage, or what have you. To the well-calibrated eye, there is order here. One must simply understand that the seemingly large variations in response show exquisite sensitivity to the stimulus.

Fantastic theories follow naturally. Small wonder: a theory to explain what is really random noise, in the experiment or in the observer's brain, must have many sorts of adjustable knobs and buttons. Moreover, simple theories immediately offer predictions that can be tested in new experiments far removed from the original ones. But with nonscience, nothing is going to work out as promised under different conditions. So the theories must be so complicated that no concrete prediction is possible. They invariably are.

Criticisms are met with *ad hoc* excuses. No matter how sincerely they believe in their results, pathological scientists are really making it up as they go. The experiment doesn't work when an outside observer is there? The sample today happens to be contaminated. The experiment does work despite the surreptitious removal of a piece said to be key to the whole thing? Well, some other extraneous factor must have temporarily corrupted these results. As Langmuir concluded, "They always had an answer—always."

Are the scientists behind the pathological science stupid? No. Then are we dealing here with rank dishonesty and outright fraud? Almost never. Pathological science, Langmuir notes, springs mainly from a "quite normal scientific desire to make discoveries and to understand things." The men and women of pathological science are "perfectly honest, enthusiastic over their work." And yet, they can be so eager to find something important and new that they latch on to something trivial and false, and then cling to it with dogged tenacity. This happens more often than even most scientists will concede, and far more often than the nonscientists can imagine.

For those familiar with the scientific process, this is neither surprising nor embarrassing. The engine of science is fueled by conjecture and publication. The bold postulate, the rough-and-dirty experiment, abounds. Results are publicized quickly. Mistakes frequently penetrate even the peer reviews that precede formal publication in professional journals. Science tolerates all this, not because mistakes are welcome, but because any demand for perfection will lead to paralysis. Trial with generous allowance for error has proved the most fruitful course in the pursuit of scientific truth. Scientists know this, and shape their behavior accordingly.

INCUBATION IN THE COURTS

Many courts, most notably in recent years, seem to have lost sight of the fact. This much is clear. The most acrimonious and troublesome areas of risk litigation today lie at what courts have labeled the "frontiers of scientific knowledge." Places where "the factual finger points" but "does not conclude." Courts dealing with scientific matters have come to love these metaphors. Yet they could almost have been lifted from Langmuir's lecture.

This much is known for sure about the frontiers of science. First, there are real and important scientific effects out there, an occasional gold mine or a Golconda diamond; hard to find, quite unexpected, and of great consequence when discovered. The second thing about the frontier is that mostly it is a barren refuge for the outlaws of science, who produce nothing. The proportions are uneven because unlike real science, pathological science is born and always remains at the frontiers; it can survive nowhere else. Its observations are always at the threshold of detectability, at the extremes of sensitivity, at the margins of what can be recorded. Below the margins, in fact.

The most refractory problems in litigation today involve risks that puzzle science because there is so remarkably little there. Not little science—little risk. And abundant, pathological, unproven, unprovable claims. The claims swirl around the health effects of Agent Orange, extra-low-frequency electromagnetic fields, ultra-low exposures to radiation, radon, asbestos, and microwaves, trace contamination from dioxin, EDB, PCBs, and TCE. There is no shortage of scientific work on these subjects; to the contrary, the volume of research is way out of proportion to the largest risks that these factors might conceivably present. Likewise, in litigation over questions of engineering design, the most troubling controversies center on very subtle, marginal trade-offs in design, not on gross, obvious defects in manufacture. Small wonder, then, that there is talk in the courts of frontiers. The issues being debated with such heat are, at worst, of small practical consequence.

Despite the smallness of issues, the frontiers of science have had great allure for legal prospectors in recent years. Courts have become steadily more willing to decide factual issues that mainstream scientists still consider unresolved, and to award judgments on the strength of scientific claims that few scientists would endorse.

But who is to say finally what is good science and what is bad? One possibility, of course, is for government to leave many such calls to others. Let people decide for themselves what is risky, what is the very opposite of risky (that is, therapeutic), and what lies in the great expanse of innocuous influences and useless nostrums in between. For a while it was considered irresponsible to suggest that, in matters of medicinal drugs, say, individuals might make their own private choices by contract, and bear their own risks, without intervention or assistance from the FDA beforehand, or the liability system later on. This is still the dominant view, though such things as tobacco, laetrile, motorcycle helmets, abortifacient drugs, and experimental AIDS therapies have spawned some revisionist thinking, now and again, about rights of privacy and autonomy even in matters bordering on the suicidal.

Nevertheless, it is still widely accepted that the individual consumer, poorly informed and too impatient with such details in any event, is a bad judge of good and bad risk science. So the state must intervene, through its agencies and its courts, to resolve these matters instead. The rough outline of the process in agencies is familiar enough. What is often not recognized is that modern tort law engages in an almost identical process, the principal difference being that the courts operate retail rather than wholesale. Under contemporary rules, safety litigation requires a jury to make essentially the same calls as the FDA would make in passing on a drug, or the FAA on an aircraft design, or the EPA on a pesticide or a waste dump.

Modern legal commentators tend to assume that this is a matter of unfortunate necessity; the courts just have to decide what causes what, on the way to resolving who should pay whom. In the welter of good science and junk, accurate correlation and rank error, insightful hypothesis and pseudoscientific fantasy, who else will do the job? We don't trust the individual. Nor professional societies, insurance company laboratories, and standard-setting organizations, for they are too close to the ones who must be controlled. Nor the expert agencies like the FDA or FAA, for they have all been captured by the industry they purport to regulate. This leaves only courts and juries.

This was not always the accepted view. Consider first the changes in products liability law. Until the early 1960s, the legal standard was negligence. The question was: Did the manufacturers' employees behave as other prudent, properly trained professionals in their field? Then, in the 1960s, the law sharply shifted its focus, from the *technologist* to the *technology*. Today, the question is whether the chemical plant, the vaccine, or the aircraft engine was designed, manufactured, and labeled in ways that can be called "defective." The jury is now to ignore the professionalism (or otherwise) of the designers and manufacturers, the quality of their training, their standing among other professionals. The jury is to pass judgment, instead, on the underlying science and technology. This subtle but important shift in emphasis has changed the tenor of litigation in suits involving services (medical malpractice, for example) and nuisances (pollution cases) as well. Across the board, the attention of the courts has progressively shifted away from human-centered norms—"negligence," "reasonable care," "activities appropriate for the place where conducted," and so on. Juries must now resolve all sorts of difficult scientific questions in cases that, in an earlier day, might have been quickly disposed of on nonscientific grounds.

In many jurisdictions, evidentiary rules have changed in similar ways. The use of expert testimony used to be controlled and limited by the Frye rule, named after the 1923 federal court decision that first articulated it. Roughly speaking, the rule allowed juries to hear expert testimony only to the extent that the testimony was founded on theories or technologies "generally accepted" among experts in the field. The yardstick for quality was thus the one established by peers in the business. Expert evidence would be accepted in the courtroom only to the extent that the evidence, or at least its scientific underpinnings, would be accepted by the mainstream scientific community outside the court. Experts, in short, were held to the same standards of reasonable prudence and caution that parties were.

In 1975, however, the Federal Rules of Evidence, which are widely emulated in the states, were codified without reference to *Frye*. Many courts concluded thereafter that they should admit any expert testimony "relevant" to the case. The subsequent trend has been toward what Federal Judge Higginbotham has called the let-it-all-in rule of expert evidence. The jury alone is to draw the final line between real science and the other kind.

The effect, once again, has been to downgrade the importance of professional standards, peer review—the industry norms, so to speak, of the scientific community. Authority has thus been taken away from scientific and professional communities, and given instead to individual scientists and professionals. Thus, science's traditional demands for replication, reinforcement, and consensus within the scientific community have gradually come to be ignored in court. Instead, litigation amplifies the poles and gives prominence to the eccentrics. It downgrades science, medicine, engineering as professional disciplines. Their consensus standards count for less and less.

So in product cases today, a jury assesses (or at least is solemnly instructed to assess) design, safety features, feasible alternatives, costs, convenience, the wider interests of other consumers, and a host of other broad-ranging societal factors, on the way to deciding whether, on balance, the design should be labeled legally "defective." In pollution cases, a jury emulates instead the epidemiologist, clinician, public health official, and zoning board, deciding whether the trace contaminant poses a risk, whether the risk materialized as injury to the plaintiff at hand, whether the activity behind the risk was reasonable for the neighborhood, and so on. All of this is done in splendid isolation. Scientists, from the mainstream and elsewhere, will be heard, of course. Then the jury will make its own call on what is science and what is not.

The courtroom has become, in short, a very congenial home for the pathological scientist.

HELP FOR THE LEGAL PROSPECTOR

In the last decade, ambitious lawyers, aided by sympathetic judges and jurors, have grown notably adept at elevating pathological science to respectability.

There is much legal solicitude, to start with, for new science and "the first case." Diseases exist long before scientists unravel their etiologies, the argument runs. Until man synthesizes PCBs, there are no PCBs to speak of. Does the first person injured by these chemicals have to wait for another thousand to suffer too, while sluggish epidemiologists count the corpses? Victim counting aside, with every new discovery, there will be a time when only one person—the discoverer—knows and believes it. So the courts must take new, fringe claims of cause and effect seriously. Brushing them off will leave the deserving uncompensated, and the guilty unpunished. Novel or otherwise, facts are what they are, no matter how many scientists may subscribe to them at first.

Quite so. Scientists, of course, recognize the importance of the first case too. "Shouldn't we pay attention to marginal results that we don't quite understand?" Robert Adair asks rhetorically. Yes. And "is it not possible that some original and unforeseen truth will emerge from such weak evidence?" Yes. And yet there is still every reason to remain highly suspicious of new science that seems to remain persistently at the fringes, resisting serious attempts over time to move it into the mainstream.

Experience teaches that even radically new phenomena that ultimately prove to be real almost never fit the Langmuir profile, even at the beginning. Langmuir himself brought up Pasteur's discovery of germs. "Everybody thought [Pasteur] was a fool—thought there couldn't be any sense to the subject. It took a long time before germs were believed in." Yet they were believed in. And by modern standards, Pasteur is an easy case. Not simply because we all believe in germs, now. But because we believe in science more than Pasteur's contemporaries did.

Modern science in fact has abundant experience with threshold phenomena and rare events. As Langmuir further noted, when Laue and Bragg put forward their theory of X rays as electromagnetic waves, "the first reports left one uncertain. But within three or four years they were making precision measurements of the wavelengths of X rays." Likewise with the first experiments of the wave theory of electrons. "The first evidence was very poor. . . . But [the] important thing is how quickly results were resolved." Until very recently, no scientist dreamed that certain metal oxides would be superconductors at quite high temperatures. When two IBM scientists first published such a claim, it was greeted skeptically; spurious superconductivity claims have been common in the past. Yet in a matter of months the effect had been documented well enough to justify a quite uncontroversial Nobel prize.

The crucial test of real science, as Langmuir pointed out, is "the test of time." Yes, the marginal result, the weak evidence, sometimes does point to something real. But once science has some reasonable inkling of where to look, it quickly works out ways to look much more precisely. Later results will soon converge on some new truth. Or they will diverge into clouds of contradiction and retraction. The new, unexpected, marginal result is important, not because it is usually right, but despite the fact it is usually wrong. "No such result is believable," Adair cautions, "until it emerges from the swamp of uncertainty and error and passes through the winnowing and sifting process. And if no 'smoking gun' appears over a reasonable period of time, we can expect that there is none."

The test of a new phenomenon, then, is what happens in the months, perhaps in the few years, after it is first reported. Is there steady convergence toward scientific consensus, with new data and emerging theory to back things up? Then the phenomenon is probably real. The defining character of pathological science, by contrast, is that its peddlers (as Langmuir put it) just "go on, and on, and on, and on," in splendid, idiosyncratic isolation.

But isn't the "test of time" grossly unfair to the injured plaintiff who is in court now, grievously injured, impecunious, and in need of help? Occasionally, perhaps, it will be. But not often. Clocks run considerably faster in science than in the law. It took the courts a solid decade after the carcinogenicity of asbestos was well established to hand down verdicts reflecting the fact. Who (if anyone) deserved the Nobel prize for discovering high-temperature superconductivity and low-temperature fusion? The scientific community reached a consensus within a year on both questions. Who owns which patents, some valuable, others valueless, in these two areas? The legal community may let us know sometime in the next decade or so. It is, in short, laughable to suggest that perhaps no one will get around to noticing an important scientific phenomenon until after it has caught the fancy of the Trial Lawyers of America. Legal paper moves as molasses compared with the bubbling mountain stream of scientific inquiry. First-case concerns, then, present little real justification for making the courts especially hospitable to science from the frontier and beyond.

The legal pundit, and even more so the litigator, next seeks refuge in solitude. So we know that the steady electrification of America has had no visible negative impact on the health of the population as a whole? Ah yes, but consider the subgroup of people who live near transmission lines. Well then, we consider them, and find no evident impact on this population either? But suppose the fields affect only children. Or only fetuses. Or only some hypersensitive fetuses. Carried only by allergic mothers. In just a few families with genetic vulnerabilities. Just one family, maybe. One fetus. One tragic injury. From one hit by one single photon, or one toxic molecule, or one alpha particle. At Langmuir's own lecture, a scientist in the audience suggested that something like an astronomical supernova might appear to fit the profile of pathological science, and yet be real. Shouldn't the courts be at least equally open-minded about claims of singular injury? Once again, it doesn't seem right to reject a claim merely because the plaintiff happens to be extraordinarily, perhaps uniquely, unlucky.

Very rare events *are* a problem for science. When things become sufficiently rare, isolated, enigmatic, and unique, science breaks down. In the end, science is the study of regularities of some kind or another. True singularities are the domain of art, and even more so of religion. One can indeed trace the rise of modern science and the decline of mysticism, with the steady confinement of religion to the domain of the singular. Science was powerless and unnecessary when gods were numerous and active meddlers in everyday affairs. Only a remote and jealously singular God leaves room enough for the rational order of science.

Moreover, whatever science may have to say in general about what doesn't cause what, it can rarely make utterly confident negative statements about the individual case. Science finds no reason to believe that cancer is caused by aliens from Mars. But who can prove that Mrs. Smith's was not caused in just that way, the first and only such case so far, a deliberate, diabolical disruption of one critical gene, in one critical cell, by a little green man, who left no trace behind? It seems unlikely, until the little green man is renamed dioxin, emanating from Monsanto rather than from Mars. Then, with the help of pathological science, we are much more willing to believe.

Pathological science, of course, has the power to make such fantasies real. The defining characteristic of pathological science is that *every* case, every observation, is really unique. The data are at the threshold of detectability and statistical significance, so one can never be heard to complain that there are too few examples or replications. The theories to explain what is going on are infinitely plastic, so that every objection, every contingency, can be covered by a different theoretical window, a unique conjunction of the "exquisitely sensitive" parameters.

This, then, is one of the most attractive ways to bootstrap pathological science into court in the one manner that will leave all honest, competent scientists all but speechless. Is the claim that spermicides cause birth defects? Why, then, all one needs is a theory to explain how that happened in this unique case, regardless of what may happen in controlled studies of larger populations. Science itself cannot deal with such results at all, for the singular and irreproducible define the domain of all that is not science.

This is not to concede, however, that courts should freely admit evidence on any claim packaged as a unique and singular tragedy. True singularities are indeed difficult, but science has in fact proved quite competent in dealing even with such occurrences, if they are sufficiently concrete. Even rare events tend to leave many footprints. We know much about the creation of the universe, singular though the event was, because there are many stars and galaxies in motion, because radiation permeates the space around us, because particle physicists can contrive experiments that replicate some of the conditions at the creation. We can develop a science of global warming, singular though our planet is, because once again we can see many footprints in the sand. A supernova near the earth occurs only once every several centuries, yet when one did occur recently it was immediately recognized. And the accidental discoverer, a previous unknown with only marginal professional experience, was immediately given full and well-deserved credit.

What science cannot grasp is the supernova that occurs only once in all history, and is observable through only one telescope, for only one second, by only one observer, who happens to be unequipped with a reliable camera. But then, it seems likely that such supernova do not really occur at all. The cautious scientist will never utterly deny the singular case, most especially when human beings are involved. People, biological things in general, are frustratingly singular—how else could we explain a single Plato, Aristotle, or Einstein? And so it is possible, in the most broad-minded sense of that word, for there to be utterly unique and unfathomable responses to common and seemingly innocuous stimuli. Possible, but highly unlikely. That is the most a good scientist will ever say. Even on the subject of Martians, or time travel, or astrology, or perpetual motion, or cancer caused by sudden trauma.

All of which suggests, supernova and their biological equivalents notwithstanding, that the odds remain heavily stacked against the new, the untested, the unorthodox claim. Overwhelmingly, such claims will be proved wrong. When ephemeral new observations do in fact point to something real and important, the mainstream scientific community will almost certainly come around to that view long before the courts.

Still bolder defenders of let-it-all-in scientific standards in court go on to argue (in effect) for equal protection of ignorance. If scientists don't claim to know what caused this or that, it's fair to send the bill for the costs on the strength of hunches, guesses, and ascientific suspicions. Why should the "innocent victim" (the standard formula) suffer from the backwardness of science? The defendant responsible for the trauma, or the diffuse chemical pollution, or radioactive fallout, is palpably less innocent, and so should pay for the cancer if we "just aren't sure." In matters of disease, let the layman's intuition and hunch substitute for the scientist's stubborn refusal to confirm what seems obvious anyway. Depend on the fake science, in short, when the real kind is unavailable. All that serious scientists can answer to this is that the odds are stacked against justice when justice proceeds along these lines. Lay hunches, guesses, and ascientific suspicions rarely track what serious science tells us about real risks.

Others present the ingenious argument that it is the very frailty of science that requires the courts to remain open-minded toward extraordinary new claims. "Science often gets things wrong," say the pathological-science skeptics. "How true," the pathological scientists and their legal defenders sorrowfully reply. "And the scientists are as likely to be wrong when they say A does not cause B as when they say that it does."

It's a smooth argument, but the odds, again, are very much against it. Rock Crystals held in the hand do not cure disease. The power of thought does not bend spoons. The alignment of Jupiter and Mars when the Moon is in the Seventh House does not cause peace to guide the planets and love to steer the stars. The overwhelming likelihood is that an item selected at random from column A (dioxin, cabbages, the alignment of the planets) does *not* cause effects selected at random from column B (cancer, hay fever, the heartbreak of psoriasis). Most things don't cause most other things.

Moreover, and despite these odds, science is inherently biased *in favor* of finding new causes. In science, proof of noncause generally comes from the accumulation of disappointed reports. Negative science is inherently more trustworthy, at least when it comes out of the academic community, than positive science, because reports of noncauses are much less personally advantageous to the scientist making them. Scientists rarely win Nobel prizes for declaring that A and B are unrelated.

Pathological science, then, often takes shelter in the shantytowns of legal procedure, the rickety refuges of presumptions and burdens of proof. If mainstream scientists are unpersuaded, but the rest of us remain deeply suspicious, perhaps we should just declare that it is up to the factory owner, the utility, or the VDT manufacturer to prove that it *didn't* cause the cancer, the miscarriage, or the migraine headaches. The magic of the burden of proof is that it smoothly converts ignorance about the facts into certainty about the verdict, and the greater the ignorance, the more certain and expeditious the verdict. The effect, once again, is simply to transform bad science into good. Why only presumptions against chemical companies and not against supermarkets? Well, because pathological science tells us (and we all sort of believe) that diffuse environmental chemicals are worse than alfalfa sprouts and peanut butter. Good science, as it happens, tells us the opposite. But through the beauty of the law of procedure, we can make things come out just the way we want, science notwithstanding.

The courts can thus become not merely refuges but active promoters of pathological science. The National Science Foundation may not give much comfort or support. Courts, however, can channel money to pathological science, cloak it in respectability, and generate alarming headlines. Each favorable verdict, each lengthy trial in which the science and nonscience are presented to a jury on cosmetically equal terms, attracts more legal capital, spawns more litigation, and fuels greater public concern. Serious clinicians and epidemiologists are quite certain that trauma does not cause cancer. To this day, however, some courts and juries persist in considering the question as open and unresolved. Thirty years ago, a medical expert declared that the theory of traumatic causation would have been long since abandoned "if it were not for the litigation which keeps it alive."[3] Litigation has ended up giving independent life and legitimacy to the pathological science on which it ostensibly depends.

Thus, $200 million—which is to say, one-fifth of $1 *billion*—changed hands in a single Agent Orange settlement, approved by a judge who then declared that the claims settled were scientifically groundless. To settle a Bendectin class action, $100 million was offered by a company that knew, and knows, and even continues to persuade most juries, that no science at all lies behind the legal claims. A prestigious federal court of appeals left undisturbed a $4.7 million verdict based on a scientifically groundless claim that spermicides cause birth defects. Cerebral palsy cases continue to revolve on claims—unbacked by serious medical science—that electronic fetal monitors or a more aggressive resort to Caesarean deliveries could substantially reduce the incidence of injury. The list could be extended for pages.

Cases of this kind, concluded in this way, successfully blur the lines between real science and the pathological kind. The credulous nonscientist, and the skillful advocate, will come back, again and again, to that tested aphorism of the ages, there's no smoke without a fire. How come serious people, over the years, report hundreds of health effects from low-frequency electric fields? How come so many people contract cancer near the place where they receive a sudden traumatic injury? How come so many women who work at video display terminals have miscarriages? How come so many suits are filed? How come they're settled for such large sums of money? It's all just too suggestive to be resisted. There has to be something going on here.

And yet there often *is* smoke, or at least what looks very much like smoke, without a fire, just as there can be fires without smoke. There is, most notably, the kind of smoke used by magicians and special-effects artists, usually blue, with mirrors to make the dying spark look like a conflagration. So much for the aphorisms of the ages.

All that can reliably be said in science is that there's rarely fire without some smoke, a quite different proposition. In most branches of science, there's always abundant smoke in the air, from quick and dirty experiments, bold speculations, radical conjectures, unorthodox theories. It's only after the smoke dissipates that one finds out whether there was anything real burning beneath.

The no-smoke-without-a-fire hypothesis fails equally badly in the courts. How could so many courts have approved so many verdicts for people claiming injury from traumatic cancer if trauma does not in fact cause cancer? The only answer is that they did, but it doesn't. There was a day, only eight generations ago, when crop blight was common near villages where unpopular elderly crones were known to reside. People applied smoke-and-fire logic here too, and the courts, similarly persuaded, responded with some smoke and fire of their own. Old women burned, but the crop blight remained.

THE COSTS OF ACCIDENTS

Yes, of course, all human institutions, dealing with human problems, are fallible. Yes, to demand perfection is unrealistic. Plaintiffs' lawyers are often the first to present this argument in defense of the system, junk-science verdicts notwithstanding. And the argument is quite valid, even if presented by advocates who show little tolerance for human error and frailty outside the courtroom. Nonetheless, the runaway potentials of junk science in court are a special problem, not to be brushed aside as one of the ordinary incidents of imperfect institutions.

A junk-science verdict is an accident in court. It is a defective legal product, designed by incompetent experts, assembled by laborers who are not up to the task. The verdict represents a failure of supervision in both planning and production. The packaging is deceptive, the public warning expressed in the verdict misleading, sometimes dangerously so. Costs are misdirected, as are profits. Junk-science verdicts encourage excess investment in a socially costly activity—litigation itself. The social burdens are not to be underestimated. No one should appreciate that better than modern-school tort scholars, who dedicate their lives to reallocating accident costs associated with cars, planes, chemicals, contraceptives, football helmets, diving boards, and peanut butter—accidents of every description, it would appear, except accidents in court.

Who exactly bears the costs of accidents in courts? Almost everyone except those most directly responsible for them, which is to say lawyers themselves.

The first and most obvious victims, of course, are those on the losing side of the bad verdicts. Wyeth Laboratories pays for a case of polio in fact caused not by Wyeth's vaccine but by a wild strain of the virus; the taxpayer pays a swine-flu judgment for "serum sickness" not in fact caused by the vaccine. Audi loses two-thirds of its U.S. business on the strength of publicity and verdicts about defects that don't exist. The manufacturer of a spermicide, or a safe IUD, pays more than a year of its profits for a birth defect it did not cause.

Next in line on the list of junk-science victims are consumers at large. It has often been asserted, and quite correctly, that liability costs come to be reflected in the prices of goods and services, and thus send a message to consumers. This is as true, of course, when the costs are unjustified as when they are justified. With junk-science verdicts, as with the other kind, prices rise and production declines. The Audi 5000, for example, almost driven off the market by junk-science lawsuits and their attendant publicity, was an exceptionally safe car. Consumers have paid a real safety price in being discouraged from buying it.

Notwithstanding their victory in court, even the ostensible beneficiaries of junk-science verdicts pay a price too. It is no kindness to inform a retirement-age asbestos worker that his problem is asbestos if in fact it's smoking; past exposure to asbestos cannot be altered, but future exposure to tobacco still can be. People who have been told they are victims of chemically induced AIDS, and who have persuaded a jury to that effect, may well persuade themselves. This will be depressing at the very least, perhaps even psychologically paralyzing. If the placebo effect is real, as it certainly is, so too is its mirror image, hypochondria. Junk-science verdicts, in short, may promote and sustain illness even when the electric fields, the microwaves, the trace pollutants, or the unmeasurable radioactivity have caused nothing but the verdict itself.

The wreckage of junk-science verdicts extends further still. Verdicts send a cautionary message to the general public too, and people tend to believe what the courts say, most especially when they say it with large amounts of money. The casual follower of jury verdicts might easily conclude that most pelvic disease is caused by IUD contraceptives and tampons, most lung disease by workplace dust and fiber, most road injuries by defects in car design, most miscarriages, birth defects, and cancers by video displays or ambient environmental pollution. But they aren't. By far the most important keys to safety and good health involve tobacco, alcohol, seat belts, diet, and sexual habits—matters very much within the individual's own reach and control. This close-to-home diagnosis is heartily unwelcome in a liability system obsessed with third-party insurance and the relentless search for accident control far from the scene of the injury. Junk science may cheerfully accommodate the send-the-bill-elsewhere preferences of many courts and juries. But when courts and juries pander to junk science, they deliver to the public a dangerously false message.

When we can, we ban the teachings of quack diagnosticians and snake oil salesmen from the doctor's office and the itinerant peddler's pushcart. Falsehood in matters touching on health and safety is investigated by the NIH, prosecuted by the FDA. Superstition is the refuge of a primitive tribe. It saps resources, misdirects energy, and discourages creativity. It can engender a sense of helplessness and apathy, and prevent people from searching out real causes and effective therapies. Now and again, superstition and its cousins will promote a violent, destructive hunt for remedies in the most bizarre places. Dignifying junk science weakens society for precisely the same reasons that promoting good science in and out of court strengthens it. This is at least as true when the junk science is peddled from the witness box, in the solemn surroundings of a court, as when it is peddled in the less serious setting of the town square.

Finally, junk science eventually weakens the courts themselves. The truth will come out, in the end. Today, most serious students of these subjects recognize the junk-science basis for the verdicts against Agent Orange, the Ortho-Gynol spermicide, and Bendectin, and for the results of countless cases involving traumatically induced cancer. The pages of *Science* magazine calmly recount the courts' rising susceptibility to junk-science claims from clinical ecologists and other fringe experts attacking the U.S. contraceptive industry. The accumulation of junk-science verdicts does not bode well for the authority of the courts. In the end, the public acceptance of judicial power depends in considerable part on the shared belief that the courts tend to get the facts right. When the real scientists catch up with junk-science verdicts, as they inevitably will, courts will end up in disrepute.

It thus remains all-important for courts to draw the line between science and superstition. For most of human experience, and in most of the world to this day, disease has been blamed either on the supernatural or on alien cultures. The plague is a scourge of God. Or else the Jews poisoned the wells. The pathological science of disease is our own, modern variation on this varied and tragic history. It is a point worth remembering amid all the proposals for looser rules on expert testimony, more ductile presumptions on cause and effect, more malleable standards on how scientific facts are to be resolved, more sweeping metaphors about frontiers and the intrepid legal system's duty to explore them. There is usually less, not more, to marginal scientific claims than meets the untrained eye.

STOPPING POINTS

But if only we had better science, more certainty. All these suggestive studies, with microwaves and transmission lines, traumatic cancer and trace chemicals, yet never anything really solidly definite! How vexing for the nonscientific bystander, most especially the one seated on the bench or in the jury box. Do another study! It too proves inconclusive? Then a major research program is in order. The problem isn't really too much pathological science; it's too little good science. While we wait for better, the courts must just muddle along, resolving uncertainty one way or the other, as the jury may see fit. Or better still, as presumptions, burdens of proof, and such may help to tilt the scales in favor of the deserving, and against the merely wealthy.

In fact, what is most desperately needed is almost the opposite of more research. Not less research across the board. But reliable ways of saying enough is enough, procedures to prevent the erection of great and costly towers of litigation on the soft, ever-shifting sands of pathological science. In law, as in science, not all frontiers are worth exploring forever. Most especially not when exploration is so unsettling and expensive, and when there are other manifestly more productive territories to be settled.

How, for example, will more research utterly prove that the morning sickness drug Bendectin is *not* thalidomide, and does *not* cause birth defects? Thirty-three million women have used the drug, and epidemiologists and clinicians have pored over the resulting data at interminable length. But suppose tomorrow morning a new, rough experiment suggests a rare effect for pregnant women who take the drug shortly after eating rare beef and pickles. Or perhaps for women of one rare genetic ancestry who have also previously used birth control pills. Well, it's unlikely that these particular combinations have been studied in detail. They could be, of course, but it would take time. Meanwhile, birth defects remain common, and if many women are using the drug some of them will also use it shortly after eating an underdone burger. Indeed, the quick study wouldn't have been done unless some of them had. So all bets are open, the cases can come to court again, and until science tracks down this new fox and proves it's only a rabbit, we can all assemble in court once again. It is an utterly endless process.

It is always possible to conduct a new experiment and detect a new effect that isn't there. Worse still, suggestive but in fact meaningless experiments can be churned out much faster than dispositive ones that lay false claims to rest. Bad science is easier than good. Faster and cheaper. Pathological science, unfortunately, is swifter than the real stuff, because it travels so much lighter. The quick and dirty new studies can always outdistance the slow and careful old ones. There will always be new variables to test, new conditions to contrive, new hypersensitive populations to define and distinguish. This does not mean that the courthouse doors must remain wide open forever. Sooner or later courts, like other institutions, must find ways to move beyond trivial or imaginary problems to more serious things.

Consider, by way of a concluding example, the hazards attributed to low-intensity microwaves, the kinds emanating from home ovens, telephone company towers, and military communication systems. Exposure to microwaves of this sort has spawned endless concern in the courts and elsewhere. Yet, as physicist Kenneth Foster observes:

> The problem is not (as is frequently asserted) that too little is known about the biological effects of microwave energy. Rather, endless exploratory research has yielded many observations the importance of which cannot be reliably judged, and which frequently cannot be independently confirmed. Because an "effect" might be reported by an exploratory study that took weeks to carry out, whereas it might require years to confirm the existence of the phenomenon and to judge its significance, there can be no end to controversy save by exhaustion or by taking the conscious decision to leave some questions unanswered. . . . Granted, society must search for hazards of its technologies. But how to cope with the scientific noise that these studies

produce? Such searches for hazards can go on too long, and guidelines for ending them must be established.[4]

Foster's suggestion has of course outraged many who build careers and make livings on microwave effects of dubious importance and reliability. But with the perils of low-level microwaves (which if they exist at all are so tiny that decades of research have uncovered almost nothing to speak of), as with other microhazards and nonhazards that occupy so much energy in the courts and elsewhere, we must find ways to stop. It is perhaps comforting to say we need more research. But to say so is always trite, and often wrong. Reflexive, uncritical calls for more research simply comfort the pathological scientist, dignifying the concerns he has raised. Believers in Martian spaceships and astrology undoubtedly would like to hear calls for more research in their fields, too.

What takes more courage, in the courts as elsewhere, is to call for an end to what, given a fair test of time, has proved to be fruitless, wasteful speculation. Malpractice is possible on the witness stand every bit as much in the clinic or operating theater. Yet the standards we routinely assert when condemning the medical defendant, we routinely ignore when qualifying the medical witness. Malpractice by mouth in court is not controlled in any serious way whatsoever. Any old doctor is qualified to be a witness, but only one who maintains mainstream professional standards is good enough to escape liability.

To their credit, some judges are beginning to address this pernicious double standard. A few have recently begun to emphasize that radical London novelty of 1660—the professional society—and that radical Paris novelty of the 1820s—the professional journal and peer review. Some have chided witnesses, or their lawyer employers, for saying and concluding "things which, in the Court's view, they would not dare report in a peer-reviewed format."[5] Still others have grown more willing to take a hard look at the mainstream scientific consensus, in an *ad hoc* application of *Frye* against doctors.[6] Still other courts are placing new emphasis on epidemiology, the most solid evidence that can be found in cases alleging diffuse toxicity. Others are giving new attention to the expert judgments of agencies like the FDA. Still others are turning away from strict liability standards altogether, at least for pharmaceutical products, and returning to a negligence inquiry in which difficult scientific questions are less likely to be at the center of the legal inquiry. But for every court that affirms mainstream science and the epidemiology of crowds, another still is quite comfortable with the idiosyncratic views of medical and scientific iconoclasts.

Thus the courts recreate a brand new epidemiology of the common law, with a healthy cluster here, a sick patient there, and no higher order behind. Hundreds of separate legal clinicians conduct their own forensic diagnoses, reach their own idiosyncratic results. And so great epidemics of traumatic cancer, or chemical AIDS, or doctor-caused cerebral palsy, periodically sweep through the courtrooms of the country. All things considered, the legal operation on Bendectin was a success, insist the pundits. But no one can conceal the fact that the patient died. Bendectin is no longer sold in the United States.

Pathological science remains for the time being like the specter in the child's nonsense poem: "As I was walking up the stair / I saw a man who wasn't there / I saw that man again today / I wish that man would go away." At a certain age, this is considered riotously funny. It ceases to be amusing when it comes to occupy the time of large numbers of policymakers, pundits, legal scholars, and jurists who could be far more usefully employed on other things. Our courts today desperately need ways to break out of self-perpetuating cycles of litigation that involve nothing and lead nowhere.

ENDNOTES

[1]R. K. Adair, *Erroneous Science: Annals of Radiation* (unpublished, 1989).

[2]I. Langmuir, *Pathological Science* (as edited and transcribed by R. N. Hall), General Electric Corporate Research and Development, Technical Information Series Class 1 Report No. 68-C-035, April 1968.

[3]L. Auster, "The Role of Trauma in Oncogenesis: A Juridical Consideration," *Journal of the American Medical Association* 175 (11) (March 18, 1961): 946–50.

[4]K. Foster and W. F. Pickard, "Microwaves: The Risks of Risk Research," *Nature* 330 (6148) (10 December 1987): 531–32; K. R. Foster and A. W. Guy, "The Microwave Problem," *Scientific American* 255 (3) (September 1986): 32–39.

[5]*Johnston v. United States*, 597 F. Supp. 374, 415(D. Kan. 1984), cert. denied, 108 S. Ct. 694 (1988).

[6]*E. G. Kubs v. United States*, 537 F. Supp. 560, 563 (E.D. Wis.1982). (Bellanti's "opinions that the swine flu vaccine causes various ailments repeatedly reject-

ed."); *Richardson v. Richardson-Merrell, Inc.* 649 F. Supp. 799 (D.D.C. 1986) ("Dr. Done [plaintiff's principal expert] remains an unbeliever and was willing to testify to his disbelief").

Stephen Klaidman

How Well the Media Report Health Risk

THE MEDIA ARE FREQUENTLY ACCUSED of reporting inadequately on health risks. But this charge is vague, sweeping, and usually unsubstantiated. Which media are being referred to? What is the standard of adequacy? Is it an attainable standard? The real focus should be on how well we can legitimately expect the elite media to cover health risks.

As it happens, criteria for judging the quality of health-risk reporting already exist. Collectively, they are called the reasonable reader standard and are based on the legal model of a reasonable person who is "prudent and careful, . . . a personification of the community ideal of reasonable behavior . . . ."[1] A reasonable reader has a need for information about the risks and consequences of what is being reported. To be optimally useful, this information must be accurate, understandable, objective, and substantially complete. Although to some observers these criteria seem beyond the reach of working journalists, good science and medical reporters come close to meeting them daily. And they apply not only to health-risk reporting but to all news reporting.[2]

Understanding what it takes to satisfy the reasonable reader standard requires explanation of its criteria. Accuracy implies reporting as fact only information for which there is good and sufficient evidence and refers to precision in quotation, paraphrasing, description, and attribution. Understandability depends on factors such as

Stephen Klaidman is Senior Research Fellow at the Kennedy Institute of Ethics, Georgetown University.

clear presentation, neutral framing of risk comparisons, sensitivity to cognitive predispositions, and inclusion of vital facts and background information. The goal of objectivity is limited to making clear distinctions between facts and justified beliefs on the one hand and personal attitudes, dogma, and the like on the other. The requirement of substantial completeness is satisfied if adequate information is published or broadcast to meet the needs of an intelligent nonspecialist who wants to evaluate the situation being reported on.

The reasonable reader standard thus answers the theoretical question of how well we can legitimately expect the news media to report on health risks.[3] In the rest of this essay I shall examine the obstacles to meeting these reasonable reader criteria and the degree to which the elite American news media succeed in meeting them. By *elite media,* I mean those with the resources and the commitment within the constraints of each medium to cover a broad spectrum of important civic issues.

Coverage of health risks by most of the daily newspapers and local television stations around the country ranges, not surprisingly, from fair to poor. They lack the audience demand for high-quality coverage, the human, technical and financial resources to provide it, and competitive pressure. The elite media, however, do significantly better, mainly because they can afford the luxury of specialized reporters, who these days frequently have advanced degrees in health sciences, including medicine. These media organizations can also afford the publication space (although rarely the air time) that it takes to deliver "substantially complete" coverage. And they can send their reporters where the information is or conduct expensive computer searches when necessary. (The time constraints and economic imperatives of television make it unrealistic to expect coverage there to be substantially complete except on rare occasions.)

But even a well-credentialed, competent staff, an ample budget, a sophisticated audience, and plenty of space or time cannot guarantee health-risk coverage that meets the reasonable reader standard. This requires a general commitment to the ideals of journalism—to sober, precise, detailed, nuanced, carefully qualified reporting—which is sometimes incompatible with the imperatives of the journalistic market—drama, controversy, human interest, brevity, and simplicity. These are imperatives of the mass audience, which keeps general-circulation newspapers and television networks in business. Despite their drawbacks, these imperatives have the virtue of making stories inviting and, on a basic level, understandable. As a result, the general-circulation media seem here to stay. But the *New York Times*, the *Washington Post*, and the *Los Angeles Times* are also here to stay, at least for as long as print media remain viable. And each of these newspapers, among others, appears to have made a commitment to covering health risks in a way that is intended to meet the reasonable reader standard. What's more, this coverage is available to any other newspaper that wants it, through the relatively inexpensive supplementary news services sold by the two *Times* and the *Post.* About 40 percent of the nation's roughly 1,650 papers subscribe to these services.

It would be unchallenging, repetitious, and virtually useless to concentrate here on examples of bad health-risk reporting from thousands of local media outlets around the country. Although such examples abound and their influence is undoubtedly malign, little can be done to improve coverage where demand for quality is low, resources are limited, and the most talented young reporters stay on the staff only a short time. A more practical project would be to identify some of the flaws in the best health-risk reporting done by the elite newspapers and television networks in the United States and to discern the causes of these flaws and how to avoid them. That they persist even when well-trained, competent journalists are furnished with the best available journalistic resources indicates that these flaws are deeply rooted, systemic institutional and psychological weaknesses and therefore highly resistant to change.

A coherent assessment of the quality of health-risk reporting in the United States must take account of the characteristics of health-risk stories that present reporting and writing problems for experienced journalists with solid backgrounds in relevant sciences, the obstacles to good reporting that derive from the objectives and culture of the elite news organizations and journalists, and the capacity or unwillingness of much of the public to understand or absorb certain kinds of information.

CHARACTERISTICS OF HEALTH-RISK STORIES

The six points listed below apply to the two most frequently reported types of health-risk stories—those concerning the disclosure of scientific findings related to health risks and those concerning hazardous events.

1. The consequences of the finding or event may be either unpleasant or unpredictable and may therefore trigger unwarranted or undesirable responses ranging from denial to irrational fear.

2. Information may be inaccessible. In the case of a scientific report in a peer-reviewed journal, for example, important data may be in a researcher's lab notes but unavailable to journalists. In the case of a hazardous event such as the release of radiation from a nuclear plant, the plant operators may be able to hide the cause and minimize the seriousness of the accident.

3. The scientific principles underlying a finding or event may be complex and hard to convey in lay language.

4. The available scientific data may be incomplete, inconclusive, inconsistent, or contradictory.

5. The results of a study or the best explanation available for a hazardous event may be ambiguous.

6. Risk estimates provided by government, industry, advocacy groups, or academic analysts may be based on assumptions and methodologies that represent different values and may yield results that vary by orders of magnitude.

Almost every characteristic on this list applies equally well to other kinds of reporting: unpleasant consequences, with apologies to Sam Spade, "are the stuff that news is made of," and there is no evidence that readers and viewers are more likely to deny virulent disease than violent crime; digging out hard-to-get information is what journalists are paid to do; arcane language and complexity are typical of arms control stories; incomplete, inconsistent, and contradictory data are what reporters regularly sift through to find news; ambiguity and inconclusiveness are commonplace to court reporters, among others; and manipulation by selective use of different methods and assumptions is a familiar technique to any reporter who covers bureaucracy, law, or finance.

If health-risk stories are inherently no more easy or difficult to write than other complex news stories, is there something about the enterprise of journalism itself that undermines good health-risk reporting?

GOALS AND CULTURE OF JOURNALISM

The overriding institutional bias of American journalism is not to the left or right; it is for "a good story." Good stories are inherently interesting to large numbers of people. They sell papers and improve ratings, usually because they satisfy more than one of the criteria that guarantee mass-audience appeal: drama, human interest, and controversy. Good stories may be tainted by political bias, but they are not dependent on it or defined by it. Excessive zeal for good stories leads to distortion through overdramatization and overemphasis on human interest and controversy.

News media are more often reactive than enterprising. This trait leads to fad coverage of relatively unimportant but effectively promoted stories, such as Alar residues in apples. At the same time, much more important stories, such as harmful bacteria in chicken and eggs, may be underreported because they lack a corporate villain or some other journalistically appealing element. Although investigative reporting is a much-discussed form of journalism, in practice it is relatively rare. Besides, much of what passes for investigative journalism is really secondhand reporting of the investigations of others working for Congress, government agencies, advocacy groups, and the like.

The elite media are biased toward the center. Their audience is overwhelmingly white and middle-class. Journalists, too, are overwhelmingly white and middle-class. Relying primarily on establishment sources, they report mainly on the still predominantly white, male, middle-class establishment. As Paul Taylor of the *Washington Post* has observed, they "don't like to go beyond . . . the mores of the [mainstream] culture . . . ."[4] Although this pattern exists for obvious reasons, some of which are unassailable, it can cause journalistic myopia. Years went by, for example, before American newspapers reported explicitly on how AIDS is transmitted and how its spread can be limited. Most AIDS sufferers were outside the mainstream—homosexuals, intravenous drug users, poor blacks and Hispanics—and their travails were believed only marginally interesting to the mainstream audience. Moreover, editors considered explicit discussion of gay sexual practices, or in many cases heterosexual practices, unacceptable to their readers or viewers.

Preoccupation with the latest developments combined with limited space and time fosters ahistorical news coverage. Stories about the progress of medical research, for example, often lurch from journal article to journal article conveying no sense of long-term trends and leaving intelligent nonspecialist readers in a poor position to evaluate whether certain chemicals constitute a threat to their health—dioxin in paper, for instance. Stories about chemical disasters are frequently written without proper characterization of the long-term safety records of the plants or industries in question and sometimes lead to misinterpreting, exaggerating, or undervaluing the importance of the latest study or event. Like science and medicine, political reporting, foreign correspondence, indeed most kinds of journalism, are susceptible to journalistic ahistoricism. The problem is compounded by the fact that many journalists, even at elite media, are handicapped by having a weak background in history and the skills in languages and statistics needed to study it.

The news media are bored by institutional and systemic problems and show little interest in incremental change. Until there is a crisis, the media rarely report persistently and in depth on subjects like regulation of the savings and loan industry. There is no obvious crisis of savings and loan proportions looming in science, but the relatively new field of risk assessment, which influences how billions of tax dollars are spent, has hardly ever been thoroughly investigated and reported on by the American press. The same is true of the system under which a handful of powerful journal editors wield what may be excessive influence over the entire enterprise of medical research. Unless a development in science or medicine can be presented as a breakthrough, if only a minibreakthrough, it will usually get scant coverage. When it does make it as news, conclusions are often inflated, either by researchers in press conferences and interviews or by reporters.

Journalists' predisposition for controversy leads to the polarization of issues. Even when responsible opinion on an issue is clustered in the center, an otherwise unassailable journalistic account will sometimes provide "balance" by juxtaposing the comments of quotable "experts" whose views seem relatively extreme. Although this tendency appears to run counter to "the bias of the center," it does not.

The sources chosen for their polar views are more often than not respectable members of the scientific establishment whose opinions on unsettled questions differ sharply only because one takes the most conservative position that can be sustained by the data, and the other, the most radical. Controversy is not quite invented by journalists, but they do exaggerate it, sometimes grossly.

All of the tendencies noted in this section are in tension with the desire of many reporters and editors to meet the reasonable reader standard, whose criteria they understand to be central to their role as journalists. As they work with editors to transmute notes and impressions into stories, however, reporters come up against irreconcilable elements and inevitably make trade-offs between such conflicting goals as nuance and brevity, drama and precision, narrative flow and context, interest and importance. As a result, legitimate expectations about the reporting of health risks sometimes go unmet. But even if the reasonable reader standard were absolutely satisfied, a substantial percentage of readers and viewers would still probably not fully benefit from it.

THE NEWS AUDIENCE

Because scientific illiteracy is widespread, any attempt to reach a broad audience requires that stories about health risks be written from a fairly elementary perspective and in layman's language. For television reports, which are oral rather than written, even greater simplification is required. Because of the need to devote space or air time to explaining fundamental concepts, no space or time may be left for explaining important matters such as the assumptions on which risk assessments are based, and important qualifying material may be left out or presented in too condensed a fashion to be easily understood.

Many in the audience are looking for impossibly clear, simple answers. They want to know whether it is "safe" to take a pill, have a procedure performed, breathe the air, drink the water, eat ice cream or eggs. They tend to reject as irrelevant theoretical qualifications like "nothing is absolutely safe."

Sometimes a risk is understood well enough to be properly labeled safe or unsafe in news accounts, but in writing complex news stories there is often a trade-off between satisfying the taste for drama and playing fair with the truth, which requires appropriate qualification. Often this involves exaggerating the risk being reported. One alternative is a story with a weak lead paragraph emphasizing the uncertainty of a finding. This kind of story is guaranteed to displease editors. If it makes the paper at all, it will run on page 40 with the truss ads.

Most members of the audience decide which risks are acceptable on the basis of personal preference. As Baruch Fischhoff, Paul Slovic, Amos Tversky, Daniel Kahneman, and others have pointed out, audience members favor risks they choose over those that are imposed on them. Since they have little knowledge or understanding of the morbidity and mortality associated with even the most common health risks, such as accident and stroke, they evaluate health risks against an unrealistic background.

The entire audience suffers from information overload. As a result, attention spans are short. Unless a story on television or in print is terse and inviting, which often means without nuance and substantially incomplete, it will not capture and hold the audience's attention. This is a special problem for television in an age when viewers easily switch from channel to channel, even from their beds. The analog for newspapers and magazines is that part of the young audience—perhaps a large part—has a low tolerance for anything printed.

This overview of the news media's audience, the goals and culture of the elite media, and the characteristics of health-risk stories provides a context for evaluating coverage. Most important, it reveals the difficulty of reconciling the ideals of health-risk reporting with the goals of the mass media, including those of the highest quality. I do not mean that the reasonable reader standard cannot ever be met. The standard was developed with constraints and conflicts in mind. Moreover, it is not blind to the virtues of traditional news-business imperatives such as brevity, clarity, and dramatic presentation, all of which can increase the readership of important stories; if not abused, these imperatives can also make stories more understandable and need not mislead or inadequately inform the audience.

What I do mean is that crucial compromises, some of which have been indicated above, and not all of which serve the audience badly, are made in preparing stories. Some of the compromises do serve the audience very badly, however, and they have far greater influence on the quality of stories than, for example, the much more widely discussed problems of inaccurate reporting and manipulation of journalists by sources. These compromises involve what is included and what is left out of news stories, what is emphasized and what is downplayed, who counts as an expert and who does not, whether an institution or an individual is treated as trustworthy or not, the overall tone of presentation, the pictures used (on television, the pictures can determine the words, and they usually determine what the audience remembers), the display given to stories, and the like. The rest of this essay is devoted to an analysis of how and why some of these news judgments are made and what impact they have on the coverage of health risks.

SHAPING THE NEWS

Something can be immensely important without being news. It becomes news only when some editor decides it is news. And if the editor is in Sioux Falls rather than New York or Washington, it is news only in the local paper's limited circulation area. The savings and loan crisis, far and away the biggest financial scandal in American history, was not news for a very long time because New York and Washington editors failed to penetrate its apparently mind-numbing opacity. Global warming, a well-known phenomenon since the end of the nineteenth century, was not news until one very hot day in June 1988, when James Hansen, a soft-spoken scientist from the National Aeronautics and Space Administration, found a newsworthy way to announce its presence.[5] Frequent failures in the plumbing of nuclear plants did not become news until one such failure in March 1979 came close to causing a disaster. Contamination of animal feed in Michigan in 1973 has been called "probably the most widespread, and the least reported, chemical disaster ever to happen in the Western world."[6] And the cancer-causing effects of smoking, though known since the late 1930s, were not news until 1964, when Luther Terry packaged the vast array of existing data as the first *Surgeon General's Report on Smoking and Health*. What was it about these stories that kept them from becoming news for so long? Apart from the savings and loan scandal, which has only indirect health implications, there are a number of answers.

In the case of global warming, there was substantial uncertainty about the magnitude and consequences of the phenomenon, in part because greenhouse-effect calculations were based on fairly primitive methodology. There was also a lack of immediacy, since whatever the consequences, they probably would not be felt for fifty years. Official administration sources downplayed the potential risk, partly because the costs of slowing the warming were so high. And no credible scientific source, until Hansen came along, would interpret and phrase the evidence in a way that made it sound like news.

Before March 1979, nuclear plants regularly issued reports on problems with pipes, pumps, valves, and other elements of their cooling systems essential to operation and safety. For the most part, these problems were routine. Collectively, however, they were important because they indicated systemic weaknesses and might have led to reporting on other problems such as poor control-room design and inadequate training of operators. Local newspapers in the vicinity of the plants usually carried brief news items on these routine problems, but the national media were not paying attention. Although the incidence of problems was frequent and in at least one case (Davis-Besse, in Ohio), dangerous, official sources minimized the risks, and opponents of nuclear power were not yet numerous, well organized, or trusted enough to effectively challenge the official version. Until the accident at Three Mile Island, the elite news media accepted the official view and treated the plumbing problems as unnewsworthy.

As for the feed-contamination situation, a researcher reported that the media "failed to function as a public watchdog because 'not until the results of contamination were glaringly obvious' did they stop 'accepting the explanations of the bureaucrats and start investigating farmers' complaints.' "[7] In other words, official sources were viewed as reliable and farmers were not.

The cigarette story is more complicated. Even though solid epidemiological evidence that smoking causes disease began emerging in 1938, there was strong resistance to believing it and publishing stories about it because more than half of all adults were addicted to cigarettes. Tobacco was a multi-billion-dollar industry. Cigarettes were effectively promoted as a home-grown, "All American" product; cigarette companies advertised heavily in newspapers and magazines; journalists were smokers; an incontrovertible cause-and-effect relationship between smoking and disease was not established; and so on. As a result, the epidemiological evidence was downplayed, cigarette-industry disclaimers and industry-sponsored research were overemphasized, and stories about the health effects of smoking were significantly underplayed. It took the surgeon general's report, which was carefully conceived as a major media event, to change the situation.

Before some observations about how coverage might improve, a few comments about sources are in order. Journalists depend on scientists affiliated with major government and private research centers because newsworthy developments are likely to come from their labs. What's more, their work appears in the handful of peer-reviewed journals that science and medical reporters rely on for stories. Journalists also depend on scientists who can express themselves clearly and provocatively in laymen's language because, to put the best gloss on it, these researchers explain science clearly for nonscientists, or at worst, speak in sound bites.

The advantages of this approach are self-evident: journalists can quickly recognize what the scientific community itself has identified as the most valuable and interesting research and can report it to the public at least partly in the words of some of those recognized as the nation's leading researchers. The problem with this approach, as sophisticated science journalists are aware, is that research results, even those of leading scientists published in respected, peer-reviewed journals, are frequently highly inconclusive: they are often based on animal data or very small and perhaps even poorly designed clinical trials; the findings may be barely significant statistically and not at all significant clinically; they may represent only the first stage in a lengthy process as, for example, in developing a vaccine, and so on. But under journalism's rules, these results need not be scientifically important to qualify as news. Even if the findings are equivocal, or barely reach the level of scientific significance, they are newsworthy if they meet some of the following conditions: they appear in a prestigious journal, the senior author of the article is well known, the subject is deemed interesting enough to capture the public's attention, or the data are interpreted provocatively by the author, which may mean suggesting more than the evidence will sustain.

This analysis should not be understood as being altogether critical of journalism. It simply supports the contention that the goals of science and of journalism are substantially different. Science seeks to advance knowledge by conducting experiments whose results are falsifiable; journalism seeks to inform the public about what is most important and/or interesting at any given moment. What journalists deem important and interesting, rather than scientific phenomena, may become the focus of reporting. A trivial development in AIDS research, for example, will probably get more space or air time than a significant development in the treatment of Lesch-Nyhans Syndrome. Rather than the science entailed, the main news angle might be the politics or policy implications of the situation, or a controversy surrounding one of the researchers, or a human-interest element relating to a patient. Any one of these elements might, from the legitimate perspective of journalism, be more important and/or more interesting than the scientific element.

CONCLUSION AND EVALUATION

Most of the problems in reporting health risks are embedded in the elite news media's conception of their role. These news organizations are dedicated to serving their audience important and/or interesting news items in the most palatable form they can manage, given the constraints of time, space, and resources. Unless this basic conception is revised, change is going to be limited and slow in coming.

Two important engines for change have already been set in motion, however. The first is the increase in the number of science and health reporters who have advanced training in the fields they cover and the growing number of reporters being assigned to cover health-risk stories. The general trend toward specialization in journalism suggests that the number of reporters and editors trained in medicine and other health sciences will continue to grow. The second is the development of a new form of journalism devoted to service rather than news. The *New York Times,* the *Washington Post,* the *Los Angeles Times,* and other daily newspapers, in response to the widespread interest in health across America, publish special pages, full sections, or both on health issues every week, and the television networks air regular health features. These special features are oriented to providing readers and viewers with information related to personal health and other aspects of the health-care enterprise without any requirement that they be connected with the latest news.

This focus on service removes much of the importance of the traditional news-business imperatives and makes the reasonable reader criteria more attainable.

As far as straight reporting is concerned, trade-offs between news-business imperatives and reasonable reader criteria will continue to be made in about the same way they are made now as long as newspaper editors and television news producers think they are satisfying most of their readers and viewers. Drama will therefore sometimes triumph over nuance and controversy will be exaggerated; scientific findings will sometimes be overstated and environmental risks understated, or vice versa. Even in this compromised environment, though, the best health reporters, such as Lawrence K. Altman and Gina Kolata of the *New York Times,* Susan Okie and Victor Cohn of the *Washington Post,* Robert Steinbrook of the *Los Angeles Times,* David Perlman of the *San Francisco Chronicle,* and Ruth SoRelle of the *Houston Chronicle,* will continue to turn out stories that come close to, or succeed in meeting, the reasonable reader standard. And television reporters such as ABC's George Strait, NBC's Robert Bazell, and CBS's Susan Spencer will, as now, frequently come as close to meeting the standard as their ratings-driven medium will allow. When other reporters come along who are as talented and well-trained as these men and women, overall coverage will improve. But as long as the goals of the elite news media remain essentially unchanged, marginal improvement is about all that we can expect.

ENDNOTES

[1]William L. Prosser, *The Law of Torts,* 4th ed. (St Paul: West Publishing, 1971), 151.

[2]Stephen Klaidman and Tom L. Beauchamp, *The Virtuous Journalist* (New York: Oxford University Press, 1987), 32–56.

[3]For the philosophical underpinnings of this argument, please see my essay "The Roles and Responsibilities of the American Press," in Philip S. Cook, ed., *Liberty of Expression* (Washington, D.C.: Wilson Center Press, 1990), 91–108.

[4]Paul Taylor, "Public Figures and Private Lives: What Lines Should Be Drawn?" symposium at the Joan Shorenstein Barone Center, Kennedy School of Government, Harvard University, 10 June 1989.

[5]James Hansen testifying before the Senate Committee on Energy and Natural Resources, 23 June 1988.

[6]Malcolm Peltu, citing another researcher, in "Media Reporting of Risk Information: Uncertainties and the Future," International Workshop on Risk Communication, 17–20 October 1988, KFA Julich, Federal Republic of Germany.

[7]Ibid.

Edward J. Burger, Jr.

Health as a Surrogate for the Environment

"I see nobody on the road," said Alice.

"I only wish I had such eyes," the king remarked with a fretful tone. "To be able to see Nobody! And at that distance too! Why, it's as much as I can do to see real people in this light."

—Lewis Carroll
From *Through the Looking Glass*

A SERIES OF POLITICAL ACTIONS has been taken under the wrong banner. Much environmental legislation and regulation has been enacted under the promise of protection, not of the physical environment, but of human health. The threat to health has been used over the past two decades for "selling" environmental legislation and regulation, often in ways or to a degree that contradicts scientific evidence. Health has been used as a surrogate; the promoters of political action—legislators, environmentalists, and professional consumerists—have been right for the wrong reasons.

On one level, this phenomenon raises the issue of the place of science and scientific fact in forming political judgment on technically complex matters. Establishment scientists and persons with training in preventive medicine have found themselves in the paradoxical position of holding back political zeal for action while trying (often unsuccessfully) to set the factual record straight. The political momentum has promoted and enlarged our national preoccupation with

Edward J. Burger, Jr., M.D. is Director of the Institute for Health Policy Analysis, Washington D.C., and Professor at Georgetown University Medical School.

health and has, in turn, aroused new expectations and fears concerning risk. At the same time, this phenomenon seems to illustrate dramatically what certain academic political scientists have been suggesting for some time: that political action is generally driven not by fact but by metaphor and myth.[1]

Rachael Carson's *Silent Spring* made the environment a national concern and also established health as a political rationale for apprehension about air pollution, pesticide residues, and ionizing radiation from nuclear energy sources.[2] A decade later, this pattern had intensified, and threat to health had become the rallying cry for political action to deal with the environment.

By the end of the 1960s, there was substantial impatience with the pace of environmental improvement. This was followed by an explosion of legislative initiatives, new government agencies, administrative action (the regulation and enforcement of regulations), and soon thereafter, judicial action. Congress entered a period of legislative activism, arrogating to itself greater accountability from the executive branch agencies through a series of new jurisdictional linkages. Taking back some of the discretionary authority it had previously granted to the agencies,[3] Congress wrote greater specificity into laws governing clean air and industrial chemicals.

Health was almost always paramount as a reason for political initiative. Health was thought to be much too important to be weighed against considerations such as costs. The 1970 amendments to the Clean Air Act specifically prohibited the consideration of anything but health in developing primary air quality standards. A commissioner of the Food and Drug Administration in the early 1970s was admonished for keeping an economist on his staff whose duty was to estimate the economic consequences of drug and food regulation.

CASE STUDIES

Five brief case studies illustrate the argument of this essay.

NTA

Tripolyphosphate "builders" used in household detergents were early recognized as substantial contributors to accelerated eutrophication, or aging, of ponds and lakes. Eutrophication is a natural process that occurs at varying rates in almost all surface waters, especially in standing waters such as ponds and lakes. Enriching nutrients lead to the growth of algae and other aquatic vegetation, which accumulate until the ponds and lakes fill in or die.

More than sixty years of study by environmental scientists revealed that eutrophication was occurring in a number of bodies of water at an accelerated pace—over a single generation rather than hundreds or thousands of years, for example. Multiple nutrients were thought to be involved in a complex chemical-biological process. Phosphates were seized upon as particularly important factors because they both controlled the rate of eutrophication in many instances and were controllable.

In 1967, a government task force was created to study the issue of eutrophication and to urge the elimination and replacement of phosphates in household detergents. This admonition was repeated two years later by the advisory board of the International (United States–Canada) Joint Commission, and 1972 was proposed as a deadline for phosphate elimination. Congressional hearings further emphasized the urgency of this substitution and elimination. The problem was a lack of suitable phosphate substitutes. Many of the alternative substances were corrosive or acutely toxic. Only one material, ultimately adopted in Sweden and Canada, stood out as an attractive, biologically inactive, phosphate substitute: nitrilotriacetic acid (NTA). NTA is an example of a chemical with the property known as chelation, the ability to combine with metallic elements. Because of this property, certain chelating chemicals are used for the treatment of acute poisoning.

Given the prospect of widespread use of NTA and its ultimate disposal in the environment, a number of scientific questions could have been raised concerning the effect of NTA on metallic elements in the earth's crust or in biological systems. Yet it was not this phenomenon but a proposed threat of cancer that eventually led to the rejection of NTA.

NTA had been tested in a series of chronic animal studies performed by the National Institute of Environmental Health Science of the National Institutes of Health. In 1971, the National Cancer Institute, another NIH organization, was asked by the surgeon general to render an opinion about whether NTA was or was not a carcinogen. The National Cancer Institute responded that, on the basis of the experimental evidence, NTA could not be ruled out as a carcinogen, for the experimental procedures by which it had been examined were not sufficiently specific to provide a definitive answer.[4] It was this theoretical proposal that NTA might be a carcinogen (which had no empirical basis) that led to a joint government announcement in September 1971 that "the limited data available do not rule out the possibility that NTA is a carcinogen" and took it out of consideration for use in the United States. (NTA has continued to be used in Canada and Sweden.)

DDT

Rachael Carson quite appropriately raised the issue of persistent and stable insecticides such as DDT in 1962 in *Silent Spring*. DDT had been introduced in the mid-1940s and was heavily relied on during World War II as a substance for controlling malaria and other insect vector-borne diseases. Following the war, insect control through a variety of pesticides, including DDT, was begun. DDT was inexpensive, long-lasting in effect, broad in activity, and low in toxicity to humans.

Some of the very features that made DDT advantageous as an insecticide raised fears among those concerned about the environment. DDT residues, found widely distributed in the earth's crust and in the tissues and organs of wildlife, appeared to be associated with abnormal forms and disturbances of animal life. The DDT issue played out for almost a decade and involved the interaction of government regulatory bodies, the Department of Agriculture, the courts, academic scientists, and professional environmentalists.

A year following the publication of *Silent Spring*, a Committee on Pesticides of the President's Science Advisory Committee recommended that "accretion of residues in the environment be controlled by orderly reduction in the use of persistent pesticides."[5] Two years later another panel of the President's Science Advisory Committee on Environmental Pollution pointed to the rapid growth in the manufacture and use of organic chemical pesticides since World War II. The panel again noted the accumulation of residues of pesticides such as DDT both in the physical environment and in human tissues found at autopsy. The aggregate accumulation in human tissues—20 tons—was indeed impressive. However, on the average, the individual accumulation was very small and no adverse health effects associated with these accumulations were recognized.[6]

In 1966, in the name of protection of wildlife and the environment, a lawyer and a small group of scientists entered litigation to stop the use of DDT by a local mosquito control commission in Long Island. Although dismissed by the court, the action was successful in blocking the use of DDT by the control commission. In October of the following year, the Environmental Defense Fund was incorporated to promote the protection of the environment through legal action. Elimination of the use of DDT was chosen as the prime objective. Within a week of incorporation, the Environmental Defense Fund successfully brought legal action against DDT and Dieldrin (another pesticide) in Michigan and, a year later, in Wisconsin.

With success in three localities, the EDF joined with the National Audubon Society, the Sierra Club, and the West Michigan Environmental Action Council to petition the secretary of agriculture in October 1969 to cancel and suspend all pesticide products containing DDT.* At the same time, the EDF petitioned the Secretary of the Department of Health, Education, and Welfare to repeal the "tolerances" for allowable residue levels of DDT in agricultural products intended for human consumption.

Between 1969 and 1972, DDT was the centerpiece of a series of lawsuits brought by representatives of the environmental community to force the executive branch agencies to reduce or ban permitted uses of DDT. Several government agencies, representing a variety of interests, were involved. The environmentalist plaintiffs petitioned the court to cancel and suspend all existing DDT registrations. The court returned the issues to the regulatory agencies, who responded with moderate action. This was followed in each case by a new cycle leading to further but still moderate response. In all, four cycles of review by the courts and remanding to the executive branch agencies took place.

By 1971, the new Environmental Protection Agency had come into being, and a third cycle of judicial review followed by administrative

*The unit of government approval of a pesticide product is a "registered use" of the product. Revocation of approval may come in the form of cancellation (a deliberate move taken after a period of study and review) or suspension (an immediate ban).

review ensued, resulting this time in some new legal principles governing the regulation of environmental hazards.[7]

On July 15, 1971, the administrator of the EPA issued notices of cancellation of all remaining registered uses of DDT. More than fifty registrants filed objections and requested a public hearing. Two registrants requested review by a specially appointed scientific advisory committee. A fourth court review ensued over the demands for immediate suspension, and again the issue was sent to the government agency for reworking.

As the law provided, the EPA both appointed a scientific review committee and held a public hearing to advise on how to respond to the challenges to DDT. In September 1971, the DDT Advisory Committee concluded that the worldwide pool of DDT was significant, was widely distributed, and had not decreased in size markedly, despite a pattern of declining usage. The committee acknowledged an association between DDT residues and effects on wildlife and, for this reason, recommended reduction in the use of DDT at an accelerated rate, leading ultimately to "the elimination of any significant addition to the environment."[8]

The public hearing on DDT began on August 17, 1971, continued over six months, and produced a transcript of 9,000 pages of testimony. Manufacturers, the Plant Protection Division of the Department of Agriculture, the secretary of agriculture, and the Environmental Protection Agency composed the 123 who testified. During the course of this testimony, DDT residues in human tissues and organs were acknowledged, but there was no clear evidence that human exposure to DDT was related to disease.

In April 1972, the hearing examiner issued a series of "decisions and recommendations" in which he proposed that all cancellations be withdrawn and that, with very few exceptions, the registered uses be continued.

Within two months, the administrator of the EPA proceeded to make his own "findings of fact" and ordered the cancellation of essentially all domestic uses of DDT. In his announcement, he acknowledged the widespread distribution of DDT in the environment and the biological accumulation of DDT residues in wildlife and evidence for the toxic effects on some forms of wildlife. He also stated that:

> DDT is found in the tissues of members of the general population. While the acute human toxicity of DDT is low, there is presumptive evidence of association between DDT exposure and cancer in man.[9]

This assertion contradicted one of the conclusions of an extensive review of the biological properties and effects on human health of exposure to DDT and other pesticides undertaken by a group of scientists convened three years earlier by the secretary of HEW—the Commission on Pesticides. It had found that:

> On the basis of present knowledge, the only unequivocal consequence of long-term exposure to persistent pesticides, at the levels encountered by the general population, is the acquisition of residues to tissues and body fluids. No reliable study has revealed a causal association between the presence of these residues and human disease.[10]

Thus, while the previous reviews of DDT and its biological effects had not indicated a human health hazard, the possibility that DDT might cause cancer became one of the prominent arguments used to justify an environmental decision.

Air Pollution

In the early 1970s, Congress leaned particularly hard on health-related arguments in seeking revision of the laws governing air pollution. Air pollution laws had existed in some form in the United States since 1881, when the Chicago city council adopted an ordinance on the subject. In the late 1940s and early 1950s public concern about air pollution rose, spurred by acute air pollution in Donora, Pennsylvania, in 1948 and in London, England, in 1952.

Recognizing its federal responsibility, Congress passed the first version of the Clean Air Act in 1953. After a four-day inversion in 1966, public sentiment again increased in favor of government responsibility, and President Johnson proposed the Air Quality Act of 1967. That law established regional "airsheds" and regional commissions, all to be governed by national standards. Thus, the initial form of government control over air pollutants was a combination of federal guidance and regional jurisdiction.

A change in political strategy in 1969 and 1970 profoundly affected national institutions—both public and private. In the Senate, principal jurisdiction over air quality lay with the Senate Public Works Committee. Frustrated with the pace of reducing air pollution in the past, this committee recommended marked changes in federal action and federal responsibility. Protection of human health was deemed *the* nominal basis for action and more important than all other factors. The committee report accompanying a new legislative proposal in 1970 stated that:

> (1) the health of people is more important than the question of whether the early achievement of ambient air quality standards protective of human health is technically feasible; and (2) the growth of pollution load in many areas, even with the application of available technology, would still be deleterious to public health. Therefore, the Committee determined that existing sources of pollutants either should meet the standard of the law or be closed down.[11]

Impatience with slow action at the state level provoked Congress to legislate aggressively to control air pollution. National standards, termed primary air quality standards, were to be established, and health considerations alone were to determine them. An additional special class of airborne contaminants, theoretically believed to have an adverse effect on public health, were singled out for special attention. Industries identified as sources of these pollutants would be obliged to prove that these emissions would not be harmful to human health.

The Senate Public Works Committee put special emphasis on automobile exhaust emissions, and Congress wrote numerical standards into the law. Again, the exclusive goal was protection of health and welfare, and references to economic and technological feasibility were struck from the legislative history. For the automotive emission standards, the committee staff borrowed from two preliminary documents. The authors of one unpublished analysis, a theoretical calculation of automotive emissions required to reach desired air pollution levels, had used Los Angeles County—the worst case—and extended their resulting estimates to the remainder of the country.[12] The other paper, published in *Science* by two economists, described a series of proposed "research" levels of emissions as "goals."[13]

Congress leaned on this scant factual record and then proceeded to build a highly conservative (risk-averse) case. The research standards were written into the law as operational standards, and the timetable for their achievement was moved to five years earlier than the scientists themselves had proposed.

Senator Edmund Muskie, then chairman of the Subcommittee on Air and Water Pollution of the Senate Public Works Committee, in a speech to the National Academy of Sciences in 1973 said:

> The health of the American people must be protected against environmental hazards . . . . And we must not allow those standards to be compromised because they are difficult to achieve, or because of cost . . . .

While Senator Muskie also insisted that environmental standards should be based on "the best evidence the scientific community can develop,"[14] it soon became clear that the legislative process was in no mood to await a deliberate judgment about the existing body of fact.

Within five years of enactment of the 1970 amendments, a senior scientist from the Department of Health, Education, and Welfare wrote:

> In my opinion the scientific basis for legislatively mandated standards did not address the uncertainties in our technical information base. Therefore, one should ask whether or not somewhat less stringent emission controls would not be more defensible and whether or not an honest technical effort several years ago would not have prevented or minimized national discord centering on this issue. It is my opinion that Federal scientists may have been too eager to support their superiors and unwilling to examine critically our scientific information base. If this opinion is correct, then most of the revisions in emission standards currently under discussion really deal not with any significant relaxation affecting public health but with the uncertainties inherent in the original emissions standards.[15]

Perhaps even more damning was a critical view volunteered a year later by an EPA scientist who described the climate surrounding the development of the 1970 standards:

> The philosophy that took shape called for scraping the barrel of experimental evidence to locate the lowest level, for a given averaging time, at which an adverse effect had been reported. Circumstantial evidence was all that was needed.[16]

This force fitting of a body of fact to accommodate a political decision had numerous consequences. One was confusion over the question of what improvements in health would follow the revision of air quality standards.[17] Another was tension between academic scientists, who were concerned about the factual basis for important policy decisions, and government representatives, who felt obliged to respond to public perceptions.[18]

Another consequence of this episode was the establishment of an oversight review process for regulatory agencies in the Executive Office of the President. By mid-1971, the amended Clean Air Act had produced a number of tensions within the executive branch of government. The executive branch had no institutional mechanism nor any political incentive for taking systematic account of the broad consequences of this or other regulatory actions for other government agencies and programs or for other aspects of national life. The narrowness of the considerations in the case of the Clean Air Act, coupled with a growing barrage of complaints from industries affected, ultimately provoked the establishment of a bureau in the Office of Management and Budget to be notified of important proposed regulations and to review those regulations before they were made public. This Executive Office oversight review mechanism, initially called the Quality of Life Review Process, has remained in place and relatively little changed to the present day.

PCBs

PCBs—polychlorinated biphenyls—are a group of 210 related chemical substances developed for commercial use in the 1920s. They have unusual chemical and physical stability as well as important electrical insulating properties. Their major use has been in electrical equipment—transformers and capacitors—particularly in confined spaces where their use has reduced the hazard of fire and explosion. Political-scientific concerns about PCBs arose in the late 1960s for two reasons: trace quantities were discovered to be widely distributed in the environment in a fashion similar to DDT and were similarly believed harmful to wildlife; as a result of an accidental leakage into rice oil being processed for cooking use in a Japanese plant, approximately 1,000 persons were made ill in 1968.

The toxicity and biological properties of PCBs had been investigated modestly in the 1930s and, by the standards of that day, they had been found biologically very inactive (nontoxic). But in 1969–1970, PCBs became the most prominent chemical material used to promote the Toxic Substances Control Act, then being considered by Congress. Between 1970 and 1972, PCBs were the subject of substantial scientific review and a barrage of newspaper stories. Government reports, including those which reflected the views of academic scientists, essentially exonerated PCBs as toxic substances and pointed to more biologically active impurities. A combination of government and private-industry announcements of restrictions on manufacture, distribution, and use were made in 1972 with the expectation that a better-informed public would be less anxious.[19]

Instead, however, the public became even more alarmed about the use of PCBs. Chosen as the paradigm of toxic substances by the promoters of the Toxic Substances Control Act, PCBs received enormous press coverage between 1971 and 1976. They were described as "deadly chemicals in American industry,"[20] "thought by many scientists to be a serious long-term danger to man and animals,"[21] and "linked to birth defects."[22]

As enactment of the proposed law grew more likely in 1975–1976, press focus on PCBs increased, this time emphasizing the specter of cancer.[23] In August 1976, the Senate approved the Toxic Substances Control Act. During that month, Representative Gilbert Gude introduced a last-minute amendment that wrote special restrictions and regulations exclusively for PCBs into the act. A story in the *New York Times* referred to PCBs as "a class of chemicals . . . linked to cancer and birth defects, water pollution and wildlife contamination" and noted that some House members believed "banning PCBs was a moral responsibility to the people."[24]

To this day, PCBs are described as cancer-causing agents, yet no scientific evidence justifies this reputation.[25]

The initial proposals for legislation for "hazardous substances" arose over a perceived need to inform the government and, where appropriate, control the introduction into commerce of otherwise unregulated new chemical products and metals thought to pose a threat to human health or ecological balance.[26] The gestation period for this legislation was nearly seven years. During this time, protection of health became the prominent political rationale for legislation. A speech in 1975 by John Quarles, deputy administrator of the EPA, to the Manufacturing Chemists Association was typical. It began with an assertion that "the potential impact of toxic substances on the health of people is frightening" and continued with references to "time bombs" and emphasized a link to cancer.[27]

The Council of Environmental Quality devoted the first chapter of its 1975 annual report to a discussion of exposure to environmental chemical substances as *the* significant contributor to human cancer. That same report discussed the need for legislation to control PCBs.

Following the passage of the Toxic Substances Control Act in October 1976, the EPA issued an information bulletin explaining the scope and background of the new law. Once again, threat to human health was emphasized and PCBs were highlighted as "the most vivid example of the danger of uncontrolled chemical contaminants."[28]

Tetraethyl Lead

Lead, a widely distributed natural constituent of the earth's crust, has been used beneficially by man for 6,000 years. The biological properties of metallic lead and of organic compounds of lead have been extensively explored and the toxicity of lead is well understood.

Because it is widely distributed naturally in the environment, human exposure to lead occurs via a number of routes, including the water we drink and the food we ingest. Industrial use of lead contributes to the redistribution of lead in the environment and to further exposure. The largest consumer of lead has been the storage battery industry and the second largest, the petroleum industry. Tetraethyl and tetramethyl lead were adopted as fuel additives in 1922 as antiknock substances in automotive gasoline. Harmful exposure of children to lead-containing paint has been recognized for years and has slowly been reduced through the use of nonlead paints and the covering or replacement of painted surfaces in buildings.

The health implications of airborne lead from engine exhaust have been a subject of scientific study and public controversy for many years. In his Harben Lectures in 1960, scientist Robert A. Kehoe reviewed what was known of the metabolism of lead and of the significance of population exposure to low-level, lead-containing emissions.[29] His conclusions (which at that point exonerated tetraethyl lead as a community hazard) were technically sound. However, they were suspect in the minds of some, for his laboratory was funded by the very fortune that had derived from the development of the gasoline engine.

In addition to concern for human health, a second issue arose in the late 1960s and early 1970s that focused national attention on lead. The automobile was recognized as a major contributor to air pollution in certain cities. If automobile traffic itself were not to be curtailed, a decrease in airborne hydrocarbons from automotive sources would have to be brought about. This required the modification of automobile engines and the addition of a catalytic device to the exhaust systems. Because lead acted as a poison to the device, a source of lead-free gasoline was necessary. The new Clean Air Act amendments of 1970 gave the EPA administrator the authority to prohibit the sale of lead-containing fuel additives if he determined that these would "endanger human health or any emission device."[30]

The scientific data relating tetraethyl lead in gasoline to human health were still inconclusive. It was the catalyst issue and the requirement to provide a lead-free supply of gasoline that prompted the regulation of lead-containing fuels.

In early 1972, a committee of the National Academy of Sciences reported that:

1. The atmosphere over large cities contained twenty times the concentration of lead found in air over sparsely populated areas of the country.

2. The consumption of lead alkyl fuel additives was increasing substantially every year while the data suggested that the concentration of lead in air, even over the largest cities, was increasing very slowly, if at all.

3. Lead paint was clearly the principal environmental source for children living in urban ghettos. Approximately 1 percent had symptoms compatible with clinical lead poisoning.

4. There had been no cases of lead poisoning due to lead as a community air pollutant.

5. Airborne lead could conceivably add to the lead burden of urban-dwelling children through the oral or the respiratory route.[31]

In the *Federal Register* of February 1972, the EPA published two regulations for lead and phosphorus in gasoline: lead- and phosphorus-free gasoline was to be generally available by July 1, 1974, and the percentage of lead in the remaining gasoline was to be steadily reduced in stages between January 1, 1974, and July 1, 1977.[32]

These proposals were accompanied by background papers dealing with health and economic questions, implications for the petroleum industry, and the relationship between these actions and other environmental controls. The basis for these proposals included the assumption that a supply of lead-free gasoline would exist along with a concern for health.

In a reevaluation of its position on the health effects of airborne lead in September 1972, the EPA proposed to further reduce lead emission from automobiles on the basis of "new" information about lead in the tissues and organs of urban children. Contrary to the judgment of the National Academy of Sciences Committee, the EPA proposed that a sizeable number of urban children, already found to have higher-than-normal blood lead levels, would be especially vulnerable to ingestion of dust containing lead.[33] With this reasoning, EPA proposed to reverse the order of its initiatives and place the health issue far in front of the technological (catalytic converter) issue.

The real purpose of this move was to use the specter of a health hazard as the political argument for reducing lead in gasoline. The EPA proposal immediately became a target of severe criticism from the secretary of HEW and from other lead experts in the government. In a letter to the EPA administrator, notable for its candor, Merlin DuVal, secretary of HEW, wrote:

> The decision [for regulating tetraethyl lead] having been made upon grounds other than those having to do with hazard to the public health, your staff now rushed to explore with us the question of whether or not a hazard to the public health could be involved as a reason for accelerating the implementation date of the primary decision. It is our view that there is no firm evidence, at this time, that lead poisoning in humans could be traced per se to the presence of lead in gasoline.[34]

On January 10, 1973, the EPA published its proposals for providing a lead-free gasoline supply and phased removal of lead from the remainder of gasoline. In October, the National Resources Defense Council sued the EPA for what the NRDC considered inadequate regulation and considerable delay in announcing fuel regulations. In November, the EPA announced its final decisions, including the eventual removal of all lead from gasoline. These decisions were challenged in court. A three-judge panel reversed the EPA on its health-based regulations because of inadequate data. This decision was later reversed by the full panel of appellate judges.

THE POLITICAL USE OF CANCER

A British senior scientist remarked during an international scientific meeting in 1985 that the United States had become "thoroughly persuaded of the teachings of the Book of Genesis—carcinogenesis, teratogenesis and mutagenesis."[35] The contribution of environmental physical and chemical agents—real or perceived—to the human cancer burden, to genetic alteration, and to the incidence of congenital anomalies has been the prominent centerpiece of legislative and administrative strategies to defend or promote environmental initiatives.

The original form of the legislative proposal that eventually became the Superfund law, designed to improve or restore chemical waste disposal sites, was based on both a concern for maintaining the integrity of property and a concern about hazards to health resulting from human exposure to soil contaminants. It initially envisioned a monetary compensation program for impacts on health attributable to residence near dump sites. An early compromise led to the dropping of the health issue in order to secure passage of the Superfund law. As a part of that compromise, a study was commissioned to determine the degree of hazard posed by chemical waste disposal sites.[36] The focus of the report from this study group was on cancer and birth defects. The study group was able to make no determination of the impact of chemical waste disposal on health but nevertheless crafted an elaborate second compensation system to accommodate such health claims.

In 1978, three government research agencies issued an unpublished report designed to estimate the contribution of the occupational environment to human cancer.[37] This document, whose analysis was later discounted by its nine contributors, stated that at least 20 percent of cancer mortality was attributable to occupational factors, of which asbestos contributed 13 to 15 percent. The message of this report became quickly translated into a political announcement in a speech by Joseph Califano, then secretary of HEW.

The estimates paper and the Califano speech brought forth a barrage of criticism from a number of scientists who found no empirical basis for the conclusions. Two British epidemiologists, Sir Richard Doll and Richard Peto, were sufficiently provoked by the estimates paper and its political consequences to develop a more rigorous analysis of the causes of cancer in the United States, in which they noted that:

> It seems likely that whoever wrote the [estimates] paper . . . did so for political rather than scientific purposes and it will undoubtedly continue in the future as in the past to be used for political purposes . . . .[38]

IMPLICATIONS

How should we think about these matters? On one level, of course, we can applaud the unquestioned success of the political strategy. Concern about health has been skillfully and successfully used to sell the environment as a political issue. The question of whether the same political outcome would have been realized without the use of the strategy is difficult to determine since the necessary social experiment was not performed.

On another level, it is proper to contemplate the long-term effects of this political strategy on public perceptions of risk and, therefore, on personal and political behavior. Have the pessimistic or even dire predictions for health accompanying each major legislative and regulatory proposal for the environment, amplified by press reports of those political activities, contributed to the public's understanding of what threatens its health? There are strong indications that the two are linked. Further, the press appears to play upon itself in circular fashion. With the government's interest in PCBs in the early 1970s, an enormous amount of new applied research was begun to illuminate further the biological properties of that family of compounds. An extensive body of knowledge was developed, wiping away uncertainties and leaving a substantial legacy of information about how PCBs do and don't interact with cells, tissues, and organs. The original estimates of PCBs as relatively biologically inert have been confirmed. However, as in all areas of science, the resolution of scientific questions through experiment always leads to a further generation of questions and new hypotheses. These new loose ends of scientific understanding have been seized upon by those who wish to indict PCBs as the paradigm of toxic chemical species. Thus, it appears that while this pattern of political maneuvering and public advertisement has been successful in promoting environmental issues, it has also contributed to a trail of both expectations and fears which promises to persist for decades. It has played a major role in setting the national agenda for public concern about health and risks to health.

This political legacy has, in turn, made possible further political action with second- and higher-order ramifications. A prominent referendum initiative in California—The Safe Drinking Water and Toxic Enforcement Act of 1986, known popularly as Proposition 65—was initiated and successfully sold to the citizens of California through the enlistment of fears of disease caused by man-made chemical substances.[39] There is no evidence that this new law will contribute anything beneficial to the health of Californians (although it has created an extensive new economic activity marked by legal maneuvering). The concern about environmental risks to health continues to shape national and governmental policies on issues such as energy, agricultural practices, and export of U.S. products.

One of the paradoxical consequences of this saga has been the cohort of academic scientists and physicians, trained in preventive medicine, who have found themselves unexpectedly opposing the very political moves that are taken in the name of preservation of health. The body of factual evidence doesn't exist, they have said, or its components don't pass elementary tests of intellectually respectable data.

Yet, there is even another level at which to consider this brief history. A traditional view has held that an informed and interested electorate was a necessary ingredient in a properly functioning democratic governmental process. It was the individual's ability and willingness to arm himself with objective information and to choose rationally that was considered a prerequisite of efficient, democratic governmental machinery. This accords with the scientist's own belief in the integrity of factual information and the importance of providing that factual basis for sound public choices.

This traditional, even sacred, view of democratic fundamentals has been placed in great doubt in recent years, notably by those students of political science who see as the basis for political choice, not fact and objective reason, but rather, myth and metaphor. Roger Cobb and Charles Elder have frankly declared that "systematic research over the last two decades consistently revealed that those high standards and historically perceived requisites for democracy were not met or even approached by any western democracy."[40] Murray Edelman has stated that "political beliefs and perceptions are very largely not based upon empirical observation or, indeed, upon information at all."[41] It is metaphor and myth, not objective or empirically derived evidence which shapes the political landscape.

According to this view, substantial political agendas are created around conflict and emotion.[42] They coalesce attachments to myths and metaphors and these, in turn, shape or become the perceptions of the political world. In this role, metaphors take on new and important powers of their own. They can evoke an altered political or physical landscape in which both anxieties and solutions are revealed. As Edelman notes, "The ubiquity of [public] anxiety and its externalization in myth are important ingredients in creating and assuring a political following."[43]

Furthermore, myths and metaphors can simplify, whereas facts tend to confuse public thinking:

> Political metaphors can vividly, potently, and persuasively evoke changed worlds in which the remedies for anxieties are clearly perceived and self-serving courses of action are sanctified.[44]

Finally, and equally important, metaphorically determined public attitude is resistant to alteration and therefore often unaffected by contrary data—from whatever quarter or however credible and objective. Thus, rather than mirroring objective reality, myth and metaphor create new prescriptions that emphasize seemingly simple solutions to a complex maze of alternatives, and resultant beliefs are remarkably immune to revision by the most rigorously considered objective data.

ENDNOTES

[1]M. Edelman, *Politics as Symbolic Action: Mass Arousal and Quiescence* (New York: Academic Press, 1971), 65.

[2]R. Carson, *Silent Spring* (New York: Houghton Mifflin, 1962).

[3]U.S. Department of Health, Education, and Welfare, "Report and Conclusions Concerning the Use of Nitrilotriaceic Acid and Other Substitutes for Phosphates in Laundry Detergents," unpublished, 15 September 1971.

[4]Ibid.

[5]*Use of Pesticides,* a report of the President's Science Advisory Committee (Washington, D.C.: The White House, 15 May 1963).

[6]*Restoring the Quality of Our Environment,* a report of the Environmental Pollution Panel of the President's Science Advisor (Washington, D.C.: The White House, November 1965).

[7]*Environmental Defense Fund v. Ruckelshaus,* U.S. Court of Appeals, District of Columbia Circuit, 7 January 1971, 439 F.2d 584.

[8]Report of the DDT Advisory Committee to William D. Ruckelshaus, Administrator, U.S. Environmental Protection Agency, 9 September 1971.

[9]W. Ruckelshaus, decision on DDT, April 1972.

[10]*Report of the Secretary's Commission on Pesticides and Their Relationship to Environmental Health,* Parts I and II (Washington, D.C.: U.S. Department of Health, Education, and Welfare, December 1969).

[11]*National Air Quality Standard Act of 1970,* report of the Committee on Public Works, United States Senate, to accompany S.4358, Report No. 91–116, 17 September 1970.

[12]D. S. Barth, J. C. Romanovsky, E. A. Shuck, and N. P. Ceransky, "Federal Motor Vehicle Emissions Goals for CO, HC, and NO_x, Based on Desired Air Quality Levels," unpublished paper presented at the Annual Meeting of the Air Pollution Control Association, 16 June 1970.

[13]L. B. Lave and E. B. Seskin, "Air Pollution and Human Health," *Science* 169 (3947) (21 August 1970): 723–33.

[14]Edmund S. Muskie, speech delivered at the National Academy of Sciences Symposium on Health Standards in the Clean Air Act of 1970, Washington, D.C., 3 October 1973.

[15]J. F. Finklea, "Setting and Revising Emission Standards for Light Duty Motor Vehicles," memorandum to files, National Institute for Occupational Safety and Health, Center for Disease Control, U.S. Department of Health, Education and Welfare, 1975.

[16]J. Romanovsky, personal communication, 26 February 1976.

[17]H. Schimmel, *Evidence for Possible Acute Health Effects of Ambient Air Pollution from Time Series Analysis: Methodological Questions and Some New Results Based on New York City Daily Mortality, 1963–1976,* a report, read in part, submitted for discussion at symposium, "Environmental Effects of Sulfur and Related Particulates," New York Academy of Sciences, 23 and 24 March 1978.

[18]B. G. Ferris, Jr. and F. E. Speizer, "Criteria for Establishing Standards for Air Pollutants," paper developed for the Air Quality Project, the Business Roundtable, New York. The authors proposed a definition of adverse health effect as "medically significant physiologic or pathologic changes generally evidenced by permanent damage or incapacitating illness to the individual." That view, interestingly, turned out to be too conservative for the business community in the 1970s, and the scientific interpretation was published without comment.

[19]Panel on Hazardous Trace Substances, "Polychlorinated Biphenyls—Environmental Impact: A Review," *Environmental Research* 5 (1972): 249–362; and Interdepartmental Task Force on PCBs, *Polychlorinated Biphenyls and the Environment,* No. ADM–72–10419 (Springfield, Va.: National Technical Information Service, U.S. Department of Commerce, 1972).

[20]H. Burchard, "Law Sought to Ban DDT-like Chemical," *Washington Post,* 25 July 1971.

[21]H. Burchard, "Millions of Children Tainted," *Washington Post,* 24 July 1971.

[22]"Dr. S. S. Epstein Warns That NTA, PCB, Thought Responsible for Birth Defects in Babies in Japan," *New York Times,* 26 September 1971.

[23]See for example G. Hill, "U.S. Agency Wages a Drive to Ban Cancer by Screening Chemicals," *New York Times,* 28 February 1976; M. Sheraton, "Consumer Cancer Grows," *New York Times,* 22 March 1976; "Anti-cancer Compromise," *New York Times,* 5 June 1976.

[24]R. D. Lyons, "House Votes Ban on Output of PCBs within 3 Years," *New York Times,* 25 August 1976.

[25]*Lake Michigan Sport Fishing: Should You Eat Your Catch?* (Washington, D.C.: National Wildlife Federation, 1989).

[26]"Control of Hazardous Substances, Need for Legislation," unpublished memorandum, Council on Environmental Quality, Executive Office of the President, Washington, D.C., 30 September 1970.

[27]J. R. Quarles, Jr., "Toxic Substances—Time Bombs, Set and Ticking," speech to the Manufacturing Chemists Association/EPA symposium, "Water and Hazardous Materials Regulations," Hotel Washington, Washington, D.C., 14 May 1975.

[28]Toxic Substances Control Act, accompanying brochure, (Washington, D.C.: Office of Public Affairs, U.S. Environmental Protection Agency, 7 October 1976).

[29]R. A. Kehoe, "The Metabolism of Lead in Man in Health and Disease," the Harben Lecture 1960, *Journal of the Royal Institute of Public Health and Hygiene* 24 (1961): 81–97; 101–20; 129–43; 177–203.

[30]The Clean Air Act as amended, 42 U.S.C., 1970.

[31]National Academy of Sciences, *Airborne Lead in Perspective* (Washington, D.C.: Committee on the Biological Effects of Air Pollutants, 1972).

[32]"Notice of Proposed Rule Making. Regulation of Fuels and Fuel Additives," *Federal Register* 37 (36) (23 February 1972): 3882–84.

[33]*Update of EPA's Position on Health Effects of Lead, The Agency's Health Position for Controlling Lead Emission from Motor Vehicle Exhaust* (Washington, D.C.: U.S. Environmental Protection Agency, 22 September 1972).

[34]M. K. DuVal, letter to William D. Ruckelshaus, 23 August 1972.

[35]*The Chemical Industry and the Health of the Community* (London: Royal Society of Medicine, June 1985).

[36]U.S. Senate, *Injuries and Damages from Hazardous Wastes—Analysis and Improvement of Legal Remedies,* a report to the Congress in compliance with Section 301(e) of the Comprehensive Environmental Response, Compensation and Liability Act of 1980 (PL 96–510) by the Superfund Section 301(e) Study Group, Committee Print, Serial No. 97–12 (Washington, D.C.: Senate Committee on Environment and Public Works, September 1982).

[37]National Institute of Environmental Health Sciences, National Institute for Occupational Safety and Health, National Cancer Institute, "Estimates of the Fraction of Cancer in the United States Related to Occupational Factors," unpublished, 15 September 1978.

[38]R. Doll and R. Peto, *The Causes of Cancer: Quantitative Estimates of Avoidable Risks of Cancer in the United States Today* (Oxford: Oxford University Press, 1981).

[39]State of California, Water and Toxic Enforcement Act of 1986.

[40]R. W. Cobb and C. D. Elder, *Participation in American Politics: the Dynamics of Agenda Building* (Baltimore: Johns Hopkins University Press, 1983).

[41]M. Edelman, *Politics as Symbolic Action* (Chicago: University of Chicago Press, 1971).

[42]M. Edelman, *Constructing the Political Spectacle* (Chicago: University of Chicago Press, 1988).

[43]Edelman, *Politics as Symbolic Action.*

[44]Ibid.

That it will never come again
Is what makes life so sweet.

Emily Dickinson (1839–1886)
From *Bolts of Melody*

Allan M. Brandt

The Cigarette, Risk, and American Culture

On Saturday, January 11, 1964, Surgeon General Luther Terry stepped to the podium of the State Department auditorium to begin a nationally televised press conference. Seated directly behind him were ten eminent physicians and scientists, the members of his Advisory Committee on Smoking and Health. This group of individuals had met regularly over the last eighteen months to evaluate the evidence about the risks of cigarette smoking. Although the results of this investigation had been held top secret, signs prohibiting smoking hung in the auditorium, a harbinger of the coming announcement. In the outside corridors, members of the press puffed away. Reporters were offered copies of the report in the closed auditorium for an hour before the press conference. At the conclusion of the session, they rushed to phones to call in the story. The next day, the report received front-page coverage throughout the country.

For the 70 million regular smokers in the United States, the report constituted bad news. It found that among men who smoke cigarettes the death rate from cancer of the lung was 1,000 percent higher than among nonsmokers. The report also cited chronic bronchitis and emphysema to be of far greater incidence among smokers. Additionally, the committee found that the incidence of coronary artery disease, the leading cause of death in the United States, was 70

Allan M. Brandt is Associate Professor in the Department of Social Medicine and the Department of History at the University of North Carolina at Chapel Hill.

percent higher among smokers. In short, cigarette smokers placed themselves at much higher risk of serious disease than did non-smokers.[1]

These findings, contained in the massive 387-page document, which cited thousands of research studies, held few surprises. In fact, the committee had conducted no new research. It had merely reviewed existing data. And indeed, since the early twentieth century and beyond, physicians had pointed out hazards of cigarette smoking. As long as there have been cigarettes there has been concern about their impact on health. By the time of the release of the report, polls showed that most Americans already associated cigarettes with cancer. If such information was widely known, what is the meaning of the surgeon general's committee report, and what was its significance? What were the social and scientific forces which led to the report and what was its impact?

The report marked the beginning of a revolution in attitudes and behaviors relating to cigarettes. In the last quarter century, half of all living Americans who have ever smoked have now quit. At the time of the 1964 report, 42 percent of all U.S. adults smoked; in 1989, only 26 percent were smokers. According to the most recent *Surgeon General's Report* (1989), approximately 750,000 smoking-related deaths have been avoided since 1964 because people have quit or not started smoking.[2] Terry's *Surgeon General's Report* signaled the beginning of a profound change in the meaning of the cigarette and spurred new interest more generally in the relationship of behavior, risk, and health.

This essay briefly traces the history of the debate about the risk of smoking and places the *Surgeon General's Report* in a broader context by examining the process by which the cigarette came to be defined as a major health risk. The report raised fundamental questions about the nature of biomedicine, public health, and especially causal inference; it profoundly altered the way we think about issues of health and disease. This was part of a broader debate in twentieth-century science about the nature of evidence, proof, and causality, a debate about the epistemological foundations of biomedicine. How do we know what we know? What constitutes "proof" in modern science? What is the nature of causal relationships? And finally, how will risks be defined, measured, and regulated?

The cigarette provides a means of tracing an important watershed in medical "ways of knowing." But the issues raised go beyond the realm of biomedicine; the debate about smoking was shaped by the meaning of the cigarette in American culture, the nature of the tobacco industry, public health, and government. In short, the process by which risk is assessed and perceived reveals deep social, cultural, and political values.[3]

THE RISE OF THE CIGARETTE

In many ways the cigarette seems such a ubiquitous part of American culture that it is difficult to imagine that it is really a twentieth-century phenomenon. Between 1900 and 1965, per capita consumption rose from 49 to 4,318.

Developments in agricultural technique, production technology, and industrial organization, as well as such factors as the introduction of the portable match, all contributed to the growth of the tobacco industry.[4] The cigarette marks the convergence of corporate capitalism, technology, mass marketing, and, in particular, the impact of advertising.[5] These forces induced new modes of individual and group behavior. With the rise of consumerism, a new behavioral ethic was defined. From a culture that promoted self-denial and self-discipline in the late nineteenth century—one condemning indulgence in all forms—Americans were now encouraged to indulge.

As individuals came to fear the loss of autonomy in an industrial world, cigarette smoking promised individual redemption. The Marlboro man was the first urban-industrial cowboy, a symbol of modernity, autonomy, power, and sexuality. Such advertising pointed away from the product toward the moral and psychological value of the patron.[6] Advertising promised consumers well-being and power.[7] Creating demand for relatively undifferentiated, nonessential items was the core of the new consumer culture, which the cigarette epitomizes. The tobacco industry boomed, as did state revenues associated with the manufacture and sale of cigarettes. When demand for cigarettes rose, so too did concern about their impact on health.

As cigarette smoking became increasingly popular in the early twentieth century, claims for its virtues and vices ran strong. Though many touted the positive and pleasureful aspects of the cigarette, the dramatic rise in smoking was accompanied by a powerful anti-cigarette movement which sought to identify both the moral and the health risks of tobacco. By the first decade of the twentieth century, concerns about the demoralizing impact of the cigarette were widely cited.

Boys were often caught sneaking off behind school buildings to smoke in groups, and "cigarette fiends" were identified as a major social problem of the growing cities. Among the most prominent anti-cigarette crusaders was Henry Ford. "If you will study the history of almost any criminal you will find that he is an inveterate cigarette smoker," advised Ford.[8] He donated the funds for the publication of a national journal which appeared under the title "The Case Against the Little White Slaver." On another occasion Ford explained, "With every breath of cigarette smoke they inhale imbecility and exhale manhood. . . . The yellow finger stain is an emblem of deeper degradation and enslavement than the ball and chain." Ford enlisted Thomas Edison to investigate scientifically the harms of smoking.

In addition to the concern expressed about young boys smoking, anti-cigarette activists centered attention on the detrimental consequences of smoking for women—now vigorously solicited as smokers—and its impact on their health and social mores.[9] As the movement for prohibition gathered momentum, cigarettes were frequently tied to the use of alcohol. By the First World War, some thirteen states had enacted legislation prohibiting or regulating the sale of cigarettes; anti-cigarette activists often cited medical and scientific experts in support of such controls.[10]

By the 1920s, as consumption continued to rise, research into the consequences of smoking intensified. Researchers focused attention on the impact of tobacco on what they called "mental efficiency." Usually in such studies, smokers fared poorly.[11] But the problem with such research was clear; as one scientist explained, "It might be either that the smoking habit induces lethargy or that lazy men are the kind that find smoking agreeable."[12] This problem of inference would continue to plague the debate about smoking into our time. Other studies concentrated on the physical growth and development of smokers; did cigarette smoking stunt growth?[13] The moralistic nature of such experiments lay just below the surface.

It could be argued that moral reformers protesting the rising use of cigarettes in America hid behind the cloak of scientific authority in offering their arguments. But this would misrepresent their ideas and tactics. They simply saw no tension in seeing the cigarette as ungodly *and* unhealthy; they equated moral dangers and health risks. Moral reformers had absolutely no compunction about employing arguments based on weak data about the physically debilitating impact of smoking. Medical doctors and researchers moved easily between citing the moral and citing the health consequences of smoking; there was no attempt to differentiate such arguments.

MODERN EPIDEMIOLOGY AND STATISTICAL INFERENCE

By the late 1920s, researchers began to focus more precisely on the *specific* health consequences of smoking. As early as 1928, in a somewhat primitive epidemiological study, researchers associated heavy smoking with cancer.[14] In addition, surgeons published clinical reports associating cancer in their patients with their smoking habits.[15] In 1931, Frederick L. Hoffman, a well-known statistician for the Prudential Insurance Company, tied smoking to cancer. Hoffman noted the difficulties of conducting epidemiological studies in this area. The basic methodological questions of statistical research—issues of representativeness, sample size, and the construction of control groups—all presented researchers with a series of complex problems. Hoffman called for the exercise of moderation in all behavior, a truism of progressive hygiene, suggesting that "extreme moderation in smoking habits would certainly be advisable."[16]

In 1938, Raymond Pearl, the Johns Hopkins statistician and biometrician, published the first significant statistical analysis of the health impact of smoking. Pearl came to the conclusion that in individuals it was difficult to assess the risks of such behaviors, especially when their impact was not immediate and when many intervening variables also affected health. Therefore, he concluded, the only precise way to evaluate their effect on health was to employ statistical methods after collecting data on large groups. Comparing the mortality curves of smokers and nonsmokers, Pearl found that individuals who smoked could expect shorter lives. He offered no explanation for why this might be so.[17]

During the 1920s and 1930s, as the first studies attempting to link cigarettes to cancer were conducted, the field of epidemiology stood at a crossroads. The bacteriological revolution of the late nineteenth and early twentieth century had directed attention away from the traditional environmental questions which had brought epidemiology to the fore. Research came to center on mechanism: identifying causative agents, universally assumed to be microorganisms. Indeed, the notion that disease was actually "caused" by hazards in the environment fell into disrepute. Public health officers were compelled to demonstrate Robert Koch's postulates, the fundamental truths of the new germ theory.[18] There were, of course, exceptions to this trend, especially in the study of industrial and occupational health. But these fields for the most part were distant from the central concerns of medicine and public health. In fact, the major statistical work of the period came from population genetics and the actuarial studies of the insurance industry, rather than from the disciplines of public health. Neither Hoffman nor Pearl would have considered himself an epidemiologist.

The municipal laboratory had become the new focus of public health. Even when researchers identified environmental or behavioral risks, they generally focused on the mechanism of disease. The whole notion of statistical inference was questioned, as research centered on the cellular level. In this respect, exposure to a carcinogen was equated with exposure to an infectious organism. Identifying the health risks of a particular behavior like smoking fitted this model poorly. The length of time before the disease developed was protracted (and equated with an "incubation period"); in addition, the large number of intervening variables confounded notions of specific causality. Everyone "exposed" did not get the disease; indeed, most did not; and some who were not exposed did. Also, there was broad cultural discomfort with notions of comparative risk assessment. How dangerous was the cigarette? How did this danger rate vis-à-vis other risks? Finally, medical theory offered few persuasive models for understanding systemic and chronic diseases; the anomalies of cigarette smoking did not fit the biomedical model's ideal of specific causality.

Changing patterns of disease, however, forced researchers to search for other models of causality. By the end of the Second World War, concern about lung cancer had intensified. It seemed to statisticians and physicians to be a striking exception to many other disease patterns of the twentieth century; deaths from lung cancer had risen from 4,000 in 1935 to 11,000 in 1945. By 1960 the number of annual lung cancer deaths would rise to 36,000.[19] By the mid-1980s carcinoma of the lung would become the most prevalent of all cancers, accounting for more than 140,000 deaths each year. Yet, at the turn of the twentieth century, the disease was a relative rarity, with less than 400 cases recorded in 1900.

There were, of course, many theories to account for this shift. Some observers attributed the rise in cases to better reporting, more sophisticated diagnostic abilities, the widespread use of X rays, and the ability to make precise pathological analyses. Others suggested that increasing life expectancy permitted the development of disease that in an earlier era would not have had the chance to wreak its havoc on victims who would die earlier deaths from other causes.[20]

But some physicians and public health officers pointed to one of the most dramatic behavioral changes in the history of American culture, the rise of cigarette smoking. By the late 1940s it was already known that prolonged exposure to certain industrial chemicals and vapors—chromate, nickel carbonyl, and radioactive dusts—could produce lung cancer. Some scientists now suggested that the inhalation of cigarette smoke might have similar effects. This hypothesis led to a series of epidemiological studies of the risk of smoking. These studies, in turn, would lead to a redefinition of risk, epidemiology, and public health.

First published in the 1950s, these investigations were based upon retrospective findings: in other words, individuals with lung cancer were identified in hospitals and interviewed regarding their smoking practices; they were then compared with a similar group who did not smoke. The findings revealed that cigarette smokers were at far higher risk for the development of lung cancer than were nonsmokers. But critics raised a series of objections to such studies. In particular, it was clear that there were a number of opportunities for bias in the construction of sample and control groups. For example, it was suggested that lung cancer patients were likely, because of the nature of their disease, to exaggerate their smoking habits.[21]

Given the methodological problems with retrospective studies, two major prospective studies on smoking and cancer were begun in 1951. Under the auspices of the British Medical Research Council,

Richard Doll and Bradford Hill sent questionnaires on smoking practices to all British physicians.[22] When members of the profession died, Doll and Hill obtained data concerning the cause of their deaths. The results were consistent with the earlier findings from the retrospective studies.[23]

A second major prospective study, conducted by E. Cuyler Hammond under the auspices of the American Cancer Society, led to similar conclusions. Total death rates were far higher among smokers than among nonsmokers. Lung cancer deaths were 3 to 9 times as high among smokers as among nonsmokers, 5 to 16 times as high among heavy smokers. Among those who smoked two or more packs a day, the death rates were 2.25 times as high as for men who had never smoked, a strong indication of a dose effect. Excess mortality was even higher for coronary artery disease than for lung cancer; rates for smokers exceeded those for nonsmokers by 70 percent. Quitting, Hammond found, reduced risk; formerly a heavy smoker, he himself now quit.[24] By 1960, a range of epidemiological studies had all arrived at consistent findings: cigarette smoking significantly contributed to lung cancer and coronary artery disease.[25]

These epidemiological studies introduced the concept of large, population-based surveys. They focused attention on the definition of comparative risk and excess mortality. Implicit in such studies was a critique of the whole notion of specific causality; these researchers recognized that there were literally hundreds of variables affecting the incidence of disease. Therefore they sought to design studies which, by including many individuals, would be controlled except for a single variable—in this case, cigarette smoking.

This mode of research touched off an important debate within the scientific community about the nature of causality, proof, and risk. At stake were the very epistemological foundations of scientific knowledge: How do we know what we know? What is the reliability of causal inference from statistical data? Those committed to hereditarian, genetic views of cancer, for example, found fault with an epidemiologic approach which centered attention on behavioral effects.[26]

At the basis of the epidemiological argument was the clear limitation of laboratory experimentation for making determinations about probability and risk. The debate about smoking and health revealed an intraprofessional battle between epidemiology and lab science, a clash of values, assumptions, and expectations. Moreover, the debate revealed a deeper discomfort with statistical logic and quantitative methods in biomedicine, a trend which persists today.[27] Before any successful anti-cigarette campaign could be waged, the legitimacy of epidemiological data concerning risk for generating health policy would have to be established.

FROM EPIDEMIOLOGY TO PUBLIC POLICY

Knowledge of the risks of smoking—which continued to accrue throughout the 1950s—did not immediately lead to the formulation of public policy. Indeed, there was considerable debate about the implications of these findings for public health authorities. What was the appropriate role of the state vis-à-vis the risks of cigarette smoking? Should the government play a role in educating its citizens about the hazards of smoking? Recognizing the gravity of the hazard, should the government take steps to regulate the sale of cigarettes more aggressively, or restrict their use? These questions, of course, were complicated by the nature of the behavior itself: no one need be exposed to the hazards of smoking unless he or she so chose; the "voluntary" nature of the risks, it was argued, militated against any governmental intervention.

The first step which the federal government took—haltingly, in 1962—was to sponsor a commission to study the evidence that cigarettes were harmful. In some respects, this was a curious way to proceed, given the quality of the evidence which already existed. But the creation of the Surgeon General's Advisory Commission on Smoking and Health revealed the political aspects of the debate.[28] First, powerful economic interests repeatedly called the epidemiological findings into question, suggesting that the relationship of cigarettes to disease was "merely statistical" and that no clear and objective findings confirmed these risks "in the laboratory."[29] The industry responded to the epidemiological data with advertising campaigns which assured the public their brands were safe, at the same time that it introduced filter cigarettes with expansive claims for health and safety.[30] The industry worked diligently to undermine, if not obscure, public perceptions of the risk of the cigarette. Second, there was no single, authoritative "reading" of the mounting evidence. Forces in the public health establishment, especially the voluntary health agencies, realized that the findings linking cigarettes to disease had to be legitimated in the medical and scientific communities, as well as among the public.[31] Identifying "risk factors" for disease would become an increasingly important aspect of the work of the "voluntaries," eager to assure the public—and especially contributors—of progress in finding "the cause" of serious chronic disease.[32]

The advisory committee, appointed in July 1962, explicitly avoided all questions of social policy; its charge was to determine whether or not smoking *caused* disease. But it conducted no new research. The committee reviewed some 7,000 publications, including 3,000 research reports published since 1950.[33] It sought to arrive at a clinical judgment on smoking. As one public health official explained, "What do we (that is, the surgeon general of the United States Public Health Service) advise our patient, the American public, about smoking?" Implicit in this question was a particular model of public health and the role of the state.

The report, despite the fact that it offered no new data, nevertheless made a fundamental contribution to the study of causal inference in epidemiological studies. What did it mean to say, for example, that cigarettes *caused* lung cancer? How should "cause" be distinguished from "associated with," " a factor," or "determinant"? Members of the committee realized the complexity of saying simply that smoking causes cancer. Many individuals could smoke heavily throughout their lives and apparently suffer no adverse consequences; "cause" implied a single process in which A, by necessity, would lead to B. Therefore, they acknowledged the complexity: "It should be said at once," the report explained, "that no member of this Committee used the word 'cause' in an absolute sense in the area of this study. Although various disciplines and fields of scientific knowledge were represented among the membership, all members shared a common conception of the multiple etiology of biological processes. No member was so naive as to insist upon mono-etiology in pathological processes or in vital phenomena."[34] Yet their conviction was clear: smoking presented a tremendous risk to health. The committee developed a set of criteria for evaluating causal relationships which has been widely applied since that time. Causal evidence had to be (1) consistent, (2) strong, (3) specific, (4), supportive of appropriate temporal relationships, and (5) coherent.[35] At the press conference announcing the committee's findings, Terry was asked whether he would now recommend to a patient to stop smoking. His answer was an unequivocal "yes."

The report served the political functions on which it was predicated. It provided power and legitimacy to the epidemiologic findings; indeed, the report was of fundamental importance in raising the stature of epidemiology as a discipline. It made clear that the government would accept broader responsibility for the determination of risks and for public education to prevent disease. The ability of self-interested parties such as the tobacco industry to disparage such findings was now delimited. With the first *Surgeon General's Report,* the battle against the cigarette was joined; less obvious was how the government would utilize this document in setting a public health agenda.

THE TOBACCO WARS

In retrospect, the immediate public and political response to the *Surgeon General's Report* appears strikingly naive. Newspapers reporting the findings speculated that the tobacco industry would wither away. The presumption was widely held that smokers—now apprised of the risks—would quickly quit. In Congress, such ideas influenced legislators, who in 1965 passed the Federal Cigarette Labeling and Advertising Act. The legislation established the National Clearinghouse on Smoking and Health to encourage health education about the dangers of smoking. In addition it required that all packs of cigarettes carry a warning: "Caution: Cigarette Smoking May Be Hazardous to Your Health." Given that the surgeon general had found that smoking *causes* lung cancer, the warning was remarkably weak, indicating the effectiveness of the tobacco lobby on Capitol Hill. It further reflected the relative lack of experience most legislators had had with scientific findings. At the hearings concerning this legislation, tobacco spokesmen challenged the findings of the surgeon general. By treating all perspectives as those of "interested" parties to be brokered in the political process, members of Congress sought compromise. Moreover, the powerful economic interests, especially of tobacco-growing states, acted forcefully to moderate any regulatory initiatives.[36] Nevertheless, as scientific studies collected in subsequent surgeon general's reports continued to indict the cigarette as a major cause of serious disease, Congress took additional action. In 1971, the label was changed to "Warning: the Surgeon General Has Determined that Cigarette Smoking Is Dangerous to your Health." And, in 1985, four rotating labels were mandated.[37]

Increasingly, the battle over the nature of the risks of smoking would be waged in the media. Luther Terry's effective control of the media, for example, greatly contributed to the success of his committee. First, Terry appointed a commission of elite scientists and clinicians to study the issue of smoking and health; he successfully obviated any easy dismissal of the report by requiring that none of its members had previously expressed positions on the dangers of the cigarette.[38] Second, he invited the tobacco industry to review a list of prospective committee members and reject anyone they desired to. This made it impossible for the industry to easily discredit the report. The "secret" meetings of the committee generated widespread speculation in the press during the eighteen months of its deliberations.[39] This interest culminated in the nationally televised press conference of January 1964. Sunday newspapers throughout the country reported the story on front pages.

By 1964, in the aftermath of televised presidential debates, a presidential assassination, and a growing war in East Asia, all powerfully portrayed through the electronic media, the expanding role of the media and possibilities of exploiting them for a range of purposes, including public health education, were increasingly recognized. Terry's report and the nationally televised press conference made the surgeon general, for the first time, into a *public* figure with access to the media. It gave the office a new meaning and authority which subsequent surgeon generals would augment. Indeed, the surgeon general's principal role—given that the office has little funding or authority to initiate programs—is to speak effectively through the media.

In the struggle concerning the "meaning" of the cigarette, control of the media was bitterly contested. The tobacco industry had considerable resources to expend in this fight, attempting to allay the growing concerns about the impact of smoking on health. Advertisements, for example, continued to suggest that smokers were youthful, healthy, attractive, and sexually seductive. Although the Federal Trade Commission took action to demand a higher level of accountability from the industry, regulations were weak and difficult to enforce. The anti-tobacco forces thus pursued other strategies. A young consumer lawyer, John Banzhaf III, decided to attempt to get the FCC to apply the fairness doctrine (for equal air time) to cigarette advertising. He formed the group ASH (Action on Smoking and Health). After a court struggle, he forced the national networks to air anti-smoking spots in prime time. Anti-cigarette ads got approximately $40 million of free air time. These public-service announcements apparently did have an impact; per capita consumption fell from 4,197 in 1966 to 3,969 in 1970.[40] Given the success of this anti-cigarette media blitz, the industry then acquiesced to a legislative ban on broadcast advertising, thus averting the fairness doctrine.[41]

Congressional anti-smoking policy proved to be decidedly limited. Modest funding for public education, requiring warning labels on packages, and banning broadcast advertising constituted the entire federal program to reduce smoking. At the same time, tobacco subsidies were maintained, placing the government in the ambiguous position of working to limit cigarette smoking while simultaneously contributing to the growth of tobacco. The limits of the federal program revealed the ongoing power of the tobacco lobby and the economic interests that it represents.[42]

TRANSFORMING THE MEANING OF CIGARETTE SMOKING

Additional research findings about the nature of the risks of cigarette smoking served to tip the balance in favor of anti-smoking forces during the last decade. Despite considerable gains in stigmatizing the cigarette, the anti-smoking forces had, by the late 1970s, foundered on a traditional American libertarian ethic: "It's my body and I'll do with it as I please." In keeping with this powerful cultural ideal, further governmental interference relating to smoking was seen as constituting unjustifiable intrusion into individual decisions.The Tobacco Institute viewed such intervention as "health and safety fascism." It was one thing for the government to inform the public about the dangers of smoking; quite another to restrict or ban the behavior.

For this reason, scientific studies of the impact of "sidestream" smoke took on special significance. With the publication of studies which demonstrated the risks of exposure to other people's cigarette smoke—in particular, a higher risk of lung cancer—the anti-smoking movement was reinvigorated on the basis of a powerful communitarian ethic: "Do with your own body whatever you like, but you may not expose others to risks which they do not agree to take on themselves." As epidemiologist Michael J. Martin explained, "Many people are willing to take on risk, even an enormous risk, themselves. But few are willing to tolerate even a small risk imposed on them."[43] With the imprimatur of a new *Surgeon General's Report* (1986), the data on "involuntary" smoking led to remarkable changes in the effectiveness of efforts to restrict smoking in public places.[44] By mid-1988, 320 local communities had adopted laws restricting smoking in public places, up from 90 in 1985.[45] Cigarette smoking was banned from virtually all domestic airline flights beginning in early 1990.

Another *Surgeon General's Report* (1988) also called into question the voluntary nature of cigarette smoking, now for the smoker.[46] By documenting the addictive qualities of cigarette smoking, the report further undermined the notion of an individual voluntarily "deciding" to smoke. Not surprisingly, the tobacco industry challenged these findings. Walker Merryman, a spokesman for the industry's Tobacco Institute, offered a socially elastic definition of addiction: "I've not heard of anyone holding up a liquor store or mugging an old lady to get the money to buy cigarettes."[47] Nevertheless, the recognition that cigarette smoking subjects individuals to well-recognized biological processes of transient mood alterations, tolerance, and withdrawal symptoms led increasingly to the inclusion of nicotine addiction as one more aspect of substance abuse, a deviant behavior.[48] Moreover, the growing recognition of the difficulty of quitting undercut the notion that smoking was simply a matter of choice.

Studies of the risks of sidestream smoke and the addictive nature of cigarettes were promoted by a growing anti-smoking coalition which included physicians, public health experts, and aggressive consumer activists. This, of course, is not to question the scientific validity of such studies, but rather to emphasize the relationship between authoritative science and its social and political context. The new research agenda facilitated the ongoing process of delegitimizing cigarette smoking in American culture. The cigarette—the icon of our consumer culture, the symbol of pleasure and power, sexuality and individuality—had become suspect. The smoker would subsequently be redefined, in a process which we continue to see played out—from the independent Marlboro man or liberated Virginia Slim to a new vision of a weak, irrational, and now, addicted, individual. The innocuous habit had become the noxious addiction. The stigmatization of the cigarette became a critical aspect of a revolution in American values about personal health and behavior.

The stigma of the cigarette is now tainting its producers. Increasingly, the production and sale of such a clearly dangerous and damaging product is being viewed as a moral issue; the cigarette companies are losing their standing as "reputable" industries.[49] Major social institutions have moved in recent months to sever their ties with an industry increasingly associated in the public mind with "marketing death." The decisions of Harvard University and City University of New York, for example, to divest their endowment holdings in cigarette companies explicitly expands the moral valence of the cigarette issue, further isolating the industry.[50] Despite the continued profitability of the cigarette, the industry is losing the tobacco wars, the battle to maintain a legitimate place for the cigarette in American culture.

It would nevertheless be premature to celebrate the decline in cigarette consumption. Cigarettes continue to exact an enormous toll on health in the United States, and, increasingly, throughout the world. According to recently revised figures, 390,000 deaths each year are attributed to cigarette smoking in the United States alone.[51] Smoking is estimated to cause 30 percent of all cancer deaths, 21 percent of all deaths from coronary artery disease, and 82 percent of all deaths from chronic obstructive pulmonary disease. Since 1986, lung cancer has become the leading cause of cancer deaths among American women, surpassing breast cancer, the epidemiological result of the rise in women smoking since the 1940s. Smoking remains the "single most important preventable cause of death" in the United States.[52] A recent federal study estimated that cigarettes cost the nation some $52 billion each year in health expenses and time lost from work.[53] Despite the decline in smoking, the tobacco industry remains highly profitable[54] and the industry continues to spend more than $2.5 billion each year promoting the sale of cigarettes.[55]

As cigarette consumption in the United States has declined, multinational tobacco companies have worked to market their product more vigorously in the developing world. Recent worldwide surveys of cigarette consumption show steep increases in Africa and Asia. The World Health Organization recently characterized the commercial marketing of cigarettes in developing nations as "intense and ruthless."[56] According to WHO, 600,000 new cases of lung cancer now occur worldwide every year; most are the result of cigarette smoking. By the year 2000, the annual number of lung cancer cases may be as high as 2 million, with 900,000 in China alone.[57] In this sense, the risks of tobacco consumption truly are global; changes in Western consumption have been a catalyst for accelerating sales in the developing world.[58]

WHOSE RISK IS IT, ANYWAY?

With cigarette smoking there remains a complex political and cultural conflict about risk and responsibility. Consensus about the risks of smoking touched off an important debate about the question of responsibility for risk: Who is responsible for the serious burden of disease imposed by cigarette smoking? In this respect, the first *Surgeon General's Report* marks an important watershed in the history of public health. The government accepted new responsibility for the elucidation of health risks through epidemiological studies. The report articulated an expanded vision of public health, suggesting that the government had an important regulatory function in protecting its citizens from harmful products by identifying risks and educating the public.

Nevertheless, the government has been caught in an ambiguous position in its efforts to control cigarette smoking. Given the history of the prohibition of alcohol, there is little support for an outright ban on cigarettes, even from the most aggressive anti-cigarette activists. Advertising remains a contested area of public policy, but even opponents of smoking have expressed concern that a total ban may conflict with First Amendment rights. Although education has been effective among the educated, the relationship between risk and behavior modification remains obscure.[59] More significant than any particular federal intervention have been the local bans on smoking in public areas and workplaces, which have created a powerful anti-smoking social environment. In a relatively short time, public space has been subdivided; cigarette smoking has become the most rigorously defined of all public behaviors.

Recognizing that the federal government's policy options regarding cigarettes are limited, some have called for a higher standard of corporate responsibility. Smokers who have incurred serious disease, acting as plaintiffs, have attempted to fix the burden of responsibility squarely on the tobacco industry itself. In the last decade, hundreds of civil suits have been filed making the claim that the tobacco companies persisted in selling a lethal product all the while knowing (and obscuring) the risks. Given the highly addictive nature of the cigarette and the slick promotion campaigns of the industry, plaintiffs' lawyers have contended that the companies should accept—in compensatory damages—responsibility for the debility and death their product has wreaked.

These liability suits have generally been unsuccessful. Although they appeal to a populist, anti-business strain of thought in American society, typically such suits have failed in spite of the ability of lawyers to portray the industry as cynical and profit driven. Within American society there is a powerful expectation regarding individual responsibility for risk taking. The labeling and educational activities of the government have served to reinforce these expectations. As consensus regarding the risks of the cigarette has grown, the industry has, ironically, been freed of responsibility for the risks of its product.

Increasingly, Americans have come to accept notions of individual responsibility for the systemic and chronic diseases. Because heart disease, cancer, and other diseases are powerfully influenced by a range of individual "life-style" behaviors, including diet, alcohol consumption, and smoking, many health care analysts have come to emphasize the significance of modifying behaviors to affect health status, and more generally, patterns of disease.[60]

Such views have particular appeal in the context of the American health culture, which has historically emphasized the significance of an individual's responsibility for disease. Americans, in this respect, have largely come to reject fatalistic explanatory models of disease and its causes. Social values have underscored norms which suggest that individuals *can* and *should* exert fundamental control over their own health through careful and rational avoidance of risks. The popularity, for example, of the "Just Say No" campaign against illicit drugs reflects an essentially "voluntaristic" notion of risk.

As effective as such values may be in serving to define healthful behaviors, they present an important political and cultural irony. According to this behavioral ethic, those who continue to take risks must be held accountable for the results; but this emphasis on individual responsibility may deny broader social responsibilities for health and disease. This view, which has developed increasingly powerful adherents in the last decade, actually misrepresents the history of cigarette smoking in the twentieth century. Smoking is a complex behavior which has reflected deep social, cultural, and economic forces, as well as a powerful biological process of addiction. Simply identifying individual behavior as the primary vehicle of risk negates the fact that behavior itself is, at times, beyond the scope of individual agency. Behavior is shaped by powerful currents—cultural, psychological, as well as biological processes—not all immediately within the control of the individual. Behaviors such as cigarette smoking are sociocultural phenomena, not merely individual, or necessarily rational.

The emphasis on personal responsibility for risk taking and disease has come at the very moment when cigarette smoking is increasingly stratified by education, social class, and race. In 1985, 35 percent of blacks smoked compared with 29 percent of whites.[61] For college graduates the proportion of smokers fell from 28 percent in 1974 to 18 percent in 1985; for those without a college degree the decrease during the same period was from 36 to 34 percent.[62] Thus, to emphasize individual accountability is to deny that some groups may be more susceptible to certain behavioral risks, that the behavior itself is *not* simply a matter of choice.

In assessments of environmental risks, we have often considered who lives nearest the hazard; the recognition that such risks are externally imposed generates social concern for their victims. Such has not been the case with risks associated with individual behaviors; individuals who "take"—note the voluntaristic bias—such risks are considered ignorant, stupid, or self-destructive. But perhaps we might begin to rethink behavioral risk; rather than simply hold individuals accountable for the risks they incur, we might ask who is at risk to become, or remain, a cigarette smoker and why.

To adequately understand the answers to such questions will, no doubt, require a new, multidisciplinary research agenda in which the relationship of social and cultural contexts (including powerful economic forces) will be related in a sophisticated way to individual psychological motivations to engage (or disengage) certain risk behaviors. We need to better understand the *meanings* of particular behaviors and risks to particular groups of populations. What are the biological, psychological, and social forces that make it possible for some individuals to quit smoking, for example, while others, eager to free themselves of addiction, nonetheless fail? And finally, how may we promote cultural shifts that enhance both personal efficacy and autonomy in the name of health? Until we can adequately answer these questions, the cigarette will continue to be a powerful, if not pervasive, risk.

ENDNOTES

[1]U.S. Department of Health, Education, and Welfare, *Surgeon General's Report, Smoking and Health: Report of the Advisory Committee to the Surgeon General of the Public Health Service*, PHS Publication No. 1103 (Washington, D.C.: Government Printing Office, 1964); *New York Times*, 12 January 1964.

[2]U.S. Department of Health and Human Services, *Surgeon General's Report, Reducing the Health Consequences of Smoking: Twenty-five Years of Progress*, DHHS Publication No. (CDC) 90-8411 (Washington, D.C.: Public Health Service, 1989).

[3]On the social and cultural nature of risk and risk assessment see Mary Douglas and Aaron Wildavsky, *Culture and Risk: An Essay on the Selection Technical and Environmental Dangers* (Berkeley: University of California Press, 1982).

[4]William Bennett, "The Cigarette Century," *Science* 80 (September-October 1980): 37–43.

[5]Michael Schudson, *Advertising, the Uneasy Persuasion* (New York: Basic Books, 1985).

[6]R. W. Fox and T. J. Lears, *The Culture of Consumption* (New York: Pantheon, 1983).

[7]Roland Marchand, *Advertising the American Dream* (Berkeley: University of California Press, 1985).

[8]Henry Ford, introduction to *The Case Against the Little White Slaver* (Detroit: 1914), 5.

[9]See Gordon L. Dillow, "The Hundred Year War Against the Cigarette," *American Heritage* 32 (February-March 1981): 94–107. On the history of recruiting women smokers see, for example, Schudson.

[10]Robert Sobel, *They Satisfy* (New York: Doubleday, 1978).

[11]See, for example, M. V. O'Shea, *Tobacco and Mental Efficiency* (New York: Macmillan, 1923), a monograph sponsored by the Committee to Study the Tobacco Problem, which was organized in 1918.

[12]J. Rossyln Earp, "Tobacco and Scholarship," *Scientific Monthly* 26 (April 1928): 335–36.

[13]See E. L. Clarke, "Effect of Smoking on Clark College Students," *Clark College Record* 4 (July 1909): 3191–98; G.L. Meylan "The Effect of Smoking on College Students," *Popular Science Monthly* 77 (August 1910): 169–78.

[14]H. L. Lombard and C. R. Doering, "Cancer Studies in Massachusetts. 2. Habits, Characteristics, and Environment of Individuals with and without Cancer," *New England Journal of Medicine* 98 (26 April): 481–87.

[15]Alton Ochsner, "My First Recognition of the Relationship of Smoking and Lung Cancer," *Preventive Medicine* 2 (1973): 611–14.

[16]F. L. Hoffman, "Cancer and Smoking Habits," *Annals of Surgery* (January 1931): 50–67.

[17]Raymond Pearl, "Tobacco Smoking and Longevity," *Science* 87 (2252) (4 March 1938): 216–17.

[18]Mervyn Susser, "Epidemiology in the United States After World War II: The Evolution of Technique," *Epidemiologic Reviews* 7 (1985): 147–77.

[19]E. Cuyler Hammond, "The Effects of Smoking," *Scientific American* 207 (July 1962): 39–51.

[20]Clarence C. Little, "Some Phases of the Problem of Smoking and Lung Cancer," *New England Journal of Medicine* 264 (June 15, 1961): 1241–45.

[21]Richard Doll and A. Bradford Hill, "A Study of the Aetiology of Carcinoma of the Lung," *British Medical Journal* 2 (13 December 1952): 1271–86.

[22]Charles Webster, *The Health Services Since the War*, vol. 1 (London: Her Majesty's Stationery Office, 1988), 233–7.

[23]Richard Doll and A. Bradford Hill, "The Mortality of Doctors in Relation to their Smoking Habits: A Preliminary Report," *British Medical Journal* 1 (4887) (26 June 1954): 1451–55; Doll and Hill, "Lung Cancer and other Causes of Death in Relation to Smoking: A Second Report on the Mortality of British Doctors," *British Medical Journal* 2 (1 November 1956): 1071–81.

[24]E.Cuyler Hammond and Daniel Horn, "Smoking and Death Rates—Report on Forty-four Months of Follow-up on 187,783 Men. I. Total Mortality," *Journal of the American Medical Association* 166 (10) (8 March 1958): 1159–72.

[25]Jerome Cornfield, et al., "Smoking and Lung Cancer: Recent Evidence and Discussion of Some Questions," *Journal of the National Cancer Institute* 22 (1959): 123–203.

[26]R. A. Fisher, "Alleged Dangers of Cigarette-Smoking," *British Medical Journal* 2 (43) (1957): 297–98.

[27]Alvan R. Feinstein, *Clinical Judgment* (Baltimore: Williams and Wilkins, 1967).

[28]A. Lee Fritschler, *Smoking and Politics: Policymaking and the Federal Bureaucracy* (New York: Appleton-Century-Crofts, 1969).

[29]Luther Terry, "The First Surgeon General's Report on Smoking," *New York State Journal of Medicine* 13 (1983): 1254–55.

[30]Thomas Whiteside, *Selling Death: Cigarette Advertising and Public Health* (New York: Liveright, 1971).

[31]Susan Wagner, *Cigarette Country* (New York: Praeger, 1981).

[32]James Patterson, *The Dread Disease: Cancer and American Culture* (Cambridge: Harvard University Press, 1987).

[33]*Surgeon General's Report,* National Archives Manuscripts, Record Group 90, Washington, D.C.

[34]*Surgeon General's Report, Smoking and Health.*

[35]A. M. Lilienfeld, "The Surgeon General's 'Epidemiological Criteria for Causality,' " *Journal of Chronic Diseases* 36 (1983): 837–45.

[36]Elizabeth M. Whelan, *A Smoking Gun* (Philadelphia: George F. Stickley Co., 1984).

[37]John K. Iglehart, "Smoking and Public Policy," *New England Journal of Medicine* 310 (8) (1984): 539–44; Iglehart, "The Campaign Against Smoking Gains Momentum," *New England Journal of Medicine* 314 (16) (1986): 1059–64.

[38]Luther Terry, "The First Surgeon General's Report on Smoking," *New York State Journal of Medicine* 13 (1983): 1254–55.

[39]Leonard M. Schuman, "The Origins of the Report of the Advisory Committee on Smoking and Health to the Surgeon General," *Journal of Public Health Policy* 2 (March 1981): 19–27.

[40]Kenneth E. Warner, "Cigarette Smoking in the 1970s: The Impact of the Antismoking Campaign on Consumption," *Science* 211 (13 February 1981): 729–731.

[41]Whelan.

[42]Harvey M. Sapolsky, "The Political Obstacles to the Control of Cigarette Smoking in the United States," *Journal of Health Politics, Policy and Law* 5 (2) (1980): 277–90.

[43]"Tobacco Company Profits Just Won't Quit," *Business Week* (22 December 1986): 66–67. For a full exposition of the ethical issues associated with cigarette smoking see Robert E. Goodin, *No Smoking: The Ethical Issues* (Chicago: University of Chicago Press, 1989).

[44]Jonathan E. Fielding, "Smoking: Health Effects and Control," *New England Journal of Medicine* 313 (8) (1985): 491–98; (9) (1985): 555–61.

[45]*Surgeon General's Report, Reducing the Health Consequences of Smoking. Twenty-five Years of Progress.*

[46]U.S. Department of Health and Human Services, *Surgeon General's Report, The Health Consequences of Smoking: Nicotine Addiction,* DHHS Publication No. (CDC) 88-8406 (Washington, D.C.: Public Health Service, 1988).

[47]"Surgeon General's Stature Is Likely to Add Force to Report on Smoking as Addiction," *Wall Street Journal,* 13 May 1988, 1.

[48]J. E. Henningfield, "Pharmacologic Basis and Treatment of Cigarette Smoking," *Clinical Psychiatry* 45 (1984): 24–34.

[49]Michael Kinsley, "Smokenders," *New Republic* (14 May 1990): 4, 53.

[50]*New York Times,* 24 May 1990.

[51]"U.S. Report Raises Estimate of Smoking Toll," *Washington Post,* 11 January 1989, A20.

[52]*Surgeon General's Report, Reducing the Health Consequences of Smoking. Twenty-five Years of Progress.*

[53]*New York Times,* 21 February 1990.

[54]"Tobacco Company Profits Just Won't Quit," *Business Week* (22 December 1986): 66–67.

[55]R. M. Davis, "Current Trends in Cigarette Advertising and Marketing," *New England Journal of Medicine* 316 (12) (19 March 1987): 725–32.

[56]Robin Herman, "Diseases of Affluence," *Washington Post Health,* 3 January 1989, 12–15.

[57]William U. Chandler, "Banishing Tobacco," *World Watch Paper* 68 (Washington, D.C.: World Watch Institute, 1986).

[58]Peter Schmeisser, "Pushing Cigarettes Overseas," *New York Times Magazine* (10 July 1988): 16–25.

[59]Howard Leventhal and Paul D. Cleary, "The Smoking Problem: A Review of the Research and Theory in Behavioral Risk Modification," *Psychological Bulletin* 88 (2) (1980): 370–405; Neil D. Weinstein, ed., *Taking Care: Understanding and Encouraging Self Protective Behavior* (New York: Cambridge University Press, 1987).

[60]John Knowles, "The Responsibility of the Individual," *Dædalus* 106 (1) (Winter 1977): 57–80.

[61]M. C. Fiore, T. E. Novotny, J. P. Pierce, K. M. Hatziandreu, and R. M. Davis, "Trends in Cigarette Smoking in the United States: The Changing Influence of Gender and Race," *Journal of the American Medical Association* 261 (6 January 1989): 49–55.

[62]Ibid., 56–60.

Roy Widdus, Andre Meheus, and Roger Short

The Management of Risk in Sexually Transmitted Diseases

INCLUSION OF SEXUALLY TRANSMITTED DISEASES (STDs) as a case study in a symposium on risk is somewhat unusual since in the last few decades risk analysis has focused predominantly on toxicological or technological risks. It is, we hope, a reflection of society's growing awareness of the importance of communicable disease as a continuing source of risk to the United States population.

STDs are cumulative over time. Each sexually active adult can potentially retain infections (apparent or not) acquired from each of his or her previous sexual partners, who may in turn have acquired infections from any of their partners. Under such circumstances one act of extramarital intercourse may expose you to a variety of infections acquired from a large number of different individuals. Since there is nothing obvious about your partner to indicate the magnitude of the risk you are running, you have to take the information your partner gives you about his or her previous sexual history on trust. Not only is your partner likely to be ill informed, but in the heat of the moment, some partners are also not trustworthy.

Human sexual behavior is heavily determined by culture: it is the society in which we live, rather than we ourselves, that determines

Roy Widdus, M.D., is Chief of Programme Coordination and Development for the World Health Organization Global Programme on AIDS, in Geneva.

Andre Meheus, M.D., is Programme Manager for the World Health Organization Programme on Sexually Transmitted Diseases, in Geneva.

Roger Short, M.D., is Professor of Reproductive Biology at Monash University in Melbourne.

who may have sex with whom, and where, and when, and how. The "natural" pattern of sexual behavior of our species—bereft of man-made, cultural constraints—bears consideration. Were we designed by nature to be a monogamous primate? The answer seems to be definitely no.[1] Cross-cultural studies of human mating systems around the world show that of the 849 societies studied, 84 percent were polygamous (83 percent polygynous, 1 percent polyandrous), and only 16 percent monogamous.[2]

Each Western man and woman will probably have more than one sexual partner in a lifetime, and the average man is likely to have more partners than the average woman. Although at any one time a man is likely to be "pair-bonded" to one woman, and vice versa, such pair bonds are often broken and re-formed. Serial monogamy may be our polygamous compromise.

Throughout the Western world, especially in the United States, improved communications and growing urbanization have loosened the grip of the strict religious and cultural constraints on our sexuality and given sexual behavior freer reign, enhancing the opportunity for STD transmission. One of the greatest changes has been in sexual behavior during adolescence. In many traditional societies in sub-Saharan Africa the pubertal initiation ceremonies allowing sexual activity to commence are more important than the act of marriage itself. But the Western world, with its prohibition of premarital sex, has been caught completely unawares by the combination of an earlier age for onset of puberty (as a result of improved health and nutrition in infancy and childhood) with a relaxation of cultural restraints on adolescent sexual behavior.

On the one hand, we are plagued by precocious fertility, which can result in teenage pregnancies, abortions, single-parent families, and the poverty trap. On the other hand, those who choose to defer marriage and childbearing—to complete their education or establish careers—may unwittingly embark on an extended period of what we might call exploratory polygamy. Sexual partnerships that do not stand the test of time are formed, and the earlier this activity commences, the greater the number of partnerships that fail.

The 1988 National Survey of Adolescent Males showed that 69 percent of black males, 33 percent of Hispanics, and 26 percent of whites had already had sexual intercourse by the age of 15.[3] In Baltimore, Maryland, 50 percent of black males were sexually active before the age of 13.[4] And by age 15, 1 out of every 5 American girls had already had intercourse. About half the unmarried adolescent women who had already had intercourse had had more than one sexual partner, and around 10 percent had had six or more partners. Only 3 percent of the women had delayed intercourse until after marriage.

As a consequence of all this sexual activity, teenagers in the United States experience higher rates of sexually transmitted diseases, including AIDS, than heterosexuals of any other age group. Nearly 25 percent of all cases of sexually transmitted disease occur in adolescents, with 2.5 million new cases a year, or 1 in 7 of all 15- to 19-year-olds.[5] In 1980, about 1 in every 100 women in the United States age 15–19 who had ever had sex was hospitalized for pelvic inflammatory disease, a relatively common consequence of STDs.[6]

Adolescents seem to have a sense of personal invulnerability and immortality, and a propensity for risk seeking and risk taking. Most American adolescents do not see themselves as being at risk of acquiring sexually transmitted diseases, so they rarely make regular use of condoms.[7] Neither do they see themselves as being at risk of becoming pregnant, and yet in 1988 there were 860,000 teenage pregnancies in the United States, the vast majority unintended, with 397,000 ending in induced abortion.[8] While there is encouraging new evidence to show that making adolescent males in metropolitan areas of the United States aware of the AIDS threat can dramatically increase their use of condoms, unfortunately those most at risk are least likely to use them.[9]

Now the most commonly occurring group of serious infectious diseases in most countries, sexually transmitted diseases are by no means confined to adolescents. More than 20 pathogens have been found to spread by sexual contact in all age groups. Some, such as *Chlamydia trachomatis* and viral agents such as genital herpes and HIV, are replacing the most common bacterial diseases (syphilis, gonorrhea, and chancroid) in importance and frequency. These newcomers, regarded as the second generation of sexually transmitted diseases, are frequently more difficult to identify, treat, and control, and can cause serious complications, some of which result in chronic ill health, disability, or death. Also, probably more than other infectious diseases, STDs result in considerable psychological distress related to their stigmatization and the physical consequences they incur.

EPIDEMIOLOGICAL TRENDS IN MAJOR STDs

Since the majority of STD infections are asymptomatic, the incidence of STDs is underreported. Some data are worth summarizing, however, and it is interesting to note that the upward trend in STDs in the United States in recent years is the opposite of the trend in most other industrialized countries.

Syphilis (Treponema pallidum): Following the World War II peak, occurrence in the United States declined to an all-time low in 1956. After a steady increase up to 1965, incidence went up and down like a roller coaster till 1985. Reported cases in homosexual men rose from 1960 to 1982 and dropped thereafter. From 1985 to 1988, incidence increased by 50 percent, predominantly in black men and women.[10] Cases of congenital syphilis rose 6-fold between 1980 and 1988. This increase has been attributed to three factors: the rise of prostitution in which drugs (especially "crack" cocaine) are purchased with sex, the widespread use of spectinomycin rather than penicillin for the treatment of gonorrhea, and the shifting of resources from syphilis to AIDS control.[11]

Gonorrhea (Neisseria gonorrhoea): It is estimated that the number of treated cases of gonorrhea in the United States in 1984 was on the order of 1.7 million.[12] Since 1984, the race differential in reported cases has been growing: in 1988, there were 20 times more cases in blacks than in whites. This finding may be due to bias in reporting practices, however. A more detailed analysis of incidence trends over the last 15 years shows that gonorrhea has increased much more among women than among men.[13] The recent downward trend in rectal gonorrhea in men has been suggested as evidence of behavior change in the homosexual community.

Chlamydial Infection (Chlamydia trachomatis): Diagnosis and reporting of chlamydial infection in the United States are not uniform, so data on incidence are extremely limited. Although trends in the incidence of proven chlamydial infections cannot yet be determined, trends in the incidence of nongonococcal urethritis in men provide a reasonable approximation, since the proportion of cases attributable to *C. trachomatis* infection has remained fairly constant at about 40 percent in various studies during the last decade. Visits to private physicians for nongonococcal urethritis are estimated at over 4 million annually, with an estimated 2.6 million in women and 1.8 million in men.[14]

Genital Herpes (Herpes simplex viruses): The incidence of genital herpes has increased dramatically during the last 20 years, although some of this rise may be due to improvement of diagnosis and reporting. In the United States, the number of physician-patient contacts for genital herpes went from 30,000 to 450,000 between 1966 and 1984.[15] It is estimated that 724,000 new cases of genital herpes occur annually, with a cumulative prevalence of 30 million infected persons as a minimum.

Chancroid (Hemophilus ducreyi): The worldwide incidence of this disease is believed to greatly exceed that of syphilis.[16] In the United States, however, the number peaked in 1947, when 9,515 chancroid cases were reported. Between 1948 and 1978, the number of cases decreased, with an annual mean of 878 in the early 1970s. This trend reversed in 1978, and the resulting increase accelerated between 1981 and 1983, when an outbreak of 923 cases was reported. In 1985, the number of reported cases rose above 2,000 for the first time since 1956; in 1986 and 1987 large increases were observed.

Genital Warts (Human papillomavirus): Infections with papillomavirus are usually asymptomatic but sometimes cause mild symptoms. Certain types of this virus are associated with cervical cancer as well as with genital warts. The prevalence of infection is known only through sampling populations at clinics or medical centers. From 1966 to 1987, physician consultations in the United States for genital warts rose from 169,000 to 1,800,000.[17]

Hepatitis (Hepatitis B virus): An estimated 200,000 to 300,000 hepatitis infections occur annually in the United States, of which a falling percentage (about 21 percent fewer cases in 1985 than in 1982) are transmitted between male homosexuals, and a rising percentage (about 18 percent more cases in 1985 than in 1982) are transmitted heterosexually.[18]

AIDS (Human immunodeficiency virus): Acquired Immune Deficiency Syndrome was first recognized in 1981. In the United States approximately 1 million to 1.5 million persons are estimated to be infected with the human immunodeficiency virus (HIV).[19] HIV inflicts progressive immune system damage that leaves HIV-infected persons vulnerable to infections and cancers that are rare in uninfected persons. *Pneumocystis carinii* pneumonia and Kaposi's sarcoma (a cancer of the blood and/or lymphatic vessel walls) are two of the "opportunistic" diseases that characterize AIDS. Some 20 to 25 percent of infected persons progress to AIDS within five years after infection, and an anticipated 50 percent within 10 years.[20]

From the present AIDS case distribution, it is estimated that most HIV transmission now occurs among homosexual men and injecting drug users; however, heterosexual transmission is increasing, especially among minority populations.[21] As of 1 June 1990, a cumulative total of 132,436 cases of AIDS had been reported to the Centers for Disease Control; approximately half of this number have already died.

Without treatment, persons diagnosed with AIDS generally die within 6 months to 2 years. Zidovudine (azidothymidine, AZT), the only treatment now available, appears to slow disease progression and may double the expected length of survival of those diagnosed with HIV infection or AIDS.

DISTRIBUTION OF STD RISK

The incidence of STD is not randomly distributed throughout the population. Several high-risk groups can be defined. These are groups in which individuals at higher risk are disproportionately represented. For most STDs, the highest incidence rates are observed in 20- to 24-year-olds, followed by the 25–29 and 15–19 age groups.

Although the overall rate of STD cases is higher for men than for women, STDs tend to occur at earlier ages among women than among men. In many industrialized countries the male-to-female ratio for some infections, such as gonorrhea, has fallen drastically during the past 25 years. The reason is not clear, but increased sexual activity of women, improved diagnostic techniques, increased tracing of female contacts of men with gonorrhea, and routine screening using gonococcal culture have all increased the number of cases detected in females.

In homosexual men, many STDs occur with increased frequency. This is illustrated by the increase in the male-to-female ratio of cases of early syphilis in the past 25 years.

The frequency of STDs is higher among single, divorced, and separated persons than among married couples. Other risk groups include prostitutes and international travelers, whose numbers have grown steadily during the past two decades, and who have played a particularly important role in the rapid spread of penicillinase-producing (penicillin-resistant) strains of *N. gonorrhoea* (PPNG) throughout the world.

The concept of *risk groups* for STD transmission is of limited usefulness except in identifying targets of convenience for prevention efforts, and it is likely to lead to stigmatization of these groups. It is incorrect to characterize all members of such groups as being at uniformly elevated risk.

A more useful concept is *risk behaviors.* While these may be prevalent in some groups defined by other criteria (such as involvement in prostitution, either as prostitute or client), they occur to a greater or a lesser degree throughout society and not necessarily uniformly or only within risk groups.

Since no group appears to be immune to STDs, the essential characteristic of elevated risk for STDs is sexual behavior that increases the probability of unprotected sexual exposure to an infected individual. Precise determination of individual risk depends upon such factors as number of partners per unit of time, number and nature of sexual acts (oral, anal, vaginal sex), use of protective measures (condoms, spermicides), partner selection, probability of infection in a partner (which depends on behavior and the availability of treatment), prevalence of STD infections in the population from which partners are chosen, and health care behavior (such as early seeking of treatment, which may forestall serious disease and curtail infectiousness).

ECONOMIC MAGNITUDE OF STD IMPACT

In 1985, the Institute of Medicine calculated the total annual financial burden of treatment of 13 potentially vaccine-preventable diseases. Gonorrhea, the major STD analyzed, ranked third in cost among all vaccine-preventable diseases in 1984, with an estimated cost of close to U.S.$1 billion.[22]

The recent rapid rise and expensive treatment of AIDS have prompted a number of cost studies. To date, estimates have varied because of lack of data and differing assumptions. Generally, hospital costs for AIDS alone have been estimated; costs for care of asymptomatic infected patients and HIV-related illness not categorized as AIDS have not been included in these calculations. Projections range from U.S. $30,000 to U.S. $75,000 for AIDS patients alive during 1992. Use of these cost estimates and the projection that a total of 172,000 AIDS patients in the United States will require medical care during 1992 suggest that AIDS will cost U.S. $5 billion–13 billion in that year.[23] This is undoubtedly a low estimate, since it does not capture the true magnitude of HIV-associated illness. It should be recognized that the number of AIDS patients requiring care will continue to rise for some years after 1992 since 1 million to 1.5 million persons in the United States are estimated to be infected with HIV in 1990. There are also likely to be improvements in survival time because of new treatments for HIV and HIV-associated opportunistic infections and cancers.

The estimates quoted above do not account for the cost of zidovudine for patients with AIDS (at present approximately U.S. $6,000–8,000 per patient per year) or the larger group of pre-AIDS patients for which zidovudine has recently been demonstrated to be effective, probably approaching 500,000 persons in the United States. Nor do these estimates take into account other treatments such as pentamidine for *Pneumocystis carinii* pneumonia, at an approximate cost of U.S. $1,000–2,000 per patient per year, for a number of pre-AIDS and AIDS patients estimated to be comparable to those who could benefit from zidovudine.

A disproportionate incidence of STD occurs among inner-city low-income and minority populations in the United States.[24] Trends in the last five years suggest that directing both treatment and prevention efforts to these populations is urgent.

The difference in the perception of AIDS and of other STD risks is illustrated by the relative magnitude of resources devoted to research on these diseases within the budget of the National Institutes of Health. In 1988, U.S. $473 million was allocated to AIDS research but only U.S. $57 million to other STD research.

As with other STDs, data on AIDS show a striking discrepancy between the resources devoted to biomedical research and those devoted to behavioral research: from 1984 to 1987, of the total U.S. AIDS research expenditures, only 2 percent was devoted to social and behavioral aspects.[25] Given that prevention through behavior change and motivating HIV- or other STD-infected persons to seek treatment will always be major aspects of AIDS or STD control, this unequal distribution warrants examination.

PERCEPTION OF STD RISK

According to the "health belief model" (a convenient framework for analyzing attitudes toward health threats and actions to enhance their avoidance), individuals will not generally take preventive health actions unless "they possess minimal levels of health-related motivation and knowledge, view themselves as potentially vulnerable to the disease, view the condition as threatening, are convinced of the efficacy of the proposed action and see few difficulties in taking the recommended actions."[26]

To our knowledge, there has been no systematic study of public perception of STD risks other than the risk of AIDS. Identifying factors important to the perception of different STDs would be useful for identifying areas amenable to change or devising public health campaigns to reduce these risks. STD threats such as cervical cancer caused by papillomaviruses, for example, may be particularly underestimated. STDs regarded as very threatening, however, could become the focus of prevention campaigns.

Although recent attention to AIDS may be heightening awareness of the risk of STD, the public, with its reticence to discuss sexual matters, may be underestimating the occurrence of STD. Also, certain consequences of STD, such as infertility resulting from pelvic inflammatory disease, are essentially "hidden." The fact that certain STDs are associated with cancer has only recently come to light and may not yet be widely recognized. Because some of the major STDs are curable, albeit with increasing difficulty because of antibiotic resistance, the public may also believe that STDs are curable or at least treatable and therefore not major cause for concern. Treatments and cures do not exist for most viral STDs, however.

Since it is likely to underestimate the seriousness and risk of STD, the public tends to minimize the benefit of behavior changes to lower STD risk, such as decreasing the probability of infecting partners or offspring. The motivation to change behavior is hindered by the perceived difficulty of negotiating the use of condoms in sexual encounters, the lack of belief that sexual behavior change is feasible in the long term, and the perception that carrying condoms implies sexual promiscuousness.

The association of STDs and groups at high risk for STDs with immorality and prostitution and the potential shame involved in acquiring an STD have undoubtedly shaped attitudes in the United States toward STDs since the late nineteenth century.[27] STDs have been used to support the viewpoints of both those who wish to control "corrupt sexuality" (usually for moral reasons but sometimes for others, such as eugenics) and those who seek to demonstrate that attempts to regulate sexuality will fail because they have in the past. The exploitation of a health problem for other purposes further complicates the setting of rational public health policy.

REDUCING RISK OF SEXUALLY TRANSMITTED DISEASES

To reduce the probability of STD infection, individuals must abstain from sex, maintain mutually faithful sexual relationships with uninfected partners, or use condoms for penetrative sexual intercourse with partners who are infected or not known to be uninfected.

For the public health policymaker, strategies to reduce STD transmission include provision of treatment to reduce the number of infected individuals and partner notification by either the patient or the health care provider. Information campaigns can be targeted at groups at high risk of STDs to encourage individuals to reduce risk-taking behavior. Condoms can be made more available, and mass-media advertising of condoms expanded. Actions to destigmatize STDs can be promoted. The message to be conveyed is that STDs are unfortunate consequences of a normal activity and that precautions can be taken to minimize STD risk.

Voluntary, confidential screening to detect infected individuals can help prevent STD transmission. Such programs need to be coupled with treatment or with measures such as counseling to reduce sexual transmission. Screening programs are effective, however, only if adequate attention is paid to the way the information obtained is to be used.

Evidence from campaigns to reduce behavioral risk from STDs and other health threats leads to the conclusion that risk-reducing behavior will be adopted and sustained by people in risk-behavior groups only if they are given information they find personally relevant in language they understand. The message must get their attention but not promote so much anxiety as to result in denial and must entail behavior changes that people at risk perceive as beneficial and within their capacity to adopt. The skills to adopt such behavior must be transmitted, and the means for adopting the behavior changes must be available. Individuals can be coached in procedures for negotiating condom use, for instance, but condoms must also be accessible and affordable.

Peer-group support for the changes must be available as well. Other reinforcement of the perceived benefits of sustaining the behavior change should occur, and societal norms must shift to sustain this reinforcement. Prostitutes, for example, must encourage each other to use condoms for personal protection, but clients must also view condom use as a positive, protective measure.

Various impediments may hinder the effective promotion of behaviors that lower STD risk, even if public health policymakers decide to pursue appropriate strategies. Information may be inadequate to permit levels and locations of risk behaviors to be identified in order to target programs cost-effectively. It may, for example, be difficult to reach clients of prostitutes or individuals in the general population with multiple sexual partners. The National Academy of Sciences has emphasized the need for improving policymakers' knowledge about sexual behavior in the United States.[28]

The underlying determinants of risk behavior may be too poorly understood to permit formulation of messages that motivate appropriate change. Information is needed on factors influencing selection of sexual partners. Further research on access channels and message design may be necessary to improve communication with risk-behavior groups. Also, other confounding factors such as drug addiction and alcohol use may not be adequately understood for campaigns to take account of their possible effects.

Opposition to giving explicit information about sexual behavior to those not thought to be at risk may arise from the belief that such information can encourage sexual activity. Producing a public health policy to reduce STD risk may be interrupted by people who want to control sexuality for moral, religious, or philosophical reasons, or to control other social phenomena such as prostitution. And because STDs are frequently associated with socially stigmatized groups, the needs of ethnic or racial minorities and prostitutes, who are not able to promote their own welfare as well as other groups can, may be neglected in policy formulation.

Focusing on the individual's control of sexual behavior may divert attention from the public health responsibility to provide all members of society with treatment services and with the information necessary to make informed choices about health issues. The group most vulnerable to STD risk, sexually active young male adults, has little contact with the health system or physicians.

Physicians themselves do not always regard counseling about appropriate sexual behavior as their responsibility and are not usually trained in STD prevention. Other potential channels of communication, such as the workplace and peer support mechanisms, exist but they have not been systematically used to any great extent.

Politicians hesitate to provide leadership in controversial areas where political will is lacking. Even if the need is recognized, there may be underestimation of the complexity of the task and of the resources and time needed to achieve the changes in norms of sexual behavior necessary to significantly decrease the incidence of sexually transmitted diseases.

AIDS has brought us to a new level of awareness: it is likely that more people now know about the cause of AIDS than the risk of other STDs. Opposition to stigmatization and inclusion of antidiscrimination measures in public health strategies have been embraced more firmly than in prior efforts to control other sexually transmitted diseases.

A variety of studies has shown that the attitudes and sexual behavior of groups at increased risk for STDs—such as homosexual men and prostitutes—*have* changed, often as a result of interventions launched by peer or community organizations.[29] Fewer thorough studies of attitudes and sexual behavior of groups at lower risk have been done; generally they suggest smaller changes in behavior than in awareness of risk. Continued refinement of interventions designed to reduce AIDS and STD risk will be needed.

SUMMARY AND CONCLUSIONS

The risk of sexually transmitted infection varies with each pattern of human sexual behavior. Both individuals and society can decrease that risk.

Since each person is likely to have more than one sexual partner during a lifetime, and since most sexually transmitted infections are asymptomatic and many are persistent and incurable, we must concentrate on education as the primary prevention of STD infection. Education programs must convey the fundamental options for STD prevention: to restrict the number of sexual partners and/or to use condoms for all penetrative intercourse outside a permanent, stable, mutually monogamous relationship.

Prevention campaigns must target those at greatest risk and should be at work before risk-taking behavior begins. Thus, developing effective sex education for young adolescents is especially urgent.

While STD risk reduction ultimately involves individual behavior change, society also has a responsibility to promote and facilitate such change. Adopting a public policy to reduce STD risk is most important in view of the economic and health impact of STDs on the community.

The community's attitude toward sexually transmitted diseases must also change. Hitherto there has been little coordination of school programs, family-planning measures, STD clinics, or AIDS-prevention campaigns. All need to act in concert to prevent STD.

Knowledge about how best to promote and sustain behavior change to reduce STD risk is still imperfect but has improved significantly in recent years. Knowledge of trends in STDs today can help us target STD intervention on the areas of greatest need. That change *is* possible should justify sustained application of resources to primary STD-prevention intervention as well as to the provision of diagnostic and treatment services.

Since the presence of certain STDs facilitates HIV transmission, control of STDs—especially those causing genital ulcers—may help limit the spread of HIV and AIDS.

ENDNOTES

[1]R. V. Short, "Sexual Selection and Its Component Parts: Somatic and Genital Selection, as Illustrated by Man and the Great Apes," *Advances in the Study of Behavior* 9 (1979): 131–58, and "Sexual Selection in Man and the Great Apes," in *Reproductive Biology of the Great Apes: Comparative and Biomedical Perspectives,* ed. C.E. Graham (London: Academic Press, 1981), 319–41.

[2]R. L. Smith, "Human Sperm Competition," in *Sperm Competition and the Evolution of Animal Mating Systems,* ed. R. L. Smith (London: Academic Press, 1984), 601–59.

[3]F. L. Sonnenstein et al., "Sexual Activity, Condom Use and AIDS Awareness among Adolescent Males," *Family Planning Perspectives* 21 (1989): 152–58.

[4]A. C. Novello, *Final Report of Secretary's Working Group on Pediatric HIV Infection and Disease* (Washington, D.C.: U.S. Department of Health and Human Services, 1988).

[5]Centers for Disease Control, "Cases of Specified Notifiable Diseases, United States, Weeks Ending November 19, 1988, and November 21, 1987 (46th Week)," *Morbidity and Mortality Weekly Report* 37 (46) (1988): 709–11.

[6]J. W. Curran, "Economic Consequences of Pelvic Inflammatory Disease in the United States," *American Journal of Obstetrics and Gynecology* 138 (1980): 848–51.

[7]S. Kegeles et al., "Sexually Active Adolescents and Condoms: Changes Over One Year in Knowledge, Attitudes and Use," *American Journal of Public Health* 78 (4) (1988): 460–61; and S. E. Keller et al., "The Sexual Behavior of Adolescents and the Risk of AIDS," *Journal of the American Medical Association* 260 (24) (1988): 3, 586.

[8]J. Trussell, "Teenage Pregnancy in the United States," *Family Planning Perspectives* 20 (1988): 262–72.

[9]Sonnenstein et al.

[10]Centers for Disease Control, "Summary of Notifiable Diseases, United States," *Morbidity and Mortality Weekly Report* 37 (54) (1987): 1–59; and Centers for Disease Control, "Cases of Specified Notifiable Diseases."

[11]Centers for Disease Control, "Continuing Increase in Infectious Syphilis," *Morbidity and Mortality Weekly Report* 37 (3) (1988): 35–38.

[12]Institute of Medicine, *New Vaccine Development: Establishing Priorities,* vol. 1, *Diseases of Importance in the United States* (Washington, D.C.: National Academy Press, 1985).

[13]R. J. Rice et al., "Gonorrhea in the U.S. 1975–1984: Is the Giant Only Sleeping?" *Sexually Transmitted Diseases* 14 (2) (1987): 83–87.

[14]R. C. Brunham et al., "Mucopurulent Cervicitis—The Ignored Counterpart in Women of Urethritis in Men," *New England Journal of Medicine* 311 (1) (1984): 1–6; W. J. Cates, "Epidemiology and Control of Sexually Transmitted Diseases: Strategic Evolution," *Infectious Disease Clinics of North America* 1 (1) (1987): 1–23; and F. N. Judson, "Epidemiology and Control of Nongonococcal Urethritis and Genital Chlamydial Infections: A Review," *Sexually Transmitted Diseases* 8 (2) (Supplement) (1981): 117–26.

[15]S. O. Aral and K. K. Holmes, "Epidemiology of Sexual Behavior and Sexually Transmitted Diseases," in *Sexually Transmitted Diseases* (New York: McGraw-Hill, 1990), 19–36.

[16]"Chancroid," *Lancet* (2 October 1982): 747–48.

[17]T. Chuang et al., "Incidence and Trend of Herpes Progenitalis: A 15-Year Population Study," *Mayo Clinic Proceedings* 58 (7–8) (1983): 436–41; and K. K. Holmes and J. Kreiss, "Heterosexual Transmission of Human Immunodeficiency

Virus: Overview of a Neglected Aspect of the AIDS Epidemic," *Journal of Acquired Immune Deficiency Syndromes* 1 (1988): 602–10.

[18]Institute of Medicine, *New Vaccine Development;* and Cates.

[19]U.S. Public Health Service, "Report of the Second Public Health Service AIDS Prevention and Control Conference," *Public Health Reports* 103 (Supplement 1) (1988): 1–109.

[20]Institute of Medicine and National Academy of Sciences, *Confronting AIDS: Update 1988* (Washington, D.C.: National Academy Press, 1988).

[21]U.S. Public Health Service.

[22]Institute of Medicine, *New Vaccine Development.*

[23]U.S. Public Health Service.

[24]Aral and Holmes.

[25]H. H. Hiatt, "The AIDS Epidemic: Social, Cultural and Political Issues in Industrialized Countries," in *AIDS 2001: Proceedings of a Symposium Held 22–23 April 1989 in Annecy, France,* ed. J. M. Dupuy et al. (Lyon: Fondation Marcel Merieux, 1989), 65–74.

[26]M. H. Becker, ed., *The Health Belief Model and Personal Health Behavior* (Thorofare, N.J.: Charles B. Stack, 1974).

[27]A. M. Brandt, *No Magic Bullet: A Social History of Venereal Disease in the United States since 1880* (New York: Oxford University Press, 1985), 245.

[28]National Academy of Sciences, *AIDS: Sexual Behavior and Intravenous Drug Use* (Washington, D.C.: National Academy Press, 1988).

[29]Ibid.; J. G. Joseph et al., "Perceived Risk of AIDS: Assessing the Behavioral and Psychological Consequences in a Cohort of Gay Men," *Journal of Applied Social Psychology* 17 (1987): 231–50; R. D. Stall et al., "Behavioral Risk Reductions for HIV Infection among Gay and Bisexual Men," *American Psychologist* 43 (1988): 878–85; and M. H. Becker and J. G. Joseph, "AIDS and Behavioral Change to Reduce Risk: A Review," *American Journal of Public Health* 78 (4) (1988): 394–410.

My candle burns at both ends;
  It will not last the night;
But, oh, my foes, and oh, my friends—
  It gives a lovely light.

Edna St. Vincent Millay (1892–1950)
From "First Flag"

Kathy J. Helzlsouer and Leon Gordis

Risks to Health in the United States

CHANGE IN LIFE EXPECTANCY has been very dramatic in the United States during the twentieth century, but the gains that have been made have varied by sex and race. Life expectancy increased from approximately 47 years at the turn of the century to the present 71 years for men and 78 years for women.[1] White women have had the longest life expectancy throughout this century. In 1900 the average was 48.7 years. By 1986, this had increased to 78.8 years, a gain of 30 years. White men born in 1900 could expect to live, on average, 46.6 years, whereas those born in 1986 can expect to live 72.0 years. Black women born in 1900 had an average life expectancy of only 33.5 years, but for those born in 1986 it is 73.5. Black men continue to show the lowest life expectancy. In 1900 it was 32.5 years; this increased to 65.2 years in 1985.

Although all race-sex groups experienced marked gains in life expectancy during this century, a discordant note comes from 1985 and 1986, the most recent years for which published data are available. The life expectancy of both black men and black women decreased by 0.3 years. Life expectancy for whites, on the other hand, increased by 0.3 years.[2] Differences in susceptibility to disease, risk of exposure, access to health care, and response to disease treatment may account for the race-sex differential.

While life expectancy continues to increase in the United States population, it is sobering to note that life expectancy in the United

Kathy J. Helzlsouer, M.D., is Assistant Professor in the Department of Epidemiology at Johns Hopkins University.

Leon Gordis, M.D., is Chairman of the Department of Epidemiology at Johns Hopkins University.

States is 3 years less than that in Japan or Iceland. The reasons for these differences are not clearly understood.

The major contributing factor to the increase in life expectancy in the United States has been reduction in infant and childhood mortality. In the early part of the century, whites had more than 160 deaths per 1,000 live births.[3] By 1984, the rate was 9.4 per 1,000. The black infant mortality rate, 18.4 per 1,000 live births, remained almost twice that of whites. The United States continues, however, to have higher infant mortality rates than industrialized nations such as Iceland, Japan, Sweden, Switzerland, Canada, Austria, and the United Kingdom.[4]

Childhood mortality rates have also declined in this century. From 1977 to 1984, the death rate for children aged 1 to 14 decreased from 42.3 to 34.1 per 100,000 members of the population. This decline is primarily due to a decrease in death from accident, the leading cause of death in this age group.[5]

As life expectancy has increased in this century, the profile of the leading causes of death in the United States has changed. In 1900 the three leading causes of death were infectious diseases: tuberculosis, pneumonia, and diarrhea and enteritis. In the 1980s the three leading causes of death in the United States were chronic and noncommunicable diseases: cardiovascular disease, cancer, and cerebrovascular disease. As we approach the end of the twentieth century, chronic diseases are the most important health risks we face. Cancer and heart disease, for instance, now account for almost 60 percent of our deaths.

Although our lives may be longer, they are not necessarily healthier. The "golden years" may be laden with morbidity. The rate of disability in the United States is rising.[6]

The years of potential life lost (YPLL) is a measure of premature mortality and has great societal importance.[7] Although it is not a measure of the association between exposure and disease, it is a useful gauge of the importance of various diseases in terms of their impact on public health. Chronic diseases such as cardiovascular disease and cancer are responsible for 60 percent of our deaths. Unintentional injury, suicide, and homicide are responsible for 40 percent of YPLL before the age of 65. This measure of disease risk focuses attention on diseases of the younger ages, when loss of life has the greatest impact on premature mortality and when preventive measures have the largest impact on average life expectancy.

PATTERNS OF DISEASE

Over the century, and even over the past 20 years, remarkable changes in the patterns of disease have occurred. Alterations in life-style and advances in the prevention and treatment of infectious diseases have dramatically reduced mortality from these causes. Chronic diseases such as cancer and cardiovascular disease are now the leading causes of death.

Infectious Diseases

While many of the risks of death from infectious disease have decreased, some new risks have emerged. Thus, the pattern of infectious disease continually changes.

Influenza and pneumonia are still among the top ten leading causes of death. The mortality rates have decreased and the age patterns have changed, however. In a report of causes of mortality in 1850, approximately 80 percent of the deaths attributed to pneumonia occurred in those under 50 years of age; 54 percent occurred in those under 20 years of age.[8] Nowadays, deaths from pneumonia occur primarily in those considerably older than 50.

Perhaps the most dramatic event in this century has been the eradication of the variola virus, the cause of smallpox. Although successfully prevented in the United States through immunization for many years, smallpox remained a health problem worldwide until the campaign of the World Health Organization to eradicate the disease was formally declared successful in 1977.

While one disease has been eliminated, several new or newly recognized infectious diseases have emerged. Acquired Immune Deficiency Syndrome (AIDS) first came to medical attention in 1981. While premature mortality from all causes declined from 1979 to 1986, from 1984 to 1986 the YPLL went up because of the increasing incidence of AIDS.[9] AIDS, however, is not yet among the leading causes of total mortality.

Other previously unrecognized infectious diseases include Lyme disease and babesiosis. Overall, these are rare; since they are concentrated in several geographic areas, though, these diseases present significant risks to individuals living there. Both babesiosis and Lyme disease are transmitted by ticks. Babesiosis is a malaria-like illness caused by a protozoan parasite that is found primarily on Nantucket Island.[10] Lyme disease is caused by a spirochete of the genus *Borrelia* and transmitted by the deer tick.[11] The disease was originally described in Lyme, Connecticut, in 1975 and has now been reported in almost every state. The highest rates of occurrence are in the Northeast, the upper Midwest, and the West. Avoidance of tick bites is the primary preventive measure.

Other patterns of infectious disease have resulted from changes in the geographic spread of existing diseases, from the development of new populations at risk, or from changes in the virulence, pathogenicity, or modes of transmission of infectious microorganisms.[12] All of these situations introduce new or changing risks. For example, as Americans have become more mobile, the incidence of diseases such as malaria has become more frequent in the United States. Malaria-infected mosquitoes may be coming into the country on aircraft returning from Asia and Africa.

In the past 20 years we have also seen changes in existing infectious organisms. Toxic shock syndrome, first recognized in the 1970s, results from a toxin produced by *Staphylococcus aureus*. This is a common organism, but the toxin was unknown prior to the initial epidemic. Legionnaires' disease is an example of a hazard resulting from a man-made change in the environment. The disease was first recognized in an outbreak of an acute respiratory illness among members of the American Legion attending a conference in Philadelphia in 1976. The causative organism was eventually identified and named *Legionella pneumonophila*. In retrospect, other previously occurring outbreaks in the 1960s and 1970s have now been attributed to the same family of organisms.[13] They are normal inhabitants of ponds and streams, and in their usual environment are not hazardous to man. Introduced into the water supply in buildings and in the unnatural environment of humidifiers, cooling towers, and shower heads, *Legionella* organisms persist and multiply to numbers far exceeding those in the natural habitat. They are now a potential environmental hazard to hosts that are susceptible to them.

Cardiovascular Disease

As the average life expectancy of the U.S. population has risen, chronic cardiovascular disease has become the predominant health risk. Mortality from this disease has declined approximately 2 percent per year since the 1960s, however,[14] and the years of potential life lost before the age of 65 because of these diseases have gone down.

Risks for cardiovascular disease are higher for blacks than for whites and higher for men than for women.[15] The greater prevalence of hypertension and cigarette smoking among blacks than among whites and inadequate access to health care contribute to these risks.

The risk factors for cardiovascular disease are both genetic and environmental. People with family histories of heart disease, particularly premature heart disease, have an increased chance of developing it. Other factors related to life-style, such as smoking, weight, and diet, are under our control and may alter the risk of developing coronary heart disease. While smoking increases the risk of heart disease only moderately, an increase of 70 percent compared with that of nonsmokers, smoking is responsible for over 15 percent of deaths due to heart disease. Factors contributing to the risk of cerebrovascular disease are similar to those for coronary heart disease.[16]

What explains the decrease in cardiovascular mortality? Improvements in both prevention and treatment. From 1970 to 1987, smoking declined 13 percent in the United States. In addition, recognition and treatment of hypertension have become more widespread and Americans have reduced the amount of fat in their diet. Although cardiovascular disease continues to be the greatest health risk in America, that risk does appear to be decreasing, and further improvements can be achieved through modification of life-style. Coronary care units, telemetry in ambulances, new pharmacologic agents for control of arrhythmias, and treatment of hypertension are therapeutic elements that have reduced mortality from cardiovascular disease in the United States.

Cancer

The disease burden caused by cancer has assumed a greater role in recent years because of the decline in mortality from infectious and cardiovascular diseases as well as the aging of the population. The person-years of life lost to cancer of all types increased 30 percent in both men and women from 1970 to 1984.[17] The person-years of life lost are measured as the difference between the age at death and the expectation of remaining years of life for the individual based on life tables published yearly by the National Center for Health Statistics. In terms of premature mortality, the most costly type of cancer for men is lung cancer, and for women, breast cancer. From 1970 to 1984, the person-years of life lost because of lung cancer in men increased 48 percent, and because of breast cancer, 28 percent. However, the most striking increase in premature mortality for women was caused by lung cancer, which went up 170 percent. It should be kept in mind that person-years of life lost may increase without a rise in the age-specific risk of death from cancer due to the aging and size of the population at risk of death from cancer.

From 1950 to 1985, the incidence of cancer in the United States increased 36.5 percent. In the same period, mortality from cancer increased only 6.7 percent and the 5-year relative survival rate went up to 50 percent.[18] These data suggest that during this time, treatments for cancer became more effective.

The risks of cancer are not distributed equally throughout the population. Its incidence has increased more rapidly for blacks than for whites, and for men to a greater extent than for women. Since cancer is not a single disease, trends must be examined by type of cancer. Both the incidence of, and the mortality from, stomach cancer, for example, have decreased steadily during this century. The importance of life-style and environmental factors in the etiology of stomach cancer is suggested by the marked international variation in the rates of disease and changes in incidence rates over a relatively brief span of time. The exact nature of the factors responsible for the decline in stomach cancer is not known.

The risk of developing other cancers has gone up. The most dramatic example is lung cancer, which for both men and women has reached epidemic proportions in the United States. Smoking is known to be responsible for 90 percent of lung cancer deaths. The carcinogenic effects of smoking are observed many years after initial exposure. Many epidemiologic studies have shown that smokers have a 10 times greater risk of developing lung cancer than nonsmokers. Since not all smokers develop cancer, other host factors must also play a role in determining who is susceptible to the carcinogenic action of cigarette smoke. However, it has been estimated that elimination of exposure to cigarette smoke would decrease mortality from all cancer by about 30 percent.[19] The elimination of smoking would also have a beneficial effect on the risk of heart disease and chronic obstructive pulmonary disease.

Age-adjusted incidence and mortality rates for invasive cervical cancer have decreased in the last 30 years.[20] The primary reason for the decrease in both incidence and mortality is the regular use of the PAP smear at the stage before tumors become invasive, when the disease is still highly curable.

Although cervical cancer mortality rates for women aged 25 to 34 have been stable since 1974, incidence in this group has increased by 32 percent. Incidence and mortality rates in blacks are more than double those in whites. The trends in mortality and incidence raise concern that either adequate control of the disease through routine screening is not being obtained in all populations or exposure to factors that increase the risk of disease may be on the rise. These factors include sexually transmitted diseases such as papilloma virus infections, which have been associated with cancer of the cervix. In either case, deaths from cervical cancer, although relatively rare, are almost totally avoidable with early detection and treatment. Therefore, adequate screening should be available for all segments of the population.

Although the risk of developing breast cancer has been increasing in recent years, it is an example of a disease in which the risk of death could be decreased if currently available technology for early detection were more widely applied. Mortality rates from breast cancer are reduced by approximately 30 percent for women who routinely undergo screening with mammography and physical examination.[21] Barriers to screening include the cost of mammography, which is not covered by insurance, Medicaid, or Medicare, as well as lack of patient and physician compliance with preventive services.

Since cancer rates vary among regions of countries as well as among countries, and since immigrant populations often develop the cancer rates of the countries in which they settle, environmental and life-style factors such as diet and smoking may be important risk factors for cancer. Japan, for example, perhaps because of diet, has the highest rate of stomach cancer yet the lowest rate of breast cancer—a situation opposite that of the United States.

The alterations in cancer incidence and mortality rates can be related to major changes in exposure and treatment. However, the rates are fairly insensitive to small changes that may occur in subpopulations but that may nevertheless reflect serious risks of disease. A rise in cases of cancer is expected to result from the radiation exposure of the Chernobyl nuclear accident, for example.[22] For the 24,000 persons who were between 3 and 15 kilometers of the plant, 131 cancers beyond the normal number are predicted. But this excess represents only a 2.6 percent increase in the cancer rate. It is unlikely that this small percentage increase, occurring over several years, could be detected by examination of incident or mortality statistics. The risk imposed by the exposure would be lost in the background of rates of occurrence of other diseases. Similarly, it is often extremely difficult to detect the hazardous effects of exposure to chemicals in occupational settings or to toxic waste sites because the risks could be missed as a result of the small size of the population exposed, which might preclude any demonstration of significant change, over baseline rates, in the risk of disease. Identifying such hazards may have important implications for the general public, however. For example, the risks of radon exposure as a cause of lung cancer was first identified in occupational studies of uranium mine workers. Only recently has attention been focused on the potential hazard from home exposure.[23]

ACCIDENTS

In the United states, accidents have been among the top ten causes of death in this century. Because their toll among the young is high, accidents also rank as the country's leading cause of premature death. However, the rate of death from all accidents has dramatically decreased, from 87.2 per 100,000 persons in 1903 to 39.0 per 100,000 in 1986.[24]

Motor vehicle accidents are the major cause of accidental deaths. Although the risk of death associated with motor vehicle accidents has markedly declined since 1912 through the use of occupant restraints and the imposition of speed limits, fatal motor accidents still make a large contribution to premature mortality. Alcohol-related traffic fatalities represent 55.3 percent of all years of potential life lost because of motor vehicle crashes. In comparison with other industrialized countries, the United States has had one of the lowest traffic-fatality rates calculated on the basis of miles traveled, but if this rate is calculated on the basis of population, the United States ranks less favorably.[25]

From 1912 to 1986, accidental work-related deaths per 100,000 of the population declined 81 percent, despite a doubling in the size of the work force and a marked increase in productivity. More than a third of work-related deaths involved motor vehicle accidents.

In 1986 deaths due to accidents at home numbered 8.5 per 100,000 people, a decrease of 70 percent from 1912. Also in 1986 the rate of accidental work deaths was 4.4 per 100,000 workers for all industries. The home environment, therefore, presents a level of risk that is somewhat higher than that of the work environment. The types of accident in the home resulting in death include falls, fires, poisonings, drownings, and firearm injuries.

Home is not only risky in terms of fatal accidents but also in terms of less severe injuries. In 1985, about 1 in 11 persons required medical attention or had some degree of restricted activity because of accidents at home.

OCCUPATIONAL RISKS

The incidence of occupational illness was 18 per 10,000 full-time workers in 1985. Agriculture had the highest overall incidence rate, 41.6 occupational illnesses per 10,000 full-time workers, followed by the manufacturing industry at a rate of 38.7.

According to the National Institute for Occupational Safety and Health, occupational cancers rank third on a list of leading work-related injuries and diseases. Cancers that can be attributed to occupational exposure are estimated to be approximately 4 percent of the total.[26] Epidemiologic studies have linked the cancers to exposure in the workplace to such substances as vinyl chloride, asbestos, radium, and benzene. These exposures may also interact with other behaviors of workers, such as smoking, to markedly increase the risk of developing cancer over what the risk would be from either exposure alone.

HOMICIDE

Homicide makes a significant contribution to the differences in mortality by race. From 1968 to 1985, the years of potential life lost to homicide per 100,000 of the U.S. population was 6 times higher for black men than for white men and 4 times higher for black women than for white women. Overall, the years of life lost to homicide increased 44 percent from 1968 to 1985.[27]

In comparison with 21 developed countries, the United States has the highest homicide rate among males 15 through 24 years of age.[28] This age group had 4,000 homicides in 1987. Three-quarters of all U.S. homicides in 1987 resulted from the use of firearms. Our homicide rate is 4.4 times higher than the rate in Scotland and more than 40 times higher than the rate in Japan. If the U.S. homicide rate could be reduced to Scotland's, more than 3,000 lives would be saved each year.

CONCLUSIONS

Life expectancy has continued to increase during this century, and years of life lost because of premature mortality have decreased. Can one conclude from these measures that risks to health in the United States are lower today than in the past? We think not. First, while on average we are living longer, certain segments of the population continue to have high rates of premature mortality. Black Americans, for example, have a shorter life expectancy than white Americans, and the gap between them is growing. Second, the increase in life expectancy does not necessarily mean we are living healthier or less risky lives. On the one hand, decreases in infant mortality and in death from injury as well as improvements in the prevention and treatment of infectious diseases have lengthened life. On the other hand, longer life predisposes us to morbidity and mortality from chronic diseases such as cancer and cardiovascular disease. While life expectancy is going up, so is morbidity, as the rising rate of disability in the United States shows.[29]

The drug problem contributes to premature mortality in all segments of the population. In addition to its impact on homicide, which is increasing, it also accounts for the numbers of AIDS cases occurring among IV drug abusers. The prevalence of drugs in all segments of the population is alarming and calls for widespread and early intervention in both the treatment and the prevention of alcohol and drug abuse.

The change in the type of health risks over the century, from acute to chronic disease, has significant health policy implications. Health care resources must be made available to handle the demands imposed on them by the growing number of people living into old age and suffering from chronic disease. Resources for research and health services aimed at preventing the onset of chronic disease symptoms must be allocated so as to minimize the time between the onset of disability and death.

Research has shown that many of the factors contributing to the onset of chronic disease are avoidable or modifiable. For example, 30 percent of all cancers as well as a significant proportion of heart disease can be attributed to smoking. The typical U.S. diet, which is high in fat and low in fiber, is also a major contributing factor to both cancer and cardiovascular disease. Although many of the risk factors for disease are modifiable, achieving life-style changes is difficult.

Early intervention is critical to success. Many disease processes begin early in life but do not show up as symptoms until much later. The 55-year-old man has the myocardial infarction, but atherosclerotic plaques are present in the 20-year-old. While avoidance of risk factors even late in life may be successful in preventing, or at least delaying, the onset of disease, the optimum time to intervene is before risky life-styles are established and the disease process starts. Avoidance of risk factors must begin in childhood.

Emphasizing prevention in health services would represent a dramatic change in health policy. To give prevention appropriate emphasis in American health care, several critical steps need to be taken. Medical education has traditionally emphasized diagnosis and treatment, often to the exclusion of prevention. Since the greatest impact on the health of the American population is likely to come from preventive programs, physicians must be educated to recognize their responsibility for prevention as well as therapy. Government agencies and third-party payers, who underwrite much of the health care in the United States, must also accept the value of prevention by increasing the number of preventive services for which they will provide adequate levels of reimbursement. Finally, the American public must be educated to see the value of prevention. Its benefits may not be as dramatic as those of medical or surgical treatment but may be much greater.

Access to care, quality of health care, and use of health services are even more fundamental than integration of preventive services into our health-care system. The extent to which access to care or quality of care is responsible for differentials in rates of disease or premature mortality among various segments of our society should be investigated. The infant mortality rate for blacks should not be twice that for whites. The United States should be able to achieve the same success as European countries in reducing infant mortality rates. The cancer survival differences between blacks and whites are unlikely to be due to biological differences and may well reflect differences in health care delivery.

The contribution of mental illness to morbidity and mortality is difficult to assess from available data and therefore may be overlooked as a serious health risk. The suicide rate reflects only a small part of the mental illness in the United States. The stigma associated with mental illness may be lessening and awareness of these diseases may be increasing, but access to care for all who would benefit is limited. Health insurers usually provide only limited coverage, if any, for mental health services. Research on effective intervention and reimbursement for preventive services need to be considered in the allocation of health care resources.

The risk of disease is changing. In the United States the average life expectancy has markedly improved over the course of this century. While we have reduced morbidity and mortality from infectious disease such as pneumonia and influenza and even completely eliminated the risk of smallpox, we are continually being challenged by the appearance of new diseases such as AIDS and by chronic disease and accidents. As life expectancy increases, our greatest challenge is to improve the quality of life through prevention and access to health services.

ACKNOWLEDGMENT

We thank Ms. Allyn Arnold of the Department of Epidemiology for her expert help in preparing this manuscript.

ENDNOTES

[1]J. F. Fries, "Aging, Natural Death, and the Compression of Morbidity," *New England Journal of Medicine* 303 (1980): 130–35; E. L. Schneider and J. A. Brady, "Aging, Natural Death, and the Compression of Morbidity: Another View," *New England Journal of Medicine* 309 (1983): 54–56; Department of Commerce, Bureau of the Census, *United States Life Tables 1900, 1901, 1910, and 1901–1910* (prepared by James W. Glover) (Washington, D.C.: U.S. Government Printing Office, 1921); and National Center for Health Statistics, Public Health Service, *Mortality, Part A, Vital Statistics of the United States, 1986,* vol. 2, DHHS. pub. no. (PHS) 88–1122 (Washington, D.C.: U.S. Government Printing Office, 1988).

[2]National Center for Health Statistics, *Mortality, Part A.*

[3]Department of Commerce, Bureau of the Census, *Birth, Stillbirth, and Infant Mortality Statistics for the Birth Registration Area of the United States, 1923* (Washington, D.C.: U.S. Government Printing Office, 1925).

[4]"1989 World Population Data Sheet," Population Reference Bureau, Inc.

[5]National Center for Health Statistics, Public Health Service, *Health, United States, 1987,* DHHS pub. no. (PHS) (Washington, D.C.: U.S. Government Printing Office, 1988), 88–1322.

[6]A. Colvez and M. Blanchet, "Disability Trends in the United States Population 1966–1976: Analysis of Reported Causes," *American Journal of Public Health* 71 (1981): 464–71.

[7]Centers for Disease Control, "Introduction to Table V, 'Premature Deaths, Monthly Mortality, and Monthly Physician Contacts—United States,' " *Morbidity and Mortality Weekly Report* 31 (1982): 109–10; and J. W. Horm and E. J. Sondik, "Person-Years of Life Lost Due to Cancer in the United States, 1970 and 1984," *American Journal of Public Health* 79 (1989): 1490–93.

[8]U.S. Census Office, *Mortality Statistics of the Seventh Census of the United States 1850* (Washington, D.C.: A. O. P. Nicholson, Printer, 1855).

[9]Centers for Disease Control, "Changes in Premature Mortality—United States, 1979–1986," *Morbidity and Mortality Weekly Report* 37 (1988): 47–48.

[10]B. Lober, "Changing Patterns of Infectious Diseases," *American Journal of Medicine* 84 (1988): 569–79.

[11]G. S. Habecht, G. Beck, and T. L. Benach, "Lyme Disease," *Science* 257 (1987): 78–83.

[12]Lober.

[13]A. B. Christie, "Infectious Disease: Epidemiology and Clinical Practice," chap. 16, *Legionnaires' Disease,* vol. 1 (New York: Churchill Livingstone, 1987): 475–91.

[14]Centers for Disease Control, "Years of Life Lost From Cardiovascular Disease," *Morbidity and Mortality Weekly Report* 35 (1986): 653–54, and "Chronic Disease Reports: Mortality Trends—United States," *Morbidity and Mortality Weekly Report* 38 (1979–1986): 189–91.

[15]T. J. Thom, "Cardiovascular Mortality among United States Women," *Coronary Heart Disease, Women,* proceedings of NIH workshop (New York: Haymarket-Doyma, 1987), 33–41.

[16]M. J. Klag, P. K. Whelton, and A. J. Seidler, "Decline in U.S. Stroke Mortality Demographic Trends and Antihypertensive Treatment," *Stroke* 20 (1989): 14–21; and Centers for Disease Control, "Premature Mortality Due to Cerebrovascular Disease—United States, 1983," *Morbidity and Mortality Weekly Report* 36 (1987): 316–17.

[17]National Cancer Institute, Public Health Service, *1987 Annual Cancer Statistics Review, Including Cancer Trends, 1950–1985,* DHHS. NIH pub. no. 88–2789 (Washington, D.C.: U.S. Government Printing Office, 1988).

[18]Centers for Disease Control, "Cigarette Smoking in the United States, 1986," *Morbidity and Mortality Weekly Report* 36 (1987): 581–85.

[19]R. Doll and R. Peto, "The Causes of Cancer: Quantitative Estimates of Avoidable Risks of Cancer in the United States Today," *Journal of the National Cancer Institute* 66 (1981): 1191–1308.

[20]W. Winkelstein and S. Selvin, "Cervical Cancer in Young Americans," letter, *Lancet* (June 17, 1989): 1385.

[21]S. Shapiro, W. Venet, P. Strax, and L. Venet, *Periodic Screening for Breast Cancer, The Health Insurance Plan Project and Its Sequel, 1963–1986* (Baltimore: Johns Hopkins University Press, 1988), 5.

[22]R. Wilson and E. A. Crouch, "Risk Assessment and Comparisons: An Introduction," *Science* 236 (1987): 267–70.

[23]National Safety Council, "Accident Facts," *Edition 1987* (Washington, D.C.: National Center for Health Statistics, 1987), 10.

[24]Ibid.

[25]National Safety Council.

[26]Doll and Peto.

[27]Centers for Disease Control, "Premature Mortality Due to Homicides—United States, 1968–1985," *Morbidity and Mortality Weekly Report* 37 (1988): 543–45.

[28]Ibid.

[29]Horm and Sondik.

George L. Priest

The New Legal Structure of Risk Control

SERIOUS EFFORTS TO IMPOSE LEGAL CONTROLS on the sources of societal risk date only from the mid-1960s. Most prominent in the public mind has been the creation of specialized federal agencies to directly regulate particular societal dangers—the Environmental Protection Agency, the Occupational Health and Safety Administration, the National Highway Traffic Safety Administration, and the Consumer Product Safety Commission as examples. But far more pervasive in scope and far more effective in impact than agency regulation has been the expansion of civil law to control risk. Since the late 1960s, our civil justice system has adopted the premise that civil damage awards enforcing liability rules and statutory rights can optimally regulate *every* source of societal risk. Building from this premise, our civil courts have become the most powerful institution of the modern state for regulating risk.

Prior to the 1960s, civil law had served a modest role in U.S. affairs. It enforced property rights and policed boundary disputes through property law, enforced promises through contract law, and provided damages for personal injury through negligence law where an individual was injured by an egregious breach of standards of normal behavior. Though the negligence standard of personal injury law proved loose enough to allow substantial subsequent expansion, prior to the 1960s courts employed this standard only where a party had shown clear moral culpability substantially antagonistic to social norms.

George L. Priest is the John M. Olin Professor of Law and Economics and Director of the Program in Civil Liability at Yale Law School.

Since the 1960s, however, our civil law has changed dramatically. Contract law, property law, and especially personal injury law have been transformed in both function and effect. The transformation occurred neither through some sudden change in legal doctrine nor through legislative statute or popular referendum. Instead, it occurred through the triumph of an idea: the acceptance by the judiciary of the proposition that civil damage judgments can serve as the most effective public policy instrument for internalizing costs to the parties that generate them. The basic conception derives from economics:[1] if a party engaging in some activity fails to take into account the full costs that the activity generates, the party is likely to engage in more of the activity than is appropriate for the society. Where the costs are injury costs, there will result higher levels of injurious activities and thus larger numbers of injuries than societally appropriate. If, however, a court internalizes injury costs by making the party compensate victims injured by its activities, the party will be led to readjust activity levels and reduce the number of injuries.

The proposition that the civil legal system could be employed to internalize costs was advocated in the legal literature from the earliest years of the century.[2] It was given increasing attention by the legal establishment after World War II, however, and by the 1960s commanded nearly unanimous support. It was first put into law by the state judiciary in sophisticated states like New Jersey and California, but the idea spread rapidly to the other states and to the federal judiciary. Today it is the principle underlying all civil law.

The causes are surely multiple, but it is clear that the transformation of civil law to regulate activities by internalizing costs is consistent with the legislative creation during the late 1960s and 1970s of the various agencies to regulate safety directly, as mentioned above. In many respects, however, the transformation of civil law toward this end is far more ambitious than the creation of regulatory agencies. All regulatory agencies have limited budgets and, as a consequence, thresholds of concern. Thus, they can effectively regulate only a few firm decisions in the small number of industries directly subject to their review. Our modern civil justice system, in contrast, aspires to internalize costs to all activities in the society. Our civil courts can entertain the question of whether the victim should receive compensation as long as it is economically worthwhile for a person feeling victimized to initiate litigation. Indeed, to perfect the system, the incentives for initiating litigation have themselves been enhanced by various statutes awarding attorneys' fees and shifting litigation costs. As a result, our courts today employ civil damage judgments to regulate all activities implicating harm, made within every industry, indeed, by every citizen. Through the daily aggregation of civil damage judgments in the thousands of state courts around the country, our courts provide fine-tuned control of all societal behavior.

Perhaps the most accurate characterization of our modern regime is that the principal function of modern civil law is to control risk. Henry Maine described the law of modern societies as progressing from status to contract, but that progression is surely now eclipsed. Property law whose purpose was to preserve status, contract law whose purpose was to preserve promise, and personal injury law whose purpose was to preserve some relationship of moral equilibrium among parties have all been redefined. The predominant function of modern law is to allocate risk.

The adoption of risk control as its central purpose has shifted sharply the focus of legal controversy in each of the subfields of civil law. In the field of contract law, for example, contract litigation only a few decades ago turned chiefly on differing interpretations of the terms of underlying written contracts. In modern contract litigation, in contrast, the issues have been completely reoriented around the question of risk. The fact that some change in conditions led one of the parties to breach the contract is only the beginning of the inquiry. The issue before the court is which party should bear the risk of the change in conditions that impelled the breach. Today, courts summon sophisticated theories of economics and risk bearing to determine whether it is more consistent with the long-term interests of the parties to assign the risk of the specific change of conditions that animated the breach to the breaching party or to the victim of the breach itself.

Similarly, in earlier years the law of corporations and of mergers and acquisitions was defined almost exclusively by the terms of corporate documents. Today, the papers of incorporation are often treated as only other obstacles that must be surpassed as part of the analysis of how to allocate risks that affect corporate ownership and structure. In the recent highly publicized litigation involving mergers and acquisitions, for example, the issue before the court is whether the market for corporate control will be facilitated by assigning the risk and the commensurate benefits of some novel method of hostile takeover to current shareholders, to current management, or to the corporate raiders who have initiated the struggle.

The development of risk control as the central function of the law has been most prominent, however, in fields involving personal injury. As in other fields, this development has led to an extensive redefinition of legal issues. In cases involving claims of medical malpractice, for example, modern litigation extends far beyond the earlier relatively simple inquiry into whether the doctor was morally culpable for breaching standards of community practice. In the most sophisticated malpractice litigation today, the issue is one of risk and its control: Did the attending surgeon have sufficient control over the determinants of the risk of the medical maloccurrence to justify liability, or should that risk be assigned to supporting physicians or to the hospital vicariously through a judgment against its staff?

The largest subfield of civil law today is products liability, a field whose existence stems almost entirely from the law's shift to concern about risk control. Where liability attaches only to acts of clear moral dereliction, there is little occasion for products liability: products that are dangerously defective are seldom produced intentionally and infrequently produced with indifference to consumer safety. But where the legal issue is risk control, the concerns of a court are broadened. The litigable question becomes whether a manufacturer has appropriately minimized the risks of product injury. Cases of earlier days involving claims that some mismanufacture resulted in a defective product are today hardly worth litigating; the manufacturer's opportunity to control the risk is so obvious that the manufacturer will typically pay compensation immediately. Instead, the most important of modern cases involve claims that the manufacturer's calculation of the risks of even inevitable product injuries was insufficiently precise, for it miscomputed relative costs and benefits.

An important implication of the adoption of risk control as the principal function of the law is that issues of motive and volition central to the legal regime that prevailed until the 1960s are rendered largely irrelevant. In modern contract law, for example, the decision of a party to intentionally breach a contract has little legal significance. It is acknowledged that the risks are omnipresent that changes in conditions will occur that might unsettle contracts and, thus, that it is inevitable that some contracts will be breached. The role of a court, as a result, is no longer to punish breach of contract, but to allocate between the parties the risks of such changes in underlying conditions. Similarly, though in earlier years it was necessary to demonstrate that a manufacturer had acted with bad motives or had behaved recklessly or negligently, such issues today are largely ignored. The concern of the courts has extended beyond specific bad motives to the broader risks of product injury. Thus, a manufacturer may have organized its production process with deep humanitarian concern for the welfare of its consumers, but if the company has miscalculated the risks and benefits of safety design, liability will follow immediately.

Many believe the derogation in the law of issues of motive and volition as indicating a decline in commitment to individual responsibility or, perhaps, a shift of expectations toward an impersonal or a collective responsibility. The shift in standards of law may indirectly have that effect as citizens revise their expectations of the ultimate consequences of misoccurrences that afflict them. But I believe that the stimulus for the shift toward risk control as the central purpose of civil law is different and that it did not derive from a diminished conviction in the importance of individual responsibility.

The legal regime that prevailed from the nineteenth century through the mid-1960s functioned chiefly by categorizing certain actions that generated loss as so particularly extreme or egregious as to deserve liability for any harm that resulted. Actions subject to legal liability were those for which there was a dramatically greater chance than normal that loss would result. According to this regime, prototypical candidates for liability were harms caused intentionally and those close to the intentional because of the high likelihood of injury.

Our modern legal regime, in contrast, has adopted a broader and more expansive conception of the sources of loss. In the view of modern law, a loss suffered in the society represents only the outcome of some probabilistic process. Actions can be said to generate loss if they increase the probability of occurrence of a loss. All loss-generating activities, thus, can be arrayed upon a continuum, from losses the probability of which is 100 percent—intentionally caused harms—to losses the probability of which is 0 percent.

These two contrasting approaches toward the sources of loss imply vastly different methods of legal analysis. A property law whose focus is boundary disputes, a contract law whose focus is breach of promise, and a personal injury law whose focus is serious moral dereliction are each regimes in which the law defines a clear demarcation between acts subject to liability and acts immune from it. If the property line is transgressed, a trespass action will follow. If the contract is not performed, or if the injurer is morally culpable, damages will follow.

According to this view of the law, there are certain clear actions for which liability will apply, but equally clear sets for which liability is unavailable. Indeed, there are large sets of injuries suffered by property owners, parties to contracts, and injured victims that not only do not justify liability, but do not justify even judicial scrutiny. For example, under such a regime, a consumer injured by a product who cannot show that the product was intentionally or recklessly mismanufactured or who cannot show clear moral negligence in the manufacturing process cannot recover damages. From the standpoint of the law, the product-related injury remains one of life's hazards to be suffered as best as possible according to the victim's resources, but without reference to the legal system. As another example, if a farmer promised to provide a broker 1,000 bushels of corn but because of drought can only provide 500, the farmer has breached the contract and must pay damages to the broker for the remainder. According to the law, the farmer must suffer the loss because it was the farmer, not the broker, who promised to deliver the corn.

This is not to suggest that the earlier regime was totally indifferent to conditions generating losses. If the probability of injury from product use were exceptionally high, the law could conclude that the manufacturer should have known of the product danger and find the manufacturer liable despite its claim of ignorance. Similarly, if the drought itself were so extreme that it prevented the farmer from delivering *any* of the 1,000 bushels, the law could relieve the farmer by rescinding the contract. Nevertheless, the method of analysis under the regime, even in these examples, was one of comparing the extremity of the factual context of the loss to some standard of normal or expected behavior.

According to this approach, some actions differ so dramatically from the normal—reckless manufacture or breach of contract—that legal liability is justified. Legal analysis under such a regime consisted of categorizing acts as either qualifying as sufficiently abnormal to justify liability or not. Obviously, intentional harm-causing actions justified liability. Beyond the intentional, unusually egregious actions may have justified liability. In almost all other cases, however, liability was unavailable, and the law allowed the loss to lie where it had fallen.

The adoption of risk control as the central goal of civil law rejects this categorical method of legal analysis. A law concerned with risk perceives losses as occurring probabilistically, with greater or lesser likelihood. Actions become subject to potential legal liability if they increase the occurrence of loss by some amount.

This shift does not reject, but builds upon, the liability of the previous regime. Losses caused intentionally or that are especially egregious remain subject to liability *a fortiori*. The frontier of liability, instead, is extended to disputes involving actions which increase the probability of loss by some dimension, though they may not make the loss inevitable or even highly likely. Thus, a manufacturer is made responsible for avoiding more than recklessly or egregiously negligent production methods; the manufacturer must monitor all potential sources of product risk and will be held liable whenever a risk eventuates that the manufacturer could readily have controlled. Similarly, liability for breach of contract induced by a drought will turn not on the simple issue of whether it was the farmer or the broker who breached the promise. Rather, the breach of promise is viewed as a probabilistic outcome of the drought. The issue in the case shifts to the question of the appropriate assignment of the risk of drought: Is it better to allocate the risk of drought to the individual farmer, locked into the specific climatic position of the farm, or to the broker, who can diversify drought risk by entering contracts with geographically disparate farmers?

A law concerned with risk control rejects a discrete demarcation between actions regarded as extreme and those regarded as normal. All actions can be arrayed on a continuum of contribution toward loss. Thus, central concepts of causation are changed dramatically. The earlier regime that imposed a sharp distinction between particularly extreme sources of harm and all others was necessarily committed to a very strict conception of causation. Actions were subject to liability for causing harm chiefly if they constituted the sole or exclusive source of the harm. In contrast, our modern law, devoted to risk control, focuses less upon strict causation than upon *contribution* to the occurrence of the harm. Some action may generate liability because of its contribution to the risk of occurrence, though it was only one of many simultaneously contributing sources of the loss.

The new regime of risk control thus vastly expands the opportunity for the attachment of legal liability as well as the importance of civil law as an instrument of social control. Many decry what they perceive as the increased litigiousness of modern society. But it is clear that litigiousness itself is a function of the underlying legal rules in force. Our modern civil law encourages litigation as an instrument for internalizing costs to control risks. Because in our society intentionally or egregiously caused harms are infrequent, the earlier legal regime that focused only upon such harms was a regime of very limited scope. In contrast, our modern legal regime, focused upon every *contribution* to risk, is a regime of dramatically greater dimension. Such a regime aspires to impose legal controls on all activities in the society that contribute to risk in any way. Thus, virtually every action by every citizen becomes subject to potential legal review because every action will increase the risk of some loss in some way.

To my mind, far from incorporating a diminished view of individual responsibility, the shift of the law's purpose toward risk control represents a vastly expanded commitment to standards of individual responsibility. Under the new regime, an individual is responsible not only for intentionally or maliciously harmful behavior, but for all behavior that increases the risk of loss, though the loss itself may be remote. Under earlier law, an individual needed to make certain only that his or her actions caused no direct injury to another individual. Under modern law, in contrast, an individual must make certain that his or her actions do not increase the risk of loss in any way. Thus, for each citizen, the potential of civil liability is vastly increased. The law charges each citizen to carefully monitor every action for its potential contribution to risk of loss.

From the standpoint of the control of risk, it is difficult to define a truly solitary act—an act that does not in some way implicate risks to others. The gardener spraying plants or the recluse reading silently before the fireplace may not be subject to liability personally for the increase in the collective social risk from pesticides or particulates, but will suffer the attachment of liability as pesticide or firewood prices rise or as the society proscribes such enjoyments directly. It is equally difficult in a society concerned with risk to truly shield or isolate oneself from others. The gardener's yield will be affected by the acidity of the rain, just as book prices will reflect the shift to acid-free paper. The centrality of risk effectively prevents all efforts of social escape.

Beyond increasing the scope of individual responsibility, the regime of risk control dramatically changes the substantive content of that responsibility. The focus of modern law on risk control diminishes the importance of moral standards in the evaluation of harm-causing activities. It is no longer useful in such a regime to distinguish between the guilty and the innocent or the culpable and the blameless. Almost every human action will increase the probability of some loss by some amount; empirically, it would be extremely rare for an action to contribute zero toward the probability of occurrence of all losses in all contexts. It follows, thus, that under the modern conception of risk, no action is ever truly innocent. Each of us must recognize that all of our actions are likely to harm others in the society in some way. As a consequence, every citizen stands in a position of continuous potential interaction with the law since every action is potentially subject to liability. Indeed, each of us must be aware that many of our specific actions may well lie close to the point on the risk continuum at which the attachment of legal liability becomes socially worthwhile. Once it is accepted that all actions can be arrayed at some point upon the risk-contribution continuum, sharp moral distinctions lose moment. It is no longer possible to clearly separate the moral quality of one's personal actions from the quality of the actions of others. On the risk-contribution continuum, there are no clear qualitative differences between actions whatsoever; all actions contribute something to risk. The only question is the extent of the contribution.

The decline in the importance of moral standards as grounds for comparing loss-contributing actions, however, should not be interpreted to suggest that our new legal regime of risk control lacks moral foundation. The moral foundation of the new regime is relentlessly utilitarian. The objective of controlling risk as effectively as possible prevails over all else.

Our courts have defined two basic principles of decision making to internalize costs to create incentives to reduce the risk level as much as is practicable. First, if the injury could have been practicably prevented, liability will be placed on that party in the relatively better position to prevent it. Second, if the injury could not have been practicably prevented, liability will be placed on that party in the relatively better position to spread the risks of the injury.

The modern regime of risk control accepts that the risks of harm cannot be eliminated entirely without imposing severe burdens on the society. In a well-known example, the only way to truly eliminate the risks of auto injuries is to totally prohibit driving.[3] Eliminating risks, thus, is out of the question. The appropriate social question must be how much to seek to prevent injuries directly and what then to do about those injuries that remain.

The first principle of modern law creates incentives for parties to invest to reduce the accident rate by defining a legal standard that threatens to charge parties with the costs of injuries if they fail to make risk-reduction investments. The underlying idea is to reduce the accident rate by making it cheaper for a party to invest in risk reduction than to pay damages for the unprevented injuries.

Though this first principle is often articulated, as above, in terms of placing liability on the party in the best position to prevent the accident,[4] more precisely it is the calculation of whether, for either of the parties to the accident, the burdens of investing in risk reduction exceed the expected benefits from such investments. Because the phenomenon of risk is continuous rather than discrete, it would be necessary under any moral standard to calculate some appropriate point of risk reduction by weighing burdens against benefits. Since the moral standard that prevails today is openly utilitarian, however, the predominant technique of calculation in our modern regime is economics. It should be no surprise that, as the legal system has shifted its focus to the control of risk, the discipline of economics has assumed a larger and larger place in legal analysis. The more precise statement of the first principle of civil liability today is that a court will hold a party to an injury liable if that party could have taken some action to reduce the risk of the injury at a cost less than the benefit from risk reduction.

The first principle of modern civil law has been widely accepted in the courts and the academy. Indeed, it is impossible to find even the speculation that the society would not benefit from its careful implementation. The second principle of modern law, however—the principle calling for liability to be assigned in order to spread the risks of injuries that cannot be prevented—is substantially more controversial.

In theory, the risk-spreading principle seems compelling. Since it is acknowledged that, in some cases it is literally impossible to prevent all injuries, and in other cases societally impracticable (because too costly) to prevent injuries, a regime devoted to risk control must deal with risks that, though reduced, remain, promising injury to some citizens. According to the second principle, for injuries that cannot be practicably prevented, liability will be assigned to the party that was in the relatively better position to spread the risk of the injury.

Here the function of the legal system shifts from what is essentially a safety mechanism, creating incentives to prevent injury, to an insurance mechanism or, at the least, a mechanism that facilitates insurance. Again, in theory, losses that cannot be prevented can only be insured against. The function of insurance is to reduce risk of loss by spreading risks over some broader probabilistic base. A rule of civil law can facilitate this function by assigning liability for the loss to that party in the best position to spread the loss either by obtaining market insurance or by spreading the loss internally through self-insurance.

The adoption of these two utilitarian principles of risk control have subtly changed the nature of modern adjudication. Modern trials have been transformed from disputes between individuals to occasions for judicial social engineering. In earlier days, the function of adjudication was to resolve specific controversies between often embittered parties. In such cases, the particular moral qualities of the parties or of their actions were of central importance, as issues of motive and goodwill were crucial. In modern litigation, in contrast, the court must evaluate, not how one individual or another behaved in a moment of crisis, but whether one party or another as representatives of generic categories of actors was in a better position to prevent injuries or to spread the costs of them. In litigation of this nature, the qualities of the actual litigants become irrelevant because the issue before the court is how best to fashion incentives for parties in such positions in the future. An obstetrician and a nurse-midwife may have dedicated their lives to serving others; in the incident before the court, they may have exerted great effort to help the injured child and suffered as deeply as the parent over the subsequent injury. But if the court determines that the risk of injury was within their control, that it was affected in any way by some technical decision made or ignored, or that the two professionals or their insurers were in the best position to spread such injury costs, liability for a lifetime of losses may be placed upon them.

In modern adjudication, the dispute between the specific litigants is of secondary, even trivial, importance to the exercise. The concern of the courts is how best to fashion broader incentives to maximize social welfare. The parties themselves and the loss one of them has suffered become mere informational inputs to the process of judicial revision of controlling rules of law. The legal claim serves only as an empirical example of a social problem for which a more specific legal rule defining behavior is needed. Frequently in modern litigation, the parties are unwitting instruments of this broader judicial purpose. But increasingly in recent years, the adversarial character of litigation has become pretended rather than real. The requirements of procedure compel the parties to defend contesting positions. Yet often the litigants and their attorneys play out their roles, not as hostile adversaries, but as characters, knowing that the drama being staged serves only to determine which of their insurers should foot the bill.

The new purpose of the law has led courts to adopt many novel and interesting rules that seem bizarre from the vantage point of earlier years. An example is the prominent 1982 decision of the New Jersey Supreme Court in *Beshada v. Johns-Manville.*[5] The case involved a claim by a worker that an asbestos manufacturer should be liable for damages because the manufacturer had failed to warn the worker that asbestos could cause cancer. The manufacturer sought to defend the claim by proving that, at the time the worker contracted cancer, it was not known and could not have been known scientifically that asbestos causes cancer. More perceptive of the contours of our modern regime, the plaintiffs challenged the defense as irrelevant as a matter of law. The court concurred, holding that the manufacturer was liable for breaching its duty to warn the worker that asbestos causes cancer though the court accepted that, at the time of the breach, it was impossible scientifically to have known that asbestos causes cancer.

The notion of liability for breach of a duty with which it was impossible to comply seems to strain the most basic notions of responsibility. But responsibility in a regime of risk control has a very unusual meaning. According to the court, the manufacturer should be liable for the loss for two reasons. First, the decision improved incentives for accident avoidance. "By imposing on manufacturers the costs of failure to discover hazards, we create an incentive for them to invest more actively in safety research." Second, regardless of the information available at the time of injury, holding the manufacturer liable will serve to distribute the risks of product injuries broadly, because manufacturers can include expected injury costs in the prices of their products. Responsibility under the regime of risk control, thus, can mean a responsibility imposed *ex post facto* to reduce or to spread the risks of injuries.[6]

Though the adoption of the objection of risk control has increased the prospect of liability for all citizens, the increase has been particularly directed at corporate, professional, and governmental defendants. Since the mid-1960s, the legal obligations of such entities have expanded dramatically in field after field of civil law. The four figures, presenting the only available data on the subject, suggest the dimensions of this expansion. Figures 1 and 2 address the field of products liability. Figure 1 shows changes over time in claims and accidents for the field of products liability in general. The top-most line slanting upwards to the right illustrates that federal products liability suits have increased sharply and continuously since the early 1970s with little indication of a leveling or a decline. The second line in Figure 1 shows that products liability actions filed in state courts have also increased, though not substantially.

Figure 2 describes the effect of the increase in lawsuits on claims dollars paid, as a result of both litigated judgments and settlements prior to litigation. Data illustrating the magnitude of claims dollars paid over time are only available for selected industries, such as the general aviation industry represented in Figure 2. The data show extraordinary increases over the past decade in the liability of general aviation manufacturers. Indeed, within the past ten years, liability in this industry has increased by nine times.

Figures 3 and 4 show trends in claims dollar payouts in the fields of medical malpractice and municipal liability, respectively. Both fields show developments similar in direction to general aviation, though not quite so severe. Figure 3 shows that medical malpractice liability has increased by four times over the past decade. Figure 4 shows that municipal liability expenses increased five times over a period of seven years.

Figure 1
Products Liability: Claims, Injuries

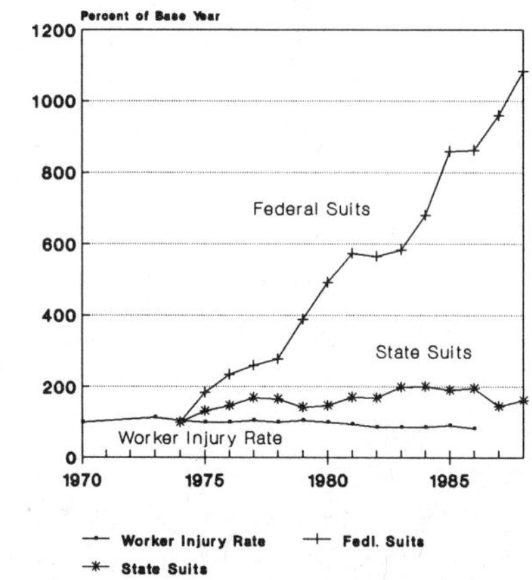

Source: Admin.Off.U.S.; CookCty.JuryVerd.Serv.; Stat.Abs.

Figure 2
General Aviation: Claims$, Accident Rate

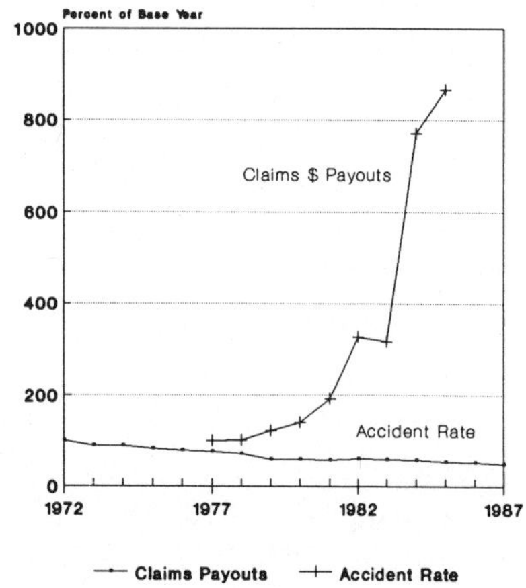

Source: Gnl.Av.Mfgs.Assn., 1988

Figure 3
Medical Malpractice: Deaths, Claims $

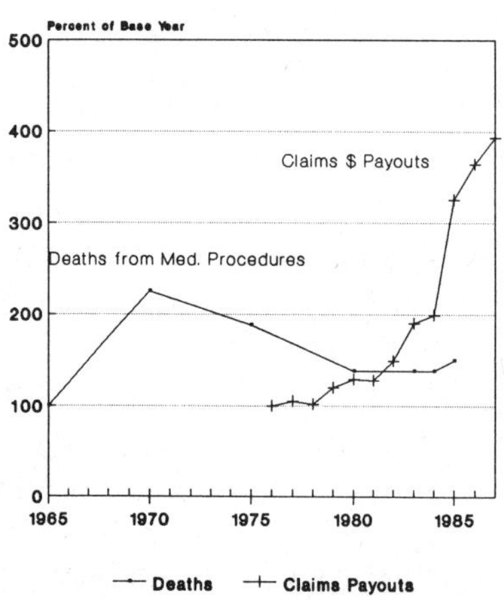

Source: U.S.Stat.Abstr.; NCSL, 1985.

Figure 4
Municipal Liability: Claims $ Payouts

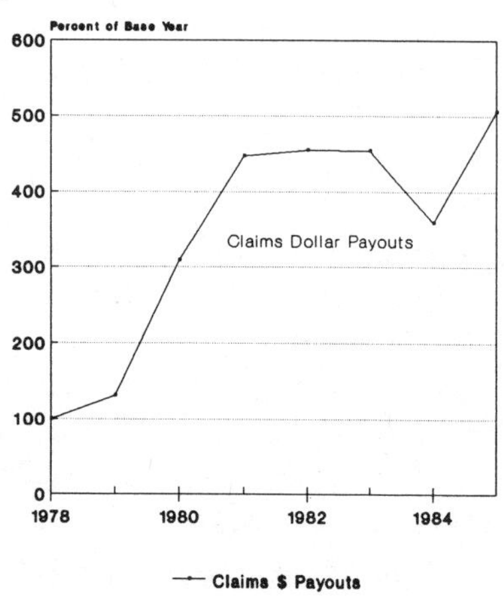

Source: Cuomo Commission, 1986

Why is it that liability costs have increased so dramatically since the 1970s for manufacturers, doctors, and municipalities, among others? Recall the two central principles of our modern risk-control regime: if the injury could have been prevented, liability will be attached to the party in the best position to prevent the injury; if not, to the party in the best position to spread injury costs. The figures describe litigation involving suits, respectively, by consumers against manufacturers, by patients against doctors and hospitals, and by other injured parties against municipalities in which there are claims that municipal supervision of public ways somehow contributed to the injury. In each of these litigation contexts, courts and juries have usually concluded that the defendant, whether manufacturer, doctor, or municipality, appears in a better position than the plaintiff—consumer, patient, or victim—both to control the determinants of risk and to spread the risks of injuries once they are suffered.

There is little reason to doubt that, at a very general level, manufacturers have more control over product safety than consumers; doctors and hospitals have more control over the outcome of medical procedures than patients; municipalities have more control over the determinants of risk on public ways than citizens. As risk control has expanded, however, litigation pressing the plausibility of this simple presumption has increased. For example, was the manufacturer or the consumer in the better position to prevent injury where teen-aged girls were burned while pouring cologne on a lighted candle to make it scented? (The Maryland Court of Appeals held the manufacturer liable for failing to warn of the risk of pouring cologne on an open flame.[7]) Was the manufacturer or the consumer in the better position to prevent injury when an employee was hit in the eye by a champagne cork as his boss waved around the bottle during a Christmas party? (The U.S. 10th Circuit upheld a jury verdict holding the manufacturer liable for failing to place a warning on the bottle informing that champagne corks can explode.[8]) Our newspapers with increasing frequency report episodes of this nature that strain the defensibility of the risk-control regime.

There are even greater reasons to be skeptical about the uniform superiority of manufacturers, doctors, and municipalities in spreading the risks of unpreventable injuries. Courts have largely presumed that defendants are in a relatively better position to spread risks because of having greater access to commercial insurance sources and because of the ability of large business enterprises to self-insure. Thus, courts have generally presumed that manufacturers can either obtain products liability insurance or can pass injury costs along in product prices. Doctors and hospitals, similarly, can either obtain malpractice insurance or can pass injury costs along to other patients, given inelastic demand for medical services. Municipalities have access to an immobile tax base allowing them to spread injury costs over the citizenry.

Many courts have also held corporate entities and municipalities liable on insurance grounds to achieve another end: to provide insurance to those members of the population—chiefly the poor—who may not have access to first-party health and disability insurance sources.[9] Thus, it has been believed that civil liability can help fill in the gaps in our society's social service safety net.

The four figures show the extent to which liability has been expanded on these risk-spreading insurance grounds. For three of the four areas of civil liability, I have been able to obtain data concerning the underlying accident rates that have generated the substantial increases in liability expenses. These data show uniformly, within each field, that accident rates have been declining steadily over exactly the same period during which claims and claims dollars have been increasing sharply.

In Figure 1, addressing products liability, for example, the bottom line shows the rate of injuries to workers requiring hospital treatment. Worker injuries constitute roughly 60 percent of all products liability claims. (Though not shown, the trend of consumer injuries is very similar to that of worker injuries.) The graph is too small to show the decline precisely, but the underlying data indicate that the rate of worker injuries has been declining steadily since 1979. Indeed, the injury rate in 1986 was 18 percent less than the rate in 1970. Figure 2 shows that the accident rate for general aviation has been declining steadily as well. Figure 3 shows a sharper decline in deaths from medical procedures, at least after 1970.

There is no mystery to the source of the relationship between a clear and steady decline in the underlying accident rate and a rapid increase over the same period in legal claims and claims dollar payouts. Increases in legal claims and claims payouts have far exceeded changes in the underlying accident rate for the clear reason that courts have been expanding liability to new contexts on grounds of risk spreading. If courts only attached liability on grounds of accident prevention, then claims and claims payouts would mirror the accident rate even if there were absolute defendant liability. The extraordinary difference in the directions of the accident trends and the claims cost trends represents the extension of liability on risk-spreading grounds to provide a form of injury compensation insurance through tort law.

There is increasing evidence, however, that the expansion of civil liability to provide insurance is proving counterproductive. From 1985 to 1987, large sectors of the society suffered from what has widely been called a liability insurance crisis. During this period, insurers drastically increased insurance premiums for manufacturers of an unusual set of products, such as vaccines, general aircraft, and sports equipment, and for an equally diverse set of services, such as obstetrics, ski lifts, and commercial trucking. In some cases—for intrauterine devices, daycare, and nurse-midwives—insurers refused to offer insurance coverage at any premium. These phenomena, however, extended beyond commercial insurance. Many municipalities, including self-insured municipalities, began to restrict and withdraw public services. Parks and forest preserves were closed; diving boards were removed from public pools; many municipalities removed slides and playground equipment from public parks.[10]

In the years since 1987, some of these services have been restored, suggesting the effects of some cyclical pattern in the liability insurance industry, though the 1985–1987 episode was surely the most severe of any cycle. Yet other evidence has suggested that these developments were more permanent. Recent surveys have uncovered that, since 1987, 47 percent of U.S. manufacturers have removed products from markets, 39 percent have decided against introducing new products, and 25 percent have discontinued new product research, all for liability reasons.[11] Other studies show that nearly 15 percent of U.S. obstetricians have abandoned the specialty because of increased malpractice liability. More generally, since the early 1980s, surveys have shown increasing numbers of doctors refusing to accept certain types of cases because of liability fears.[12]

In a market economy, products and services are withdrawn from markets only when an increase in production costs makes providing the product or service at a profit impossible. Why would the modern expansion of liability make so many products and services unprofitable? There are only two possible reasons: a cost increase attributable to increases in underlying accident rates or to increases in insurance costs.

It is unlikely that the widespread withdrawal of products and services can be attributed to sudden increases in the accident rate. First, as a general matter, accident rates have been declining, not increasing. Moreover, it is most implausible that accident rates would have increased dramatically in the mid-1980s for doctors and municipalities and simultaneously for 47 percent of U.S. manufacturers. Of course, in recent years some products have been discovered to be so greatly injurious as to merit removal from the market: asbestos and the Dalkon Shield are prominent examples. But products of this nature cannot account for the generality of the effects. There have been no discoveries of previously unknown toxic damage from diving boards or playground equipment.

There is more precise evidence available on the point. Over the past decade there has been an extraordinary decline in the production of general aircraft because of the expansion of liability. In 1978, the nation's general aircraft manufacturers produced 18,000 planes; in 1987, 1,100. Figure 2 shows clearly, however, that the accident rate for general aircraft declined steadily over the same period.

Can the product and service withdrawals be plausibly attributed to increases in insurance costs? The sharp differences shown in Figures 1–3 between accident rates and liability costs illustrate the increased extent of insurance provided through modern tort law. Employing the law to spread risks in this way surely increases manufacturer production costs. But the increase in insurance costs alone still does not explain why so many products and services have been made unprofitable. The very large majority of American consumers possess first-party health and injury insurance. In the first instance, the expansion of civil law to spread risks only shifts the insurance burden from first-party Blue Cross insurance or its analogues to third-party tort law insurance. It is not clear that the expansion of civil law to spread risks creates substantial new insurance obligations. The expansion of law to provide insurance could only make products and services unprofitable, thus, if the costs of providing insurance through tort law were substantially greater than the costs of similar first-party insurance.

There are strong reasons to believe that tort law insurance is substantially more costly than equivalent first-party insurance and that this cost difference is the underlying cause of the widespread product and service withdrawals. First, because of the way damages are measured in tort law, for similar losses the benefits provided through the law are roughly twice to three times the benefits provided under any first-party insurance system. Second, the operational costs of providing insurance through an adversarial tort system are roughly five to ten times the operational costs of first-party insurance. Third, the ability of insurers to differentiate among the insured population in order to reduce insurance costs is vastly constrained where insurance is delivered through tort law rather than through first-party coverage. For these reasons, tort law insurance is conservatively estimated to cost five to ten times more than first-party insurance for coverage of the identical injury.[13]

There is an additional disadvantage of providing insurance through the legal system. Regrettably, exactly contrary to the well-meaning ambitions of many courts, spreading risks by expanding civil liability compels the low-income workers and the poor in our society to subsidize the insurance costs of the high-income earners and the wealthy. Again, many courts have believed that making manufacturers and other defendants provide insurance to their consumers would help the poor by providing an insurance source that was otherwise unavailable. These courts, however, have neglected the role of Medicaid, Medicare, and state assistance, far more effective in insuring the poor.[14] More importantly, they have failed to think through what the terms of civil law insurance would be. Unfortunately, insurance provided through the legal system is a very bad deal for poor consumers.

All consumers of a particular product pay the same product liability insurance premium. The liability insurance premium tied to the sale of a product or service must be set according to the average expected liability payout. Damages in tort law comprise past and future income, obviously related to the wealth category; medical expenditures, which also are typically greater for high-income patients; and pain and suffering damages, which are highly correlated with lost income since it is typically sustained job loss, rather than short though intense hospital expense, that signals disruption of a victim's life. The high correlation of each of these damage elements with income means that the premiums set equal to the average damage payout will undercharge high-income consumers and overcharge low-income consumers. The provision of liability insurance tied to the sale of products and services requires the low-income to subsidize the high-income earners.

This regressive redistributional effect is inconsistent with the objective of the judiciary who thought that the expansion of liability would aid the poor. More important, it is glaringly inconsistent with any coherent and defensible social policy. It is the equivalent of charging each worker in the society the same premium for disability insurance, but compensating those previously earning high incomes substantially more than those previously earning low incomes. It is the equivalent of charging all homeowners the same fire insurance premium regardless of home value. It is the equivalent of not merely the repeal of the progressive features of the income tax but the repeal coupled with the provision of higher governmental benefits to those with high incomes. The expansion of tort liability on risk-spreading grounds, thus, has both caused the widespread removal of products and services from markets and directly harmed low-income consumers.

These effects suggest that the achievement of the risk-control objectives of our modern legal system is more difficult than has been imagined. Most clearly, the effects suggest that the two principles of our risk-control regime are not as closely linked in terms of the assignment of liability as has been thought. As described above, the vast expansion of the liability of manufacturers, professionals, and municipalities has derived from the belief that these defendants were almost always in the relatively better position *both* to prevent injuries and to insure for them. The widespread withdrawals of products and services consequent to the expansion of liability shows this presumption to be wrong.

This defect in our risk-control regime, serious though it is, is not likely to be fatal. Many call for the reform of tort law, but few for its abolition. The widespread withdrawals of products and services, however, are compelling grounds for the reanalysis of how the law can best control the risks of modern society. It is clear that our rules need refinement and our judiciary a firmer understanding of how legal rules contribute to or defeat the social goal of internalizing costs to spread risks.[15] The transformation of the law around the conception of risk, thus, is only in an initial stage. There is little chance that our judges will retreat from the objective of risk control but substantial need for them to learn how better to achieve it.

ACKNOWLEDGMENT

I am grateful to the Program in Civil Liability, Yale Law School, for support.

ENDNOTES

[1]A. C. Pigou, *The Economics of Welfare,* 4th ed. (London: Macmillan, 1948).

[2]For a detailed history of the development of the approach, see George L. Priest, "The Invention of Enterprise Liability: A Critical History of the Intellectual Foundations of Modern Tort Law," *Journal of Legal Studies* 14 (1985): 461–527.

[3]Guido Calabresi, *The Costs of Accidents* (New Haven: Yale University Press, 1970).

[4]An approach emphasized by Dean Calabresi.

[5]*Beshada v. Johns-Manville Prods. Corp.,* 90 N.J. 191, 447 A.2d 539 (1982).

[6]The *Beshada* opinion generated substantial criticism, and the New Jersey Supreme Court limited its scope to asbestos cases in *Feldman v. Lederle Labs,* 97 N.J. 429, 479 A.2d 374 (1984). Several other jurisdictions, however, have adopted the approach.

[7]*Moran v. Faberge, Inc.,* 273 Md. 538, 332 A.2d 11 (1975).

[8]*Shuput v. Heublein, Inc.,* 511 F.2d 1104 (10th Cir. 1975).

[9]This principle was first announced by the California Supreme Court in the seminal case, *Greenman v. Yuba Power Prods., Inc.,* 59 Cal. 2d 57, 377 P.2d 897, 27 Cal. Rptr. 697 (1963).

[10]For further examples and an explanation of these phenomena, see G. L. Priest, "The Current Insurance Crisis and Modern Tort Law," *Yale Law Journal* 96 (1987): 1521–90.

[11]Table 30 in E. Patrick McGuire, *The Impact of Product Liability* (New York: Conference Board, 1988), 20.

[12]Priest, "The Current Insurance Crisis."

[13]Ibid.

[14]Of course, when the insurance rationale was first articulated by the California Supreme Court in 1963, neither Medicaid nor Medicare was available.

[15]For an initial formulation, see G. L. Priest, "Internalizing Costs," mimeograph, Program in Civil Liability, Yale Law School, 1990.

The history of every country begins in the heart of a man or a woman.

Willa Cather (1873–1947)
From *O Pioneers!*

Geoffrey C. Hazard, Jr.

The Role of the Legal System in Responses to Public Risk

A DEVELOPED LEGAL SYSTEM IMPORTANTLY SHAPES the nature of risks to which the community is exposed and the procedure and content of the responses that occur when a specific risk evolves from potential threat to actual injury. Legal rules allocate initial responsibility for identifying and controlling various risks and allocate corresponding responsibilities when injuries result. A legal system is, in short, a system of authority and accountability.

A HYPOTHETICAL CASE

It is difficult to appreciate the complexity of a modern legal system, for such a system addresses in one way or another virtually all relationships within the society. However, the myriad ways in which the legal system of a modern political economy influences the responses to public risk can be illustrated through the daily journal of a hypothetical associate general counsel of a hypothetical large paper manufacturing company, Paper Products Company (PPC). The office of the associate general counsel in many large organizations is the center for traffic management of the organizations' legal problems. The entries in the imaginary journal, although fictitious, are essentially true to fact.

Monday morning: Workers' compensation insurance coverage review. (The public risk is that of injury to workers in the course of their employment and consequent burden on the taxpayers. Workers' compensation is a legally imposed scheme of health

Geoffrey C. Hazard, Jr., is Sterling Professor of Law at Yale University.

and income replacement benefits required of every employer for all of its employees concerning injuries sustained in the course of employment. "In the course of employment" includes virtually all injuries at the work site and any off site injury connected to employment, for example, injury at a company picnic. It also may include long latency disabilities that can be causally related to the workplace, such as hearing loss from high noise levels in a factory. The statutory schedule of benefits is periodically revised upward, and the cost is a significant factor in employers' total labor costs. Insurance rates move accordingly. The review by a PPC staff committee aims at controlling exposure, claims, severity of loss, direct payments, and administrative cost, all of which have legal aspects.)

Monday afternoon: Review of pending employment discrimination litigation. (The public risk is unfair treatment of people in the work force and consequent loss of individual income and of productivity in the community as a whole. Law prohibits discrimination in hiring, promotion, and terms of employment on the basis of race, gender, nationality, religious affiliation, age, and disability. Some localities in which PPC has facilities also prohibit discrimination on the basis of sexual orientation. Claims of discrimination can be asserted through the company's internal personnel management system, which includes a hearing procedure; through grievance filed with state or federal equal opportunity employment agencies, which entails a quasi-judicial administrative hearing; and suits in court for restoration to position and damages. At any given time a dozen or so such cases are pending against PPC. The review with the personnel department aims at identifying any patterns in the cases, estimating the monetary damages exposure, and reevaluating the possibilities for settlement of various cases.)

Tuesday morning: Antitrust prevention training program. (The public risk is impairment of the competitive market, and the increase in prices and reduction in availability and quality of paper products that could result. The antitrust laws prohibit business competitors from price-fixing, allocating market share, agreeing upon standards of product and service, and any other "restraint of trade." Other laws prohibit "unfair competition," including unjustifiable differentiation in prices charged to customers. The paper business is very competitive, involving many suppliers and small price differentials at every level. Sales forces face continual pressure to increase sales and to find out what the competition is doing, but also to "live and let live." The PPC antitrust training program provides indoctrination in the ground rules on such matters as gathering price information and attending trade conventions.)

Tuesday afternoon: Selection of litigation counsel to defend a recently filed environmental pollution lawsuit. (The public risk is impairment of the environment. Environmental legislation imposes complex restrictions on effluent that can affect the air, streams, groundwater, and soil conditions. Some of the legislation operates prospectively, but other provisions impose liability for site pollution against all companies that had previously operated on a site; most paper manufacturers have been sued concerning one or another of their plant sites. PPC was just served with process in a rural county in a southern state, in a case that could involve multimillion dollar liability. The law firm that has handled local PPC matters does not have the strength for such a case. Another law firm must be found that has the necessary big case capability, has no disqualifying conflicts of interest, and which can function effectively before a small town jury.)

Executive employment agreement for division manager to be hired away from competitor. (The public risk is impairment of productive capacity by deterioration of a company work force. The company uses the contract mechanism in the labor market to upgrade its work force. The law governing contracts, labor relationships, and competitive relationships permits—with certain limitations—an employer to hire away employees of other companies. However, care has to be taken against infringing on a competitor's trade secrets. Consideration also has to be given to pension and profit-sharing benefits, relocation expenses, and legal exposure if the new manager turns out to be unsatisfactory.)

Wednesday morning: Review of presentation to be made before Internal Revenue Service concerning disallowance of company's claim of rapid depreciation of certain plant equipment. (The public risk is unjustified tax avoidance and tax evasion; the special depreciation provisions of the tax law aim at increasing investment in plant and thus increasing international business competitiveness. In prior years' tax returns, the company claimed rapid depreciation for certain equipment, but the IRS initial review has disallowed the claim. The matter is now in an administrative appeal within the IRS. PPC's presentation will be made by its outside accounting firm and outside tax law firm, assisted by PPC staff accounting and legal people.)

Further negotiation with Swedish manufacturer of paper production equipment for cross-licensing of patents that reduce acidity in manufacturing process. (The public risks are inadequate encouragement of invention, which is the rationale of the patent laws, and injury to the environment, which is threatened by acids used to dissolve wood fibers in making paper. Licensing of PPC's new technology permits partial recovery of the development cost of the technology; obtaining cross-licenses permits PPC to gain the benefit of technology developed by others. International law facilitates the exchange of patent rights across national legal systems.)

Wednesday afternoon: Criminal prosecution for overweight company truck. (The public risk is damage to the highways. Legal limits on truck weights are variously enforced. The state police of a strict enforcement state last night arrested a PPC driver and have charged the company with overweight loads. The local prosecutor is threatening forfeiture of the vehicle because a repeat offense is involved.)

Land use permit has to be obtained to enlarge a loading dock at a company plant site. (The public risk is traffic congestion and deterioration of values of nearby property. Land use restrictions limit the uses to which various classes of land can be put (zoning) and require special permission for significant change in established use. A public hearing is required upon the demand of an owner of nearby land. In recent years a local environmental group has been very active in opposing enlargement of industrial uses.)

Subpoena demanding production of company pay and pension records of executive involved in divorce. (The public risk is inadequate postdivorce support for the children and the divorced spouse of a principal family income earner. Law requires divorcing spouses to provide each other with accurate reports of income and assets, and permits verification from a spouse's employer. A subpoena is a court order demanding specified information. However, law prohibits disclosure of personal confidential employee information. Finance and personnel staff wish to know what information to release.)

Thursday morning: Health cost control review. (The public risk is inadequate health care for employees and their families. State law requires all employers with more than 15 employees to provide a specified minimum schedule of health coverage benefits. The insurance premiums for health insurance have been increasing by 9 percent per year over the last decade, pushing up the PPC's labor cost accordingly. The company is considering a company-managed health care center at its headquarters and main plant. However, operating such a center entails the legal risk of exposure to liability for medical malpractice and may result in a benefit that cannot be later modified except through collective bargaining with the union representing plant employees. Staff from various departments are convening for a preliminary review of the problems involved.)

Thursday afternoon: Preliminary review of 10-Q filing. (The public risk is inadequate financial information about shares that are publicly traded. Federal securities laws require elaborate periodic disclosure statements covering financial condition and ongoing operations. It is illegal to file a statement that is materially misleading because of misstatements or omissions. The 10-Q is a report filed with the Securities and Exchange Commission each quarter of the year.)

Friday: First draft of offer to purchase a paper wholesaler. (The public risk is that a company's competitive capability may deteriorate by failure to adjust its operations to changing market conditions. Subject to the limitations of the antitrust laws and other legal restrictions, law permits private companies to change the configuration of their business by contracting with others. The company has decided that it needs to integrate "downstream" in the distribution of paper products but that a prohibitive start-up cost would be involved in trying to build a wholesale distribution system from the ground up. Hence, it is seeking to buy established wholesalers. The proposal will cover the first contemplated acquisition. A wide variety of legal problems have to be considered, including tax consequences, antitrust restrictions, financing, effects on other existing contractual arrangements, and competing offers from other manufacturers.)

Monday: Another week.

LEGAL SYSTEM AND POLITICAL SYSTEM

A society's legal system is both a mirror of its political, economic, and social institutions and a determinant of the structure of those institutions. The American legal system presupposes that control of the means of production is based primarily on capitalist ownership. Our legal system gives expression to this method of controlling production through corporation law and other bodies of law which define responsibilities regarding enterprise risk among stockholders, management and employees, and third parties including the general public. According to the law governing private business corporations, primary responsibility and accountability for enterprise risks is imposed on the owners of the enterprise involved. If the owners are many, as in the case of a large publicly held corporation, direct responsibility is delegated to corporate management; immediate responsibility is subdelegated within the corporation, eventually to a plant manager.

In contrast, in a statist system the political convention calls for vesting direct control of the means of production in the state. The subunits in which production is carried out are called state enterprises, approximately corresponding to business corporations in the capitalist system. A statist legal system reflects the concept of state ownership through the definition of jurisdiction and authority of various ministries and bureaus. Primary responsibility and accountability are imposed on the ministry having jurisdiction of the particular industry, for example the paper industry. Immediate responsibility is subdelegated to lower ministerial levels and eventually to plant managers. The source of ministerial jurisdiction is some kind of a constitution. The royalist Old Regime of Europe reflected one kind of statist constitution, the Soviet required another. The modern Western European regimes still another.

Neither a capitalist system nor a statist system works perfectly or consistently. In any system at any given time, a source of risk, for example a paper manufacturing plant, may inflict continual injury on others without anyone being actually held accountable. Moreover, no system is a pure expression of either private ownership or state control. Even in highly socialized economic systems the family has retained substantially effective "private" ownership of its living quarters, and hence can be legally responsible for such risks as igniting bedclothes with cigarettes. On the other hand, in capitalist societies the state operates many production facilities. In the present American configuration, such enterprises as airports, water supply, and primary and secondary education, for example, are carried out through state enterprises. The state accordingly is legally responsible for risks resulting from the activities of these enterprises. In any event, all systems frequently malfunction in the sense that they fail to control risks which, from an objective perspective, certainly could be better controlled.

However, there are important differences between the legal institutions based primarily on private property and contract and those in which production is based primarily on government control. These differences are specifically manifested in differences in substantive law and legal procedure. This essay outlines these differences.

The conclusion to be drawn is that policy analysis of control of public risk—both the identification of such risks and implementation of means of response—should take account of legal institutions and procedures as they actually exist. This conclusion seems rather obvious. Nevertheless, it appears that much technical and scientific policy analysis addressed to public risk in this country implicitly adopts a "command and control" perspective. This perspective is appropriate to a political system based on direct government control of production. A command and control perspective also is an obvious and direct way in which popular political sentiment can be given expression. If "public opinion demands" tighten control of environmental risk, for example, then direct controls of specific environmental risks would seem to be indicated. So also for risks to health, safety, adequacy of food supply, or sufficiency of housing. Yet use of direct controls often takes inadequate account of the institutional regime in which a large role is played by private control of the means of production. Thus, there is often a mismatch between typical technical, scientific, and political analyses of public risk and the legal institutions and procedure through which responsibility for public risk is actually allocated in a capitalist system such as ours. A better-integrated perspective could reduce the mismatch.

In developing this theme illustrations are drawn from many historical, geographical, and institutional settings. The illustrations also cover a wide range of scale, from risks originating in the household (such as fires) to societywide events (such as plagues). This breadth of illustration is intended to suggest the ubiquitous and complex nature of public risk and possible responses to it. Such a background in turn facilitates an understanding of the complex functions of a legal system in responding to public risks.

Public Risks

As a preface to considering how legal systems provide for response to public risks, it is useful to consider what is meant by *public risk*. In conventional policy analysis usage, the term *public risk* usually denotes large-scale menaces to the general community's welfare. The term is therefore ordinarily understood to mean such risks as an explosion of a nuclear plant (as at Chernobyl), a flood (the Johnstown flood in western Pennsylvania in the late nineteenth century is a classic), areawide environmental pollution (for example, in the Mexico City basin), a disease that has reached proportions of a plague (for example, AIDS), contamination of the food or water supply, or a general breakdown of law and order.

However, reflection about these dramatic examples suggests that *public risk* is defined too narrowly if it is limited to possibilities of common injury that are large in scale and sudden in occurrence. To be sure, some public risks are distinctly of this character, involving a concentrated large-scale event that was difficult to forecast. In old-fashioned parlance, these risks are "Acts of God." However, even some events of this character can be foreseen and guarded against. Large floods can be anticipated from the experience of small floods; general air pollution can be anticipated by taking account of slow but progressive smaller degrees of environmental deterioration; and nuclear power plant failure can be anticipated from the lessons learned in developing nuclear technology in the first place. This relationship between large-scale risk and a community's earlier experience with lesser misfortunes makes the more important point: "Public" risk is usually if not invariably "ordinary" risk on a larger or broader scale.

Hence, the concept of public risk, properly considered, includes all significant possibilities of unbargained-for injuries to third persons that are incurred as the result of an actor's conduct. This includes small-scale risks as well as large ones.

Account must also be taken of the multiplicity of risks that a specific activity entails. Thus, operating a paper plant near someone else's residence or place of business obviously creates some risk that noxious vapors will visit injury on those neighbors. It also creates risks of noise, traffic congestion, and reduction in the value of the nearby properties. However, *excluding* paper plants from all neighborhoods also involves risks, such as the necessity for shipping raw material and finished products over longer distances, thus increasing pollution of the air and the risk of traffic accidents, to say nothing of the risk of loss of jobs. In regulating production facilities of all kinds, these various and conflicting risks are taken into account in zoning restrictions and other legal controls. The risk posed by noxious vapors is the basis of legal requirements that paper plants be located in a well-ventilated environment. (Of course, this requirement transfers the risk to the places to which the vapors waft.)

By way of further example, allowing entry of visitors from another community creates a risk that the visitors will bring with them diseases to which the local community is not immune. It was by this mechanism that many native Americans were exterminated through the arrival of the Europeans following Columbus, and it apparently was by this mechanism that AIDS was transmitted from Africa to America and Europe. This kind of risk is the basis of modern health controls on immigrants, symbolized in the WHO yellow book, and is the basis for rules requiring quarantine and immunization. In smaller scale, the same risk is the basis of the rule that children must stay home from school when they are sick.

Public risk therefore should be conceived in terms of all kinds of risks of adverse consequences to other members of a community, whatever the scale of the risks and whatever their dynamics and their consequences.

Conceptualizing public risk in this comprehensive way facilitates analysis in several important respects. First, it reveals the enormous range of activities that have to be taken into account in considering social control of public risks. Second, a comprehensive definition of public risk reveals the excruciatingly complex interrelation of the various kinds of public risks. Since there are no simple problems of public risk, there can be no simple solutions. The difficulties posed by these interrelations become very evident when it comes to devising specific controls on any specific risk.

Third, and most significant for comparison of legal systems, a comprehensive view of public risk takes into account the smaller scale risks entailed in decentralized activity as well as the large-scale risks that come into view when social systems are considered in aggregate. That is, a comprehensive view of public risk avoids the bias of thinking of public risk solely in terms of centralized responsibility and control. It also avoids the bias of thinking of public risk only in terms that can be comprehended in mass political sentiment that can be captured in sound bites.

This is not to say that it is inappropriate to assess public risk in terms of centralized responsibility and control. It is only to say that public risk must also be assessed in terms that apply all the way down to the millions of individual actors and the choices of action they confront—the operator of a specific mechanical apparatus, the user of a specific pharmaceutical (such as a doctor), the operator of a specific manufacturing plant, or a specific visitor moving from one community to another. In one context it may make better sense pragmatically to think of a public risk primarily in terms of general threat to the community as a whole. If so, it makes corresponding sense to think of controlling that risk in terms of centralized responsibility. In another context, however, it may make better sense to think of a risk in terms of decentralized activity—what we often call "private" conduct. In virtually all contexts, however, a good response requires visualizing the problem of responsibility and control at all levels of activity in the community, from top to bottom. This becomes particularly evident when we consider a legal system. Legal systems themselves work—or fail to work—at all levels of social activity, from top to bottom.

Multiple Social Ordering Systems

A legal system is only one of several synergistic social ordering systems. In modern society at least four coexistent and interacting ordering systems can be distinguished. One is the order emanating from tradition and custom; another the order achieved through markets; a third is the order imposed by governmental bureaucracy; and a fourth is the order sought through a constitutional legal system.

Tradition and custom are exemplified in the ordering of relationships within the family and extended family. By tradition and custom within a household, the parents have authority to define priorities and duties vis-à-vis children and have responsibility to provide food and shelter for children at least until young ones can fend for themselves. Tradition and custom similarly define priorities and duties in relationships in an extended family, family groups, and villages. Tradition and custom also define the basic structure of elementary markets found in all stable societies, for example, the days on which markets are held, the location of various stalls, and the settlement of accounts. Present international markets are to an important extent the product of tradition and custom evolved over the centuries from more primitive antecedents.

Tradition and custom continue to pervade human relationships in modern societies, despite their industrialization, bureaucratization, and legalization. Concepts of individuality, propriety, and hierarchy vary from one modern society to another, more or less independent of markets, government structure, and legal systems. The conventions in many "traditional societies" require that women and children be subordinate to paternal authority. There are manifest differences of this kind between American and Japanese societies, and discernable if more subtle differences between American society and those in Canada or Mexico. Such differences in custom and tradition have to be taken into account in considering public risk, such as the adaptability to this country of Japanese industrial policy or the Canadian system of health insurance.

Markets are another ordering mechanism. In their immediate operation, markets permit each party to a market exchange to improve his portfolio of goods and services over that which he held before the exchange: A farmer exchanges an excess holding of grain or milk in return for the service of having his horse better shod by the farrier or his tractor put in better running condition by a mechanic; the farrier or mechanic in return obtains grain or milk in substitution for his available labor. This improvement in both portfolios is accomplished without violence, without subjugation, and without the directorial interference of the local bureaucracy. In a modern economy the managers of a business enterprise, such as a paper manufacturer, exchange their production for a wide variety of goods and services needed to sustain the operations of business.

Secondarily, the market system gives signals to prospective producers and purchasers about future exchange possibilities. If grain brings a good price in the market—exceeding the cost and financial risk of production—the farmer is encouraged to produce more for next year; if it brings a bad price, the farmer is led to consider directing his efforts otherwise, for example, into dairy products or into becoming a part-time mechanic. The same point holds for regional and global markets. As Adam Smith noted two centuries ago, the wider the market the larger the possibilities offered by the market mechanism for increase in wealth and well-being of all concerned.

An ongoing market system requires support from a concurrent ordering system that recognizes and defines property interests. Markets involve the exchange of property rights—grain for horseshoes, for example—but markets themselves do not define the property rights to which an exchange refers. Recognition of the property rights comes forth from tradition and custom, from assignments made by bureaucratic ordering (for example, a patent or a broadcasting license), and from a legal system.

As is well-known, markets are imperfect, often egregiously so. The market ordering mechanism suffers inherent failures from the effects of externalities—costs that cannot effectively be imposed on the enterprise whose activity generated the costs. Markets also suffer failure from abuse of the market, such as fraud, price-fixing, and monopolization. These risks of failure invite the imposition of controls on the market, particularly government regulation and controls exercised through legal rights.

A third ordering system is governmental bureaucracy. A governmental bureaucracy is a specialized corps of persons invested by higher authority with special directorial powers and responsibilities. Bureaucratic administration was epitomized by government under the Egyptian pharaohs and the mandarin system in classical China; modern Western bureaucratic administration derives primarily from that established by Louis XIV of France. Government bureaucracies are employed for all sorts of control purposes, including production (the classic example is control of irrigation), transportation (the classic example is toll roads and bridges), and commercial markets (a classical example is control of coinage). The mechanisms of bureaucratic control include licensing, imposition of record-keeping requirements, enforcement of regulations through criminal prosecution, and direct action by government functionaries.

Two important forms of government bureaucracy, often overlooked as such, are the army and the police force. An army is a bureaucratic armed force designed to prevent invasion of a community and to maintain control over adjacent borderlands. A police force is a bureaucracy designed to prevent violent disorder within the community. In many societies, the army and the police are closely interrelated if not identical. Implicitly and often explicitly, the effectiveness of other government bureaucracies is partly dependent on the coercive power of the police or the army, even in a liberal democracy. Marginal use of the coercive power of the police is essential to effective government, and the immediate efficacy of coercion makes possible the mechanism of central command and control. However, pervasive use of coercion threatens the basis of constitutional legality.

The Legal System

The fourth social ordering system is the legal system. A legal system includes rules and procedures by which activity in the community can be initiated and controlled through general norms of conduct that are formally articulated by government and administered by judicial authority (courts) that invokes those norms of conduct as its basis for decision.

The term *general norms* refers to norms that apply to the population at large or to specific subsectors of the population that are defined in categorical terms. Promulgation of general norms presupposes governmental authority over the community as a whole. General rules as a practical matter have to be expressed in written form; indeed a written medium is virtually essential for expressing rules in general form. Application of general written rules, in turn, requires specially knowledgeable officials—judges—to give the rules coherent and consistent interpretation. A modern legal system therefore is based on written general rules, including constitutional law, whose final interpretations are rested in a system of courts.

Modern systems also include various specialized institutions developed around this core mechanism. These include the legislature, which enacts general norms; rule-making agencies of government, which enact subordinate regulations to explicate and implement statutes; administrative officials, who are responsible for interpreting and enforcing the statutes and regulations in the first instance (law enforcement agencies); and private legal specialists knowledgeable in the interpretation of the regulations who can give guidance to the citizenry as to how to conduct themselves accordingly (a legal profession). Thus a modern legal system includes legislative bodies, administrative agencies, court systems, and a legal profession.

Two Components of Modern Legal Systems

A modern legal system can be considered as the product of an evolutionary process having its origin in tradition and custom and the need for regulating markets. The legal system can also be considered as originating in the control rules internal to government bureaucracies. The first view emphasizes the relationship between law and the community at large and thus the aspects of law that are democratic, spontaneous, and reciprocal. This view concentrates on certain subject areas of the law, particularly the law governing property and contract relationships. The second view emphasizes the relationship between law and government, and considers the legal system as an extension of bureaucratic rules originally designed to give direction from the top down. This view also concentrates on the areas of the law through which governmental authority is expressed, particularly the criminal law, the laws regulating business, and the organic and procedural law of the government itself.

The legal system of a modern industrialized democracy in fact incorporates both views. The object of legal rules in a constitutional regime is to permit control from two directions. One is control from the top down. In this direction of control, legal rules authorize specialized government bureaucracies to monitor various sectors of activity and to enforce standards of conduct addressed to that activity. Many of the rules are directed at private enterprise activities that create public risk such as fraud and other misconduct in the market; contamination of food, water supply, and the environment and other threats to public health; and theft and assault and other threats to public safety. An auxiliary set of rules, called *administrative law*, is designed to control against corruption, inefficiency, and officiousness on the part of the government bureaucracies themselves.

The other direction of control proceeds from the bottom, at the level of ordinary citizens and private business. The legal rules at this level seek to control against exploitation of one private interest by another private interest and against exploitation of private interests by the government. These risks are respectively controlled by private law, such as the law of property and contract, and public law, particularly constitutional law.

Two Modes of Legal Response

With the foregoing considerations in mind, two basic kinds of legal institutions offer themselves as a means of response to public risk. One is "command and control" through public law; the other is the interactive private law system based on property rights. The command and control conception contemplates a system of legal rules asserting control from the center through government regulations that define limits on risky activity, empowering officials to monitor compliance with the limits, and responding to noncompliance through criminal and regulatory penalties on offenders. The command and control system can be viewed simply as rational public administration.

The legal rules in a command and control system seek to implement the system's rational purposiveness. Legal rules of bureaucratic jurisdiction define the powers of public agencies and enterprises, for example, operating agencies such as the Port Authority of New York or the Texas Department of Highways and regulatory agencies such as the Federal Securities and Exchange Commission or Environmental Protection Agency. Legal rules also define the authority of officials within the bureaucracy and the terms of their financial and operational power and responsibility. Accountability is expressed in rules that define hierarchical authority, whereby higher echelons can overrule lower officials, and rules that authorize quasi-penal sanctions—particularly demotion or dismissal from office—and criminal penalties such as those against bribery and conflict of interest.

The private law system based on property rights is formally more complex. It contemplates a system of legal rules that defines responsibility for risk-producing activities in terms of ownership of the facilities that produce those risks. The basic rule is that an enterprise which inflicts costs on others is legally liable for those consequences. Correlatively, those who are injured have rights against the proprietor of the risky activity. Thus the paper manufacturing enterprise in our hypothetical case was under the ownership of a business corporation, which in turn was bound by legal obligations to its employees, shareholders, competitors and customers, and persons in the vicinity.

This system of rules defines responsibility in terms of legal liability and addresses noncompliance by allowing an injured person to seek compensatory damages under the law of torts (i.e., the law of private wrongs). The rules of tort law thus are an implication of the rules of property governing the risk-producing activity. Furthermore, this regime permits a party engaging in a risky activity to contract with potential victims to rearrange the terms of responsibility for the activity. For example, an enterprise wishing to operate a paper manufacturing plant that would inflict noxious odors on adjacent residences could pay a continuing fee to the owners of the residences, or buy up the residences and thereby eliminate the adjacent property right itself.

As indicated earlier—but is important to repeat—no legal system is a pure version of either a command and control regime or one of property and contract. All legal systems use a command and control system to preserve basic peace and order within the community. This sector of the legal system includes the criminal law, which defines minimal standards such as the prohibitions against homicide, assault, and theft; the law of criminal procedure, which specifies how criminal prohibitions are enforced; the establishment of police and prosecutorial authorities, which are the specialized governmental agencies empowered to administer the criminal law; and the courts having jurisdiction over regulatory and criminal prosecutions. These make up the legal mechanism of direct regulatory coercion.

Correlatively, all legal systems recognize a regime of property and contract system in at least some part of the economy. The Soviet system even in its phase of most intensive command and control permitted a limited degree of individual farmer production and informal market exchange of the resulting product. Moreover, within the most highly bureaucratized systems, such as the former Soviet regime and the present People's Republic of China, there exist informal subsystems of exchange that amount to regimes of property, tort, and contract. These informal subsystems are manifested in terms of bureaucratic "turf," the "clout" of various officials, and the continuous need for interagency "coordination." Similar informal exchange systems are also at work in the bureaucracies of constitutional regimes.

ENFORCEMENT MECHANISMS

The mechanism for bureaucratic enforcement of public law is familiar. It includes police in the broadest sense—uniformed street patrol, inspectors and compliance officers, tax collectors and auditors, and other such officials. These are linked to regulatory and investigative staffs and prosecuting attorneys. In a modern legal system thousands of administrative tribunals function through one aspect or another of public law, either directly managing publicly owned enterprises or regulating enterprises in the private sector.

Enforcement machinery in the domain of private law is less visible, but it is ubiquitous. Private contracts typically specify sanctions that are to be available if a party defaults or renders defective performance. The most common sanction is the termination of future contract rights, for example, where equipment sold under a time-payments contract may be repossessed if the buyer fails to make payments, or where an employee is fired for nonperformance. These sanctions are recognized in legal rules such as employment law, mortgage law, and the law governing the sale of goods. Additional or alternative sanctions may be established by private contract. For example, many contracts stipulate that disputes under the contract must be resolved by arbitration rather than court proceedings. However, contractually stipulated sanctions must comply with limitations imposed by public law; a private sanction that amounts to an unconscionable forfeiture may not be legally enforced.

Judges and lawyers are the personnel of the legal system, administering both public law and private law. Under direction of their clients and superiors, lawyers draft the public regulations and the private property dispositions through which the legal system expresses itself. In adjudicative proceedings, lawyers usually serve as advocates for the parties. Judges apply, interpret, and remake the law.

Legal Complexity

All social activity in a modern industrial society is facilitated or constrained by a complex legal system. Legal complexity is the institutional detail of a constitutional structure and an inevitable characteristic of a regime that has sustained itself over a long time. Not all these complexities are purposive or positive in effect. It is familiar that governmental bureaucracies become entangled in their own complexities of jurisdiction. Procedures designed to control bureaucratic abuse themselves become sources of abuse. Conflict of authority in such a system can lead to gross inefficiency (i.e., process for its own sake) and eventual paralysis. The debacles of the Eastern European economies and public administration in New York City come to mind.

Counterpart obstacles to risk control exist in regimes based on private ownership. Our constitutional regime accords strong legal protection to personal interests, private property, and contract, and rights of private association in business, social, and civic endeavors. These rights enable the property and contract system to respond to risk, but they also constrain that responsive capability. Long before a source of risk is perceived as such by the general public, it will have been noticed and taken into account by individuals in positions to know and to act. For example, if city air is noxious, some citizens will sell their city houses and move to the suburbs. If water is acrid, some people will contract for a private water supply. These market responses are accomplished through the low visibility exchanges of property, through which incremental adjustment is made to incremental risks. The traditions, customs, and legal rules permitting these adjustments also entrench the resulting relationships. Once a person has sold his home or business, ordinarily the government cannot later intercede to reverse the transaction. Once people have enlarged their own medical coverage, they may have legally protected disincentives to support broader public health coverage.

In perspective, virtually all forces eventually classified as "public risk" have already influenced decentralized choices and market prices, and resulted in legally significant changes of position. Considerations of health and safety are major factors in the existing structure at any given time of residential patterns, modes of transportation, plant and office location, education, and health services. Suppressing private responses to public risk would require virtually dismantling the structure of society itself.

The complexity of a modern legal system regime is also a source of strength, however. The system generally permits some kind of response, even if imperfect, before a risk rises to catastrophic proportion. The legislature in a constitutional regime responds to risks perceived on a larger scale, through new legislation that readjusts authority, responsibility and liability, or risky activities. The American legal system also includes an activist judiciary—that is, a judiciary willing to devise new legal premises as the basis for new rights and remedies and allocations of authority. The judicial process in this country therefore is readily available for ventilating grievances and obtaining redress. Indeed, litigation has become a standard mechanism for dealing with early manifestations of risk—environmental pollution, financial fraud, maladministration of criminal justice, and so on. The instrument of litigation affords litigants an autonomy comparable to that afforded by the market, and a power of legal compulsion comparable to that of government. Sometimes, however, the result is command and control from below.

REFERENCES

The range of relevant legal, political, and economic literature is enormous. The following are indicative:

K. Arrow, *The Limits of Organization* (New York: Norton, 1974).

G. D. Brewer and P. DeLeon, *The Foundation of Policy Analysis* (Chicago: Dorsey, 1983).

B. Fischoff, "Managing Risk Perceptions," *Issues in Science and Technology* (Fall 1985): 83.

C. Gillette and J. Krier, "Risk, Courts, and Agencies," *University of Pennsylvania Law Review* 138 (1990): 1027 and references therein.

J. W. Hurst, *Law and Markets in the United States* (Madison: University of Wisconsin Press, 1982).

C. E. Lindblom, *Politics and Markets: The World's Political-Economic Systems* (New York: Basic, 1977).

R. Posner, *Economic Analysis of Law*, 3d ed. (Boston: Little, Brown, 1986).

M. Shubik, "Political Risk: Analysis, Process, and Purpose," in R. Herring, ed., *Managing International Risk* (Cambridge: Cambridge University Press, 1983).

G. Stigler, "The Theory of Economic Regulation," *Bell Journal of Economics and Management Science* 2 (1971): 335.

Andreas Teuber

Justifying Risk

OUR ATTITUDES TOWARD RISK VARY according to what has happened to us, what we expect, what we feel, what we know, and what we care about. We ignore some risks, overestimate others. Our perceptions are selective and change as social life changes.

Nothing illuminates this last point so well as the evolution of life insurance. In the sixteenth and seventeenth centuries, it was conceived primarily as a wager. Short-term bets were taken out on the lives of a third person, usually a prominent figure like the pope. The custom seems to have originated in fifteenth-century Spain and spread to Italy, Holland, France, and England. The 1570 Code of the Low Countries lumps life insurance together with other "abuses, frauds, and crimes," and by the end of the seventeenth century it was illegal everywhere in Europe except Naples and London. Throughout the early modern period, life insurance was "betting on life," not planning for it.

Changes in the concept had to await the arrival of a new group, those with newly acquired wealth, who had something to lose if their fortunes reversed. An early prospectus of the Equitable Society for the Assurance of Lives, founded in London in 1762, extols the benefits of life insurance for the head of the household by painting a vivid portrait of the "indigent and deplorable situation" that could be brought about by his unexpected early death. Playing upon the anxieties of family members, it makes much of the "catastrophe" that would occur were they suddenly "catapulted out of the middle ranks of society," which by dint of their own "industry and thrift" they had struggled so hard to attain.[1]

Andreas Teuber is Professor of Philosophy at Brandeis University.

The transformation in the conception of life insurance from betting on life to security against its loss illustrates dramatically that our attitudes toward risk are bound up with what else we believe and value. They make sense only against a certain social background.

RISK AND CONSENT

We live in a culture that prizes autonomy. Against that background, our responses to risk acquire their meaning. We respond differently to risks that we choose for ourselves and over which we believe we have some degree of control than we do to risks that we do not choose or believe we control. In technical discussions, risks are negatives, and in calculations of costs and benefits, risks are usually considered costs. To a mountaineer, however, the risk of a climb or a particular route up a rock face, ranked in terms of its DP, or "death potential," is part of what makes that climb a challenge, even what makes it worthwhile.

The mountaineer's attitude toward risks is tied, surely, to the degree of control he believes he has over the risks he must bear. Our judgment, too, about when it is permissible to expose a person to risk or injury is tied to notions of individual responsibility and human agency. The source of an injury is often as important to us as its extent. It makes a difference to us whether a harm was due to natural causes or brought about by the action of another person. If it was caused by another person, we usually want to know if he knew what he was doing, and if he did, whether he acted deliberately. These preoccupations are reflected in our legal codes and moral practices. From a moral point of view, the key question to ask is not "What should we do about risk?" but "Which risks do we want to have on our conscience?"[2]

In the following pages I shall focus on risks imposed on us by others, on what might be called risk impositions. Under what conditions are risk impositions justified? Having devoted almost exclusive attention to the conditions under which it may or may not be permissible to cause another person harm, philosophers have paid surprisingly little attention to the permissibility of risk impositions. If, as we seem to believe, it is wrong to cause another person *harm* without that person's consent, is it wrong to impose a *risk* of harm without consent?[3]

In light of our commitment to autonomy, it is not unreasonable to think that consent plays a role in the legitimation of risky activity. Its role is important in our political process, which relies on the participation of the governed for legitimacy, and in the marketplace, where the ideal transaction is represented as one of *voluntary* exchange. Consent is also thought to be necessary in cases of medical experimentation. Detailed procedures have been developed for the use of consent forms and for obtaining a patient's "explicit, informed consent."

Given that our intuitions are fairly well grounded about the conditions under which we think it permissible to expose patients to the risks of experimental drugs or surgery, it is tempting to take such cases as models for the justification of risky activity in general. This, in turn, suggests a minimal first principle:

> Imposing risks on people is justified if and only if it is reasonable to assume that they have consented to those risks.[4]

PROBLEMS OF CONSENT

But as workable as such a principle appears to be in the context of doctor and patient, can it be extended to less clearly circumscribed risk impositions: exposure to pesticide drift, the venting of radioactivity from a nuclear power plant, carbon monoxide fumes from congested traffic, acid rain from coal-burning power plants located many miles away, or chemicals entering the water supply from abandoned toxic waste sites? In nearly all of these cases the risks to which people are exposed are not distributed singly from one individual to another, but spread in small increments over a very large population or as the result of the actions of a great many individuals, each of whose actions, taken alone, causes little harm but, in combination, poses a very grave threat indeed. Distributing consent forms to all those who might be at risk is surely an insuperable task, to say nothing of the difficulties of measuring the small magnitudes of risk to each person affected. To complicate matters further, many risks have multiple sources and interrelate, so that it is difficult, if not impossible, to figure out who is doing what to whom, let alone draw up contracts among the relevant parties.

Even if the practical difficulties of obtaining people's consent could be overcome, it is widely reported that people are notoriously poor judges of risk. People's perceptions frequently fail to match up with the actual dangers risks pose. Few people have a "feel" for what a chance of dying, say a chance of one in a million, really means. Research by psychologists Amos Tversky and Daniel Kahneman has shown that we are regularly led astray in our assessments of probabilities by rules of thumb. Faced with a judgment that requires even a minimal familiarity with statistics, we frequently avoid the statistical information and rely instead on a description which feels less strange.[5] We tend to overemphasize low probabilities and underestimate those that are high. We have to struggle to resist the gambler's fallacy: the belief that after a series of losses the odds must favor a win. We are also poor judges of outcomes. We appear to be more concerned about avoiding losses than receiving equivalent gains, and this asymmetry can be exploited in the way choices are presented. Retailers, for example, know enough about our susceptibility to the way options are framed to represent a surcharge for credit card customers as a discount to those who are willing to pay cash.[6]

The influence of framing on judgments about risk is systematic and pervasive. Health care professionals are no less susceptible to the effects of framing than their patients, who have less experience and lack expertise, as Tversky and Kahneman report. They put the following hypothetical case to a group of physicians:

> Imagine that you have operable lung cancer and must choose between two treatments: surgery and radiation therapy. Of 100 people having surgery, 10 die during the operation, 32 are dead after one year, and 66 after five years. Of 100 people having radiation therapy, none die during treatment, 23 are dead after one year, and 78 after five years. Which treatment do you prefer?[7]

Given these options, 50 percent of the physicians said they preferred radiation treatment. However, when the same options were presented in terms of survival rates rather than mortality rates, 84 percent said they would prefer surgery.

It is generally believed that consistency in judgments is a minimal condition of rationality. Since our judgments about risk are apparently inconsistent, it is hard not to draw the conclusion that our attitudes towards risk are irrational. These findings have disturbing implications for public policy, especially in a society which relies on a democratic process. If we are irrational in our judgments about risk, the policies we enact will reflect a similar bias. Given our untrustworthy attitudes, a consent-based approach to legitimating risk-imposing activities can only lead to irrational public policies.

COST-BENEFIT ANALYSIS AS A SUBSTITUTE FOR CONSENT

But if we cannot rely on a consent-based approach because it is either unworkable or not to be trusted, how are we to decide which risks to accept?

Some believe that we should rely on cost-benefit analysis to tell us what to do in our public policies involving risks. But cost-benefit analysis is regarded with some suspicion by the general public. No matter how efficient such analytic methods may be, they are believed to require the technical expertise of well-trained professionals for their operation. Therefore, policies that emerge from their application may seem less legitimate than policies that evolve, however clumsily, from a more participatory political process. Indeed, cost-benefit analysis appears to be as far removed from a consent-based approach as we could find.

However, a powerful case in favor of cost-benefit analysis, put forward recently by policy analysts Herman Leonard and Richard Zeckhauser, suggests that we may have less to fear from such a method than we imagine.[8] They admit the moral appeal of consent-based solutions and go on to argue that—contrary to popular opinion—cost-benefit analysis can be grounded in a form of consent after all. Assumptions about its narrowly technocratic character are misplaced.

Their argument, in brief, runs as follows. Cost-benefit analysis incorporates into its calculus the criterion of economic efficiency as well as an assumption of rationality. Since people want to act rationally and prefer efficiency to inefficiency, they will consent to public policies concerning risks to health and safety that are based on cost-benefit analysis, because the outcomes generated by the analysis are the same as the outcomes that they would choose if they could go through the process themselves.[9] The method measures and compares all relevant factors, incorporating all our values and assigning them weights that we would give to them were we making the decisions ourselves, or more exactly, were we making the decisions on our rationally best behavior. In this sense, risk cost-benefit analysis is our most reasonable self writ large. It is not an impersonal, narrowly technocratic method for calculating outcomes. It simply specifies choices that we—at our rationally best—would choose. It fills the vacuum created by the unavailability of market solutions and the impracticality of obtaining the explicit, informed consent of all parties to a risk decision. And it fills this vacuum in an ethically appropriate way, according to Leonard and Zeckhauser, since the ethical underpinnings for the defense of cost-benefit analysis ultimately rest, if not on actual consent, on hypothetical consent. What are we to make of this?

Commensurability of Risks

The strength of cost-benefit analysis is its capacity to order and rank a variety of options. Hence, it must be based on a measure that is sufficiently abstract and general for the costs and benefits of various alternatives to be lumped together and added up. However, the homogenization that takes place often results in the glossing over of differences and the production of outcomes that offend common sense.

Of course common sense itself is not always a reliable guide. But the measure adopted to represent all factors on a single scale must yield comparisons that are in some way recognizable and not so counterintuitive as to appear arbitrary. As Leonard and Zeckhauser themselves make clear, benefits and costs must be "appropriately" measured. Part of that appropriateness is the intuitive appeal of the comparisons, in their connecting up, however dimly, with common sense. For a comparison to yield the right intuitive "feel," the measure we choose will have to take some of the particularities of the cases into account. Although we may be able to come up with a common measure in a specific case that will yield intuitively acceptable results, this works against the grain of the analysis as a useful tool at the level of public policy, where there is incentive to come up with more and more general measures in order to compare the greatest possible variety of options. It is hard to avoid the conclusion that no matter what scale of measurement is chosen, any *general* measure of comparison will inevitably produce intuitively unacceptable results.

The technique also does not pay sufficient attention to different human responses to risk. Individual responses to risks that are treated as numerically equivalent sometimes turn out to be significantly different despite their numerical equivalence. Too often these differences are allowed to disappear in some general formulation, or get written off, if they cannot be made to fit, as simply irrational.

The Distribution of Risks

For cost-benefit analysis to be of use in the formation of public policy, some way of assigning a value to the risks is necessary, so some sensitivity to the ways in which risks are distributed throughout a population is in order. But there are different ways to identify the magnitude of risk to a population. We can, for example, estimate the chance of dying from a nuclear accident as the likelihood of a number of deaths throughout a given population, or we can spread that risk equally over individual members of the same population to estimate the average risk per individual.

Imagine that we are faced with estimating the risks of radiation-related deaths from a nuclear accident of the same magnitude as the one at Chernobyl. Those within the plant and in the area immediately surrounding it are in danger of losing their lives instantly, whereas those living further away have a considerably lower risk of delayed death from cancer. If we translate the expected number of deaths likely to result from such an accident throughout the area into the average individual risk, we seriously underestimate the risks to those who reside in the immediate vicinity of the plant. If we estimate the average individual risk to members of the population within a two-mile radius of the plant, we ignore the risks to the larger population. Which population we choose as the population at risk is not merely a matter of convenience. If we know, for instance, that the chances of dying from a nuclear accident are close to 100 percent for those working within the nuclear plant, whereas those who live furthest away face no risk at all, it is misleading to spread this risk over the entire population as an average risk per individual.

The Value of a Human Life

Human life has a special value in our culture. Many of us feel that our lives ought to be treated differently from other things we value. To some policy analysts it has therefore seemed useful to try to determine a single value for a human life. There is little agreement, however, over how to arrive at such a figure. Since there is no market in human lives, inferences are frequently drawn from situations in which people reveal what they are willing to pay for their own safety. An investigation into consumer purchases of smoke detectors, for example, estimates the value of a life at $175,000;[10] whereas a study that looks at the decisions by drivers to wear seat belts puts the figure closer to $593,000.[11] Yet another study analyzing wage differentials received by workers on dangerous jobs gives an estimate of $3,200,000.[12] The inferences vary so widely that the most determined policy analyst despairs of ever being able to put a single value on a human life.

More troubling is the assumption by policy analysts that their calculations bear relation to what we understand that value to be. Putting a price on life is sometimes seen as an example of the large-scale computations that have become so much a part of modern politics. These computations "bring with them," as the philosopher Stuart Hampshire has written, "a coarseness and grossness of moral feeling, a blunting of sensibility, and a suppression of individual discrimination and gentleness."[13]

To this charge, the policy analyst can reply that governments cannot avoid the trading of lives for money, because governments are responsible for programs in public transportation, national defense, and environmental protection, in which lives are saved or lost at a price. Since governments cannot avoid trading lives for money, they might as well set the terms under which that trading takes place. Indeed, we need not get all worked up about putting a price on life, because the lives for which we seek to find a value are statistical. As Thomas Schelling has explained, "what the government buys if it buys health and safety is a reduction in individual risks. The lives saved are usually a mathematical construct, a statistical equivalent to what, at the level of the individual, is expressible as a longevity estimate but not a finite extension of life."[14] By deciding to adopt this or that public program, say, to raise or lower auto-emission standards, a decision is made about the number of lives that are likely to be saved or lost, but no decision is made, so the claim runs, about the life or death of identifiable individuals. To the charge that putting a price on life allows government agencies and their officials to "play God," the policy analyst has this reply:

> The specification of the value of life does not give powers over life and death to the administrators of public sector projects. It takes such

> powers away. Having placed the responsibility for road-building and medical care in the public sector, we have, knowingly or not, compelled ourselves to decide between your life or mine. We can allow administrators to act as they see fit. . . . Or we can bind these decisions with rules that make those decisions less arbitrary, less subject to political influence, and less tragic. Specification of a uniform value of life constrains the choices of administrators of public sector programs and avoids many situations where one man must give or withhold the life of another.[15]

Risky Situations of Relative Urgency

Still, many are nervous about putting a price on life. Somehow it misses the more fundamental point that life is beyond price. Faced with the imminent death of persons whose actual (nonstatistical) lives are in danger, we respond as if we believed that life were sacred and not just another commodity. In efforts to save a small child caught in a well, or miners trapped in some passageway far beneath the surface of the earth, or passengers lost at sea, people are willing to go to almost any lengths, without much concern for "cost," to save the lives of those at risk.

Suppose that we are faced with determining policy in the long term for, let us say, mining safety. We might very possibly conclude that "in some cases, for the price of a rescue, we could save a much larger expected number of lives through various safety measures."[16] From the perspective of cost-benefit analysis, "fewest lives would be lost if the entire budget . . . [were] spent on prevention of accidents and on easy rescues, and no heroic or extraordinary rescues . . . attempted in case of disaster."[17]

But now imagine that we adopt such a policy. Any attempt at heroic rescue of miners will divert resources from the installation of safety equipment, which will save more lives in the long run. But what would it be like to stand by while several miners were lost who might otherwise have been saved but at a cost that had been calculated to be not worth the price?

Here the prescriptions of cost-benefit analysis diverge from what we urgently feel is the right thing to do. We appear to be willing to accept a considerable amount of inefficiency or cost-ineffectiveness in pursuit of what we believe is more important: saving the lives of those who are immediately at risk. Why not then include in a cost-benefit analysis, not only lives saved and lost, but also some measure of the psychological effects and mental disturbances that persons are likely to experience as a result of being barred from attempts at heroic rescue? There are at least three objections to be made to this proposal.

First, the significance to oneself of being the kind of person who cares enough in situations of extreme urgency is not the sort of thing that can be captured by the narrowly economic values employed in cost-benefit analysis. To capture this significance, the method would have to expand in conception of value.

Second, being the kind of a person who comes to the rescue of someone in distress tends to be experienced as part of what makes life itself worth living, as valuable for its own sake, apart from what good it may produce. Whatever value assigned to it by cost-benefit analysis, there will always be something more of value (i.e., the intrinsic worth of being this kind of person) that the analysis fails to capture.

Third, when we respond to others in situations of distress, we do so without too much thought about how else we might spend our time. We respond sympathetically and spontaneously. Stepping back to make these decisions by cost-benefit analysis may endanger these more or less spontaneous acts of human fellowship, "may profane things that must be held sacred," as Alan Gibbard has suggested, "things that, because of who we are, we must hold sacred if our lives are to be deeply rewarding."[18]

Anyone who wishes to defend cost-benefit analysis as a reliable guide to policy concerning risks with an argument based on hypothetical consent cannot simply dismiss cases of heroic rescue as yet more examples of the failing of common sense. Indeed, Leonard and Zeckhauser look for ways to accommodate our feelings of urgency. They acknowledge that "some social values will never fit in a cost-benefit framework and will have to be treated as 'additional considerations' in coming to a final decision."[19] But since they offer no principled way of how to bring in our feelings of urgency, their solution is inadequately *ad hoc*. If some values cannot be handled by the cost-benefit criterion but are still to be given some weight as "additional considerations," the method begins to look less and less like a neutral procedure that can be applied more or less automatically.

Risks and Rights

Individual rights make up another area with which cost-benefit analysis is ill equipped to deal. There are, of course, many decisions we make in which rights play no role. But in the arena of risks to life, health, and safety this is not so: rights play a very critical role indeed.

Rights constitute what might be called a minimal respect for persons and constrain persons from treating others in certain ways. Rights do not allow trade-offs. They cannot be brought together into one homogeneous total. Each person's rights count separately and have their own moral value. My rights are incommensurable with your rights; each places limits on the exercise of the other.[20]

Imagine that we are faced with the task of developing a national policy concerning secondhand cigarette smoke in enclosed public spaces. If we think of the effects on smoker and nonsmoker alike, there are clear costs and benefits on both sides. There is the irritation from the tobacco smoke felt by the nonsmoker as well as the discomfort and frustration experienced by the smoker who is asked to refrain from smoking. There are also long-term health effects on both.

We live in a culture that takes rights seriously, in particular rights to persons and property. If a person is in an enclosed space from which she cannot easily walk away, the tobacco smoke she experiences from someone else's cigarette is not only a cost, but a violation of her right not to be harmed without her consent. As Peter Railton has put it, "each time I send some of my tobacco smoke your way, you suffer some small physical change, not for the better."[21] On a rights-based view, each person's rights set up a boundary across which others are not permitted to go. And although the change that a person suffers from the tobacco smoke imposed upon him may be very small, on a rights-based view what matters is "whether or not a boundary was crossed, not the magnitude of the consequences: shoplifters have been prosecuted for stealing a pack of chewing gum."[22] Of course, smokers can claim that they have rights too, and they do, but each person's rights are brought up short when they bump up against the boundaries of somebody else's rights. Smokers are free to smoke in the confines of their own rooms. In enclosed public spaces, their right to smoke stops, like the right to swing one's arm at the tip of somebody else's nose.[23] Rights are not "additional considerations" to be taken into account in some *ad hoc* manner as a supplement to maximizing total benefit. Rights enter into the making of policy at the most basic level, and other considerations such as the comfort of smokers can be entertained only after the rights of nonsmokers have been taken into account.

Workplace air pollution presents similar problems to the risks of secondhand smoke, only here there are obvious benefits to be gained from the polluting activity. There is great incentive, no doubt, to keep production costs as low as possible. Nonetheless, there appears to be general agreement that "workplace air pollution violates workers' rights."[24] Current public policy, reflected in the Occupational Safety and Health Act, is rights based: permissible exposure levels for any toxic substance must ensure that "no employee will suffer material impairment of health or functional capacity."[25]

However, if we were to extend a rights-based solution into other areas, such as outdoor air pollution, most risk-imposing activities would have to be prohibited. The extremity of rights-based public policies concerning risks to safety and health have inclined some policy analysts to disregard rights considerations altogether. Since cost-benefit analysis is unsuited to handle these sorts of considerations anyway, such an inclination may be more self-serving than considered. Nonetheless, it is true that rights leave little room for balancing or compromising, and perhaps in the arena of outdoor air pollution we arrive at the limits of their usefulness in setting policy concerning risk. But if rights place an unusually strict limit on the levels of risk to which citizens may justifiably be exposed, it is also true that risks to which people are exposed are permissible if it can be shown that the bearers of those risks have given their consent. Only consent can turn a potential violation of a right into a permissible act.[26]

BRINGING CONSENT BACK IN

Impositions proposed by cost-benefit analysis are justified because reasonable people prefer alternatives where benefits exceed costs and would therefore choose the same outcomes as the analysis recommended if they could go through the process themselves. But this defense of the technique works only if the costs and benefits that are the input of the analysis are appropriate and comprehensive. Since they are neither, a defense of cost-benefit analysis as a form of consent does not succeed.

Because it fails to respect the distinctiveness of people's responses to risks, or to do justice to the morally significant ways in which risks can be distributed, or to give proper weight to the importance we attach to human life in situations of felt urgency, or to capture the special significance of our concern for autonomy and rights, cost-benefit analysis cannot yield the same result as individual consent. For these reasons we should not be persuaded to allow cost-benefit analysis to determine public policy—to do, as it were, our talking for us.

What we need are not improved analytic techniques or more finely tuned ways of calculating costs and benefits, but greater opportunities for participation in the decision-making process by those affected by public policies concerning risks. That process is, of course, a political process, and some policy analysts despair of our ever coming to any sort of decision, let alone a reasonable one, by that means.

"Muddling through" may be the only *just* way to make public choices involving risk because these decisions raise questions of equity to which cost-benefit analysis is blind and about which it is has nothing to say. Our responses to risks presuppose divergent interests and ideals that cost-benefit analysis neither accommodates nor grasps. These divergent interests and ideals are best dealt with by a pluralist approach, not merged into one homogeneous total as they are under cost-benefit analysis. A democratic political process works in an essentially pluralist manner and is designed to handle, however messily, the divergent interests and ideals of different people. It is also important to recognize that we want not only a method that will help us to achieve the right outcomes, but also a method that achieves its outcomes in appropriate and fair ways. "It would not do, for example," as Douglas MacLean has observed, "to replace trial by jury or democratic elections with technocratic analytic decision-making techniques, even if these techniques . . . would achieve better results."[27] And it would not do because the legitimacy of the outcome in these cases depends in part on the openness and fairness of the process.

But if people are to become more involved in making public policy decisions concerning risks to life, health, and safety, how are we to respond to the psychological studies which show that our judgments about risks are frequently "irrational, if not perverse"?[28] First, we must make every effort to educate citizens to be better at probabilistic reasoning and to supply them with relevant information in terms they can understand. We must be careful to frame options in a number of different ways, to counteract our susceptibility to framing effects.

Second, we should note that the findings of risk perception studies show that people are irrational in their attitudes towards risk only by assuming a narrow conception of rationality. Some of our presumed irrationalities and inconsistencies can be explained in other ways, so that on a broader view of the findings our choices turn out to be quite reasonable.

The control people believe they have over risks has sometimes been offered to explain the apparently irrational preference many people show for driving rather than flying. But people are not concerned merely about the chance of dying, but about "what life is like while they are living it."[29] We may indeed underestimate our chances of survival in situations where we believe we have some degree of control over the risks we bear, but we also *value* that control. As most of us know too well:

> Trade-offs between quality and quantity of life are made all the time in personal decisions about health and safety: Mark Twain, told that he could add five years to his life by giving up smoking and drinking, reportedly quipped that five years without smoking and drinking weren't worth living.[30]

Redescribing an option can lead people to reverse their preferences, as the research of Tversky and Kahneman shows. But a number of these preference reversals are also open to alternative explanations, suggesting that there may be more to our ways of thinking and reasoning than is to be found in the conception of instrumental rationality.

We are not only *end*-oriented; we are also *ideal*-oriented. We do not care just about where we end up; we care about the kind of people we have to become in order to end up in one place or another. When, for example, the life of an identifiable individual is in imminent danger and there is some chance, however remote, of saving that person, to stand idly by disturbs our sense of self. There is not only value in lives saved; there is value in being the kind of person who will go to heroic lengths to rescue another. To stand by is not only costly; it is also *dehumanizing*.[31]

CONSENT-BASED JUSTIFICATION

Although I am convinced that a consent-based approach is the only fair and appropriate way to justify risky activity, it is not without problems.

First, it is by now obvious that our minimal first principle cannot hold in the form in which it was originally stated. If we require actual consent to each and every risk of harm that is imposed, much of what we do in the course of our daily lives will have to be ruled out, since it will be impossible to obtain that consent. Some have argued that many of the risks to which we are exposed are too trivial or at least are not sufficiently important to require consent. Thus, it has been claimed, for instance, that "you are not morally required to obtain the permission of everyone who might be in the path of your car should it go out of control on your way to the post office . . . ."[32] We shall need some way of distinguishing the trivial cases that do not require consent from the nontrivial ones.

Second, once we eliminate the trivial cases, if indeed there are such cases, it remains obvious that we shall not be able to obtain the actual consent of persons in most cases of risk imposition. Many risks, such as those imposed on people by the operation of coal-burning and nuclear power plants, involve externalities and public goods. In these cases, risk-imposing decisions will be centralized and public policy will partly determine levels of risk, by setting standards for, say, the venting of radioactivity by nuclear power plants or the release of toxins into the atmosphere by chemical factories. The model of doctor-patient, in which a doctor seeks the prior consent of the patient before, say, imposing the risks of operating on his left lung, cannot serve as a paradigm for most risk decisions. If cost-benefit analysis is not the answer, we shall need to be clearer about the ways people can participate in public decisions that impose risks on them.

For consent to play a legitimating role in the making of these risk decisions, it cannot come into play only in the final stages of the decision-making process. Potential risk bearers will have to be involved at every stage of the process, in formulating, implementing, and adopting public policy. Mark McCarthy has suggested the creation of labor-management health and safety committees—to help enforce federal standards and address unregulated workplace hazards—and the incorporation of health and safety concerns in the collective bargaining process.[33] He also makes the recommendation that there be greater participation by the affected parties in the drafting of regulations at the federal level.[34]

Third, we need to become clearer about what forms of participation make for morally acceptable decisions. Some believe, for instance, that merely by consenting to work in a factory where one knows in advance that there are airborne hazards, a worker thereby gives his consent to the risks he will bear, or that by purchasing a home near a nuclear power plant, the buyer consents to the risks to which he may be exposed. No doubt for this sort of *tacit* consent to be meaningful, it must be true that one has had an opportunity to choose among a set of alternatives that are viable and risk-free and that one has been fully informed about potential risks. But even if these conditions are met, it is unlikely that consenting to work at a factory where one knows there are risks constitutes consent to those risks. Judith Thomson has argued,[35] persuasively I believe, that in consenting to walk late at night through a park that one knows to be unsafe, one does not thereby consent to being mugged. We need to become clear about what counts and what does not count as "consenting to a risk."[36]

Finally, we must acknowledge that in looking for ways for potential risk bearers to participate more fully in the decision-making process, we may be calling on skills and habits of mind with which citizens have little experience or experience of the wrong kind. In negotiations interested parties often see themselves in a trial-like process, inclined to assert their positions in the most extreme ways; they may be neither capable of nor open to arriving at a consensus on public policies concerning risk. No doubt there is some truth to the charge that we live in an adversary culture.[37]

A vision of citizenship as largely a defensive strategy and chiefly a matter of rights designed to protect the citizen from too-powerful governors can be traced back to the founding of the republic. For a consent-based approach to the problem of risk impositions to work in the ways I have outlined, this vision of citizenship may itself have to undergo transformation. Many of us will have to learn a new set of civic virtues if we are to arrive at a consensus on pressing public policy questions concerning risk to our health and safety.

ACKNOWLEDGMENTS

I am indebted to all the participants at the Working Session at Georgetown University Medical Center, Washington, D. C., September 21–24, 1989, for their criticisms of an earlier draft and to Sissela Bok, Stephen Graubard, Eli Hirsch, Owen Flanagan, Jerry Samet, and William Talbott for their helpful suggestions.

ENDNOTES

[1]The examples are drawn from Lorraine Daston, who offers a brilliant analysis of the attitudes toward life insurance, security, and risk in the early modern period in "The Quantification of Risk in the Enlightenment," unpublished manuscript.

[2]Annette Baier, "Poisoning the Wells," in Douglas MacLean, ed., *Values at Risk* (Totowa, N. J.: Rowman & Allanheld, 1986), 49.

[3]Robert Nozick, who gives a sophisticated account of rights in his book *Anarchy, State and Utopia* (New York: Basic Books, 1974), 75, notes that "no natural-law theory has yet specified a precise line delimiting people's natural rights in risky situations," but does not go on to offer such a theory himself. Samuel Scheffler observes that "while traditional lists of individual rights do typically restrict harmful activity, they are generally silent on the question of risk," in *To Breathe Freely,* ed. by Mary Gibson (Totowa, N.J.: Rowman & Allanheld, 1985), 81. Judith Thomson makes a modest but wonderfully sensitive beginning in her essay "Imposing Risks," also in *To Breathe Freely,* 124–40. Both *To Breathe Freely* and *Values at Risk* contain essays that focus on ethical issues raised by government policy concerning air pollution and the meaning and assessment of risk. These two books are among the best treatments of these subjects of which I am aware, and I have benefited from them greatly.

[4]See Patrick Derr et al., "Worker/Public Protection: The Double Standard," *Environment* 23 (9) (1981), for a similar proposal.

[5]Amos Tversky and Daniel Kahneman, "The Framing of Decisions and the Psychology of Choice," *Science* 211 (1981): 453–58.

[6]See Richard H. Thaler, "Towards a Positive Theory of Consumer Choice," *Journal of Economic Behavior and Organization* 1 (March 1980): 39–60.

[7]Originally reported by Barbara J. MacNeil, Stephen G. Pauker, Harold C. Fox, Jr., and Amos Tversky in "On the Elicitation of Preferences for Alternative Therapies," *New England Journal of Medicine* 306 (May 1982): 1259–62, described by Amos Tversky and Daniel Kahneman in "Can Normative and Descriptive Analysis be Reconciled," Center for Philosophy and Public Policy project funded by the National Science Foundation, grant number SES–8317726, RR–4 (March

1987), and summarized in *Philosophy & Public Policy Report* 8 (1) (Winter 1988): 4.

[8]Herman B. Leonard and Richard J. Zeckhauser, "Cost-Benefit Analysis Applied to Risks: Its Philosophy and Legitimacy," in *Values at Risk,* 31–48.

[9]Ibid., 36.

[10]R. Dardis, "The Value of Life: New Evidence from the Marketplace," *American Economic Review* 70 (December 1980), 1077–82.

[11]Glen Bloomquist, "Value of Life-Saving: Implications of Consumption Activity," *Journal of Political Economy* 87 (June 1979): 540–58.

[12]C. A. Olson, "An Analysis of Wage Differentials Received by Workers on Dangerous Jobs," *Journal of Human Resources* 10 (Summer 1981): 165–85.

[13]Stuart Hampshire, "Morality and Pessimism," in *Morality and Conflict* (Cambridge: Harvard University Press, 1983), 86, quoted by MacLean in *Values at Risk,* 85.

[14]Thomas Schelling, "The Life You Save May Be Your Own," in *Problems in Public Expenditure Analysis,* ed. Samuel Chase (Washington, D. C.: The Brookings Institute, 1968), 142

[15]Dan Usher, "The Value of Life for Decision Making in the Public Sector," *Ethics and Economics*, ed. Ellen Frankel Paul, Fred D. Miller, Jr., and Jeffrey Paul (Oxford: Basil Blackwell, 1985), 191.

[16]Alan Gibbard, "Risk and Value," in *Values at Risk,* 101.

[17]Ibid., 97.

[18]Ibid., 102.

[19]Leonard and Zeckhauser, 42.

[20]For a further discussion of some of these issues see the introduction by Amartya Sen and Bernard Williams to their edited volume *Utilitarianism and Beyond* (Cambridge: Cambridge University Press, 1982).

[21]Peter Railton, "Locke, Stock, and Peril: Natural Property Rights, Pollution, and Risk," in *To Breathe Freely,* 92.

[22]*Philosophy & Public Policy Report* 5 (3) (Summer 1985): 2.

[23]Ibid.

[24]Ibid., 3.

[25]Ibid.

[26]It is sometimes thought that a violation of a person's rights might be justified if one compensated him afterwards. If this were so, this could become another way to turn a potential violation of a right into a permissible act, implying yet another way to justify risk impositions. In this view consent would not be required and risk impositions would be justified so long as one compensated each and every person for any harm that occurred as the result of one's having exposed that person to the risk of harm. But to harm another without his consent, so long as one compensates, pre-empts his right to decide things for himself, treats him as a

mere means to one's own ends, and enables those who have sufficient resources to engage in harmful activities more readily and with less compunction than those of lesser means. One way not to deal with the risks imposed on nonsmokers from secondhand cigarette smoke is by placing an excise tax or a surcharge on cigarettes, which would simply allow those who could afford the increased cost of cigarettes to pay and pollute. An argument for regarding standards of safety and health in the workplace as a matter of workers' rights, violations of which are permissible only with their consent, is to block the option otherwise open to firms to pay compensation costs rather than make the workplace a safe and healthy environment within which to work. For a related discussion of these issues, see Railton, especially 112–17.

[27]Douglas MacLean, introduction to *Values at Risk,* 4–5.

[28]*Philosophy & Public Policy Report,* 8 (1) (Winter 1988): 2.

[29]Ibid.

[30]Ibid.

[31]Gibbard, 102.

[32]Mary Gibson in the introduction to *To Breathe Freely,* xi.

[33]Mark McCarthy, "Reform of Occupational Safety and Health Policy," in *To Breathe Freely,* 201–21.

[34]Union officials are not always pleased by proposals for joint labor-management committees and are reluctant to include safety and health concerns in the bargaining process. Their worries are also not completely without reason and need to be taken into account if any restructuring of present relationships between labor and management were to occur. Union opposition is expressed on a variety of grounds by saying that health and safety are rights and workers ought not to have to give up wages or other benefits to pay for them, that safety committees are a way to co-opt workers, that management does not take occupational safety and health seriously enough and ought to be compelled to improve conditions by stricter national regulations, that unions have neither the power nor the legitimacy in this country (where only 20 percent of the workforce is unionized) to negotiate with management to improve health and safety conditions in the workplace, and that negotiated agreements on health and safety between labor and management open unions up to liability suits from disabled workers. See McCarthy, 216–17.

[35]Judith Thomson, "Imposing Risks," in *To Breathe Freely,* 139.

[36]Since certain cases of *tacit* consent may be thought to be morally invalid, and may not count as consent, it should perhaps be noted that there are also circumstancess in which *actual* consent is thought to be morally invalid. Thus, in contractual relationships there are a number of conditions that are generally taken to invalidate the actual agreement among the parties, even if both parties have given their consent, to say nothing of the more complex cases in which courts have refused to uphold workers' agreements to exempt their employers from liability due to negligence. For a potential risk bearer's consent to justify a risk imposition, the conditions under which both tacit *and* actual consent are morally vaild will have to be fully and clearly set out.

[37]For accounts of the contrast between adversary and consensus culture, see Steven Kelman, *Regulating America, Regulating Sweden: A Comparative Study of Occupational Safety and Health Policy* (Cambridge: MIT Press, 1982), and Michael Thompson, "To Hell with the Turkeys! A Diatribe Directed at the Pernicious Trepidity of the Current Intellectual Debate on Risk," in *Values at Risk,* 113–35.